中国新疆36年国際協力実録
キジル・ニヤ・ダンダンウイリク

一帯一路实践图典
克孜尔 尼雅 丹丹乌里克

Silk Road
Kizil Niya Dandanoilik

小島康誉
Yasutaka Kojima

東方出版

献　辞

王恩茂（1913-2001 中国共産党新疆ウイグル自治区委員会書記 中国政治協商会議全国委員会副主席）：1986年、筆者のキジル千仏洞への修復保存資金寄付申し出を承認いただき、以降の活動につながった。また各種活動を全面的に支持いただいた。

塩川正十郎（1921-2015 運輸大臣 文部大臣 内閣官房長官 自治大臣 国家公安委員会委員長 財務大臣）：1987年に筆者が日中友好キジル千仏洞修復保存協力会を設立する際以来、日中共同ニヤ遺跡学術調査などでも格別の指導と厚情をいただいた。

上村晃史（1924-1997 上村工業株式会社社長）：1987年に筆者が設立した日中友好キジル千仏洞修復保存協力会の会長として、技術講習会を開催しその収益を寄せていただくなど募金活動に尽力をいただき、目標額を達成することが出来た。

水谷幸正（1928-2014 佛教大学学長 佛教教育学園理事長 浄土宗宗務総長）：1988年より開始した日中共同ニヤ＆ダンダンウイリク遺跡学術調査を支持いただき、真田康道佛教大学教授・井ノ口泰淳龍谷大学名誉教授に参加を呼び掛けるなど尽力いただいた。

張徳勤（1933-2015 中国国家文物局局長）：中国と外国との共同調査として最大規模の日中共同ニヤ遺跡学術調査を予備調査段階から支持いただき、1992年には正式許可を1994年には発掘許可を発出、中国政府としてニヤ調査を全面的に支持いただいた。

田辺昭三（1933-2006 京都造形芸術大学教授）：1994年より日中共同ニヤ遺跡学術調査に一門多数を率いて参加いただき、95年より第二代学術隊長として尽力をいただいた。報告書第二巻編集にも尽力、沙漠考古学に大きく貢献いただいた。

俞偉超（1933-2003 中国歴史博物館館長）：2000年、ウルムチで開催した日中共同ニヤ遺跡学術調査国際シンポジウムに参加いただくなど中国考古学界トップの立場よりニヤ調査を全面的に支持いただいた。

李遇春（1921-2003 新疆ウイグル自治区博物館副館長）：1959年、自治区成立まもない不十分な条件の中、自治区博物館隊を率いて、ニヤ遺跡調査を敢行。日中共同隊の参考にさせていただいた。

謝　辞

　日中共同ニヤ遺跡学術調査の名誉主席としてニヤ調査を全面的に支持いただき、絶大な協力をいただいた**鉄木尓・達瓦買提**元新疆ウイグル自治区主席・元中国全国人民代表会議副主席は91歳と高齢のため療養中。長寿を念じるばかりである。

中国新疆36年国際協力実録
キジル・ニヤ・ダンダンウイリク

一帯一路实践图典
克孜尔 尼雅 丹丹乌里克

Silk Road
Kizil Niya Dandanoilik

2016年「キジル千仏洞修復保存協力」開始30周年

2018年「日中共同ニヤ遺跡学術調査」開始30周年

「日中共同ダンダンウイリク遺跡学術調査」では法隆寺壁画の源流壁画発見

感謝するばかり

世界には約3300の民族、約76億人、約200の国家

宗教・歴史・体制・文化・国益は異なり

戦争・紛争・テロ・差別が頻発

相互理解はたいへん困難

だからこそ相互理解の努力が求められる

その一環として国際協力の意義は大きい

平和を守る一環でもある国際協力に老残微力を捧げる

ご指導ご支援を引き続きお願いします

（はじめに——感謝をこめて）

小島康誉

　筆者は1982年以来、中国新疆ウイグル自治区（以下新疆と略す）を150回以上訪問し、文部科学省・中国国家文物局（文化庁相当）・新疆人民政府・新疆文化庁・新疆文物局・新疆档案局・新疆文物考古研究所・ウルムチ市人民政府・新疆大学・佛教大学はじめ多くの方々のご指導ご協力をえて、新疆にのこる世界的文化遺産の調査・保護・研究、さらには人材育成事業などを実践してきた。関係者諸氏に心からの感謝を表したい。

　活動の一例を示せば、キジル千仏洞修復保存・ニヤ遺跡調査・ダンダンウイリク遺跡調査・同壁画保護・中国歴史文化遺産保護網運営・歴史档案史料刊行・新疆大学奨学金提供・新疆文化文物優秀賞提供・希望小学校建設・児童育英金提供・各種代表団派遣・招聘・各種仲介・各種寄付などである。「一帯一路」での国際協力であり、「一帯一路」の歴史交流の一端を明らかにしてきた。

　新疆人民政府は2001年に「小島康誉氏来訪20周年記念大会」、2011年に「小島康誉氏来訪30周年記念大会」を開催した。国家文物局機関紙「中国文物報」は一頁特集をくみ、ニヤ・ダンダンウイリク両遺跡の調査保護研究事業を「中国外国間共同事業と学問交流の模範例」、「多領域学問で西域考古の合作研究と保護を実施」、「中国外国学者の共同努力の傑出事業」などと最大級の評価で報道した。また同報は「小島康誉：新疆に全人生を投入する感動的日本人」と一頁ちかい大型記事、あるいは人民日報・新疆日報・NHKなど日中両国の新聞やテレビで度々報じられた。光栄なことである。

　修復保存に取り組んだキジル千仏洞は28年後の2014年世界文化遺産となり、日中共同で展開したニヤ調査では開始から7年後に中国の国宝中の国宝ともいわれる「五星出東方利中国」錦を発掘し、ダンダンウイリク調査では法隆寺金堂壁画の源流の実物資料ともいわれる屈鉄線壁画「西域のモナリザ」などを発掘し、それらの成果を何冊もの報告書や佛教大学・ウルムチ環球ホテル・北京大学での国際シンポジウムで公開し、研究保護した遺物は東京・京都・大阪・神戸・岡山やウルムチ・北京・上海・杭州・香港・台北をはじめイタリア・アメリカ・韓国などでの文物展に出陳されるほどの水準であった、更には奨学金など提供が6000人余に及び、博物館建設・農業用井戸掘削・街路灯設置……などへの評価であろう。

　私たちは、これまでにも『日中共同ニヤ遺跡学術調査報告書』・『日中共同ダンダンウイリク遺跡学術調査報告書』・『ニヤ遺跡の謎』・『新疆での世界的文化遺産保護研究事業と国際協力の意義』・『Kizil, Niya, and Dandanoilik』などを出版、あるいはWeb「ADC文化通信」・「中国歴史文化遺産保護網」に公開してきたが、専門的で文字中心なので、ビジュアル的なものをとの声が寄せられていた。そこで、大量の写真・資料から選び出し、日・中・英文を付した活動記録が本書である。そのため略している部分もあり、上記書籍なども合わせてご覧いただきたい。本書では初公開の写真・資料も多数ふくんでいる。

　一昨年は「キジル千仏洞修復保存協力」開始30周年であった。今年は「日中共同ニヤ遺跡学術調査」を開始して30周年にあたる。来年は「日中共同ダンダンウイリク遺跡学術調査」で発掘した「屈鉄線」壁画と関係深い法隆寺「鉄線描」壁画焼損70周年にあたる。このような縁ある時に本書を上梓することができ感謝するばかりである。

　世界には約3300の民族、約76億人が住み、約200の国家がある。宗教・歴史・体制・文化・国益は異なり、各地で戦争・紛争・テロ・差別が頻発している。相互理解はたいへん困難であり、だからこそ相互理解の努

力が求められる。その一環として国際協力の意義は大きい。筆者は研究者でなく、いわば国際協力手弁当長期実践家である。平和を守る国際協力に老残微力を捧げたい。皆様のご指導ご支援を引き続きお願いしたい。

　出版に際して、浅岡俊夫・安藤佳香・田中清美・吉崎伸各氏よりエッセイを寄せていただいた。周培彦・高田和行両氏には中・英訳で尽力いただき、浅岡俊夫氏には各遺構番号を確認いただいた。東方出版の今東成人会長・稲川博久社長・装丁家濱崎実幸氏はじめ諸氏にはこれまで同様お世話になった。心から感謝いたします。

2018年7月　ニューヨークにて

序言—衷心致谢

小岛康誉

　　笔者自1982年以来，已经访问中国新疆维吾尔自治区（以下简称新疆）150余次，在文部科学省、中国国家文物局（相当于日本文化厅）、新疆人民政府、新疆文化厅、新疆文物局、新疆档案局、新疆文物考古研究所、乌鲁木齐市人民政府、新疆大学、佛教大学等众多人士的指导和支持下，一直致力于考察、保护、研究新疆的世界性文化遗产，以及人才培养事业的实践活动。在此向各位相关人士表示衷心的感谢。

　　具体事例有：修复保护克孜尔千佛洞、调查尼雅遗址、对丹丹乌里克遗址的调查及壁画修复、运营中国历史文化遗产保护网、出版历史档案史料、提供新疆大学奖学金和新疆文化文物优秀奖、捐建希望小学、提供儿童育英金、派遣或邀请各类代表团、各种斡旋以及各类捐款等。是"一带一路"上的国际合作，揭示了"一带一路"上历史交流的部分史实。

　　新疆人民政府于2001年召开"小岛康誉来新疆20周年纪念大会"、2011年又召开了"小岛康誉来新疆30周年纪念大会"。国家文物局机关报"中国文物报"刊登了整版报道，高度评价尼雅、丹丹乌里克两遗址的考察保护事业是"中外合作与学科沟通的范例"、"多领域开展西域考古的研究合作与保护"、"中外学者共同努力的杰出事业"。该报同时整版刊登题为"小岛康誉：一个感动全新疆的日本人"的文章，人民日报、新疆日报、ＮＨＫ等中日两国报纸和电视多次予以报道，我倍感光荣。

　　参与保护修复的克孜尔千佛洞于28年后的2014年成为世界文化遗产；中日共同开展的尼雅考察在第7年出土了堪称国宝中的国宝的"五星出东方利中国"织锦；通过丹丹乌里克考察，发现了当为法隆寺金堂壁画之源的史料实物—届铁盘丝壁画"西域的蒙娜丽莎"等，上述成果都通过多册报告书以及在佛教大学、乌鲁木齐环球酒店、北京大学召开的国际研讨会上发表，研究保护的文物也在东京、京都、大阪、神户、冈山、乌鲁木齐、北京、上海、杭州、香港、台北以及英国、美国、韩国等地的文物展上展出，水平很高；向6000余人提供了奖学金等；捐建博物馆、挖掘农业用井和安装路灯等，所有荣誉应该是对我上述实践的表彰吧。

　　我们通过出版《中日共同尼雅遗址学术调查报告书》、《中日共同丹丹乌里克遗址学术调查报告书》、《尼雅遗址之谜》、《新疆世界性文化遗产保护研究事业与国际合作的意义》、《Kizil, Niya, and Dandanoilik》等书，或者通过网络"ADC文化通信"、"中国历史文化遗产保护网"公开研究成果，有读者指出多以文字为主，希望加些图像，于是从大量的照片和资料中精心挑选并配上中日英解说编辑成了这本活动记录书，所以有些部分省略了，请大家结合上述书籍一起阅读，本书中含有大量首次公开的照片和资料。

　　前年是"克孜尔千佛洞修复保护协力"30周年，今年又值"中日共同尼雅遗址学术调查"30周年，明年将迎来与"中日共同丹丹乌里克遗址学术调查"发现的"届铁盘丝"壁画渊源很深的法隆寺"铁线描"壁画烧毁

70周年，能在这样一个有缘之时出版此书，感恩不尽。

世界上约有3300个民族、76亿人口、200个国家，宗教、历史、体制、文化、国情各不相同，各地战争、纠纷、恐袭、歧视频繁发生。相互理解十分困难，因此才需要为相互理解而努力，作为其中一环的国际合作意义深远。笔者不是学者，应该说是"国际合作长期自费实践家"，愿为守护和平之国际合作贡献绵薄之力。希望各位继续予以指教和支持。

值此出版之际，浅冈俊夫、安藤佳香、田中清美、吉崎伸各位执笔作文；周培彦、高田和行二位倾情翻译；浅冈俊夫仔细确认各个遗迹编号；东方出版社的今东成人会长、稻川博之社长、滨崎实幸装丁家等各位一如既往予以支持，深表感谢。

2018年7月　于纽约

Preface
With Gratitude

Yasutaka Kojima

I have visited the Xinjiang Uyghur Autonomous Region of China, hereafter called Xinjiang, more than 150 times since 1982 and made the researches, the conservations, and the studies of world-class cultural heritages having survived in Xinjiang, as well as developed human resources there, with mentors and supports of people at the following institutions: the Ministry of Education, Culture, Sports, Science and Technology of Japan, the Chinese State Administration of Cultural Heritage (hereinafter called as SACH Chinese) which is corresponding to the Cultural Affairs Agency of Japan, the People's Government of the Xinjiang Region, the Xinjiang Cultural Agency, the Xinjiang Cultural Assets Bureau, the Xinjiang Archives Bureau, the Xinjiang Archaeological Institute, the People's Government of Urumqi, Xinjiang University, and Bukkyo University. I would like to express my hearty thanks to those who have been involved in the initiatives as mentioned above.

Take some projects for example: the restoration and conservation of the Kizil grottoes, the research of the Niya ruins; the research of the Dandanoilik ruins and the preservation of its murals; operation of the websites to conserve Chinese historical, cultural heritages, the publication of the archaeological archives, funding for scholarship for Xinjiang University, the presentation of the awards for outstanding performances for Xinjiang cultures and relics, construction of Kibo Elementary Schools, funding for education of grade-schoolers, dispatching or inviting various delegations, serving as an intermediary in various affairs, and contributions for various events. Those projects have embodied international cooperation in light of "One Belt, One Road" and demonstrated part of historical interactions in the course of "One Belt, One Road."

The People's Government of the Xinjiang Region held the 20th and the 30th anniversaries of Mr. Yasutaka Kojima's visit in 2001 and 2011, respectively. The official paper of SACH Chinese, or Chinese Cultural Resources News, has featured the research and conservation projects both in Niya and Dandanoilik devoting to one full page to report with such superlatives as "the role model for joint projects and academic interactions between China and other nations," "the collaborative research and preservation work on the archaeology of the Western Regions in multiple academic areas," and "the outstanding project with enormous efforts made by Chinese and overseas scholars." The same paper has also devoted almost a full page to feature "Yasutaka Kojima: the inspiring Japanese who has been dedicating his entire life to Xinjiang," which has been repeatedly reported in various newspapers and by television, including People's Daily, the Xinjiang Daily, NHK, and so forth, both in Japan and China. I am really honored.

The Kizil grottoes became the World Cultural Heritage in 2014 after I had tried to restore and conserve it for 28 years. As a result of the seven-year Japan-China joint research of the Niya ruins, the silk brocade "Five stars appearing in the east bring good fortune to China" was excavated and reported as national treasure among national treasures. Then, the Dandanoilik research excavated the mural drawn by wire line called "The Mona Lisa in the Western Regions" which is said to be the real-life material from which the Horyuji mural painting originated. Those achievements have been publicly released by a number of reports and shown in the international symposiums at Bukkyo University, Urumqi World Plaza Hotel and Peking University. The researched and conserved relics have reached a level so high enough as to be exhibited in cities like Tokyo, Kyoto, Osaka, Kobe, Okayama, Urumqi, and other cities in Italy, America and Korea. On top of all that, I have been engaged in such projects as 6,000 or more scholarship recipients, construction of a museum, digging wells for agricultural use, placement of street lamps and a good many others, all of which may have led me to receiving a high admiration as such.

We have so far produced a fair amount of publication, such as The Report of Japan-China Joint Scholarly Research of the Niya Ruins, The Report of Japan-China Joint Scholarly Research of the Dandanoilik Ruins, The Mysteries of the Niya Ruins, The Projects to Preserve and Research World-class Cultural Heritages in Xinjiang and the Significance of International Cooperation, and Kizil, Niya, and Dandanoilik, or publicly released them via websites like info@adcculture.com and www.wenbao.net. Whereas those are meant for character-oriented specialists, we have had many requests for more visual formats. Thus, this book is intended to show the activity log carrying many photos selected from a huge number of materials written in Japanese, Chinese, and English. That's why, as some parts are skipped, would you enjoy it along with those books mentioned above. There are a number of photos and materials released for the first time in this book.

Two years ago, we celebrated the 30th anniversary of the founding of the association to help restore and conserve the Kizil grottoes. This year falls on the 30th anniversary of the start of Japan-China joint scholarly research of the Niya ruins. Next year falls on the 70th anniversary of the fire damage of the Horyuji temple's mural "drawn by iron-line." It originated in the mural drawn by "flexed iron-line" which was excavated in the course of "Japan-China Joint Scholarly Research of the Dandanoilik ruins" I am very pleased to be given an opportunity to publish the book on this kind of meaningful occasion.

The world consists of approximately 3,300 races, has about 7.6 billion people, and comprises around 200 nations. There exist different religions, histories, institutions, cultures, and national interests, which have frequently given rise to wars, conflicts, terrorism, and discrimination. As mutual understanding is too tough to achieve, efforts to achieve it is all the more called for. International cooperation can be a crucial part of those efforts. Indeed, I am not a scholar, yet I am, as it were, a lifelong volunteer for international cooperation. Though being aged, I would like to devote myself to international cooperation to secure peace. I would like to ask you for further guidance and assistance.

On the occasion of publication of this edition, essays are contributed by Mr. Toshio Asaoka, Ms. Yoshika Ando, Mr. Kiyomi Tanaka, and Mr, Shin Yoshizaki. Chinese and Japanese translations are handled by Ms. Zhou Pei Yan and Mr. Kazuyuki Takada, respectively. Mr. Toshio Asaoka kindly reconfirms the number of each relic. As always, I owe much of this publication to Chairman Narihito Imahigashi, President Hirohisa Inagawa, Designer Saneyuki Hamazaki and others of Toho Shuppan.

July 2018   In New York

目次　目录　Contents

はじめに 008
序言　Preface

I　中国・新疆ウイグル自治区 ……………………………………… 015
新疆维吾尔自治区　Xinjiang Uygur Autonomous Region

II　キジル千仏洞修復保存協力 ……………………………………… 019
克孜尔千佛洞修復保存协力　Cooperation Restore and Conserve the Kizil Grottoes

III　日中共同ニヤ遺跡学術調査 ……………………………………… 055
中日共同尼雅遗址学术考察　The Japan-China Joint Scholarly Research of The Niya Ruins

IV　寄稿エッセイ ………………………………………………………… 152
随笔投稿　Contributed essays

V　日中共同ダンダンウイリク遺跡学術調査 ……………………… 157
中日共同丹丹乌里克遗址学术考察　The Japan-China Joint Scholarly Research of The Dandanoilik Ruins

VI　関連活動 ……………………………………………………………… 221
相关活动　Related Projects

VII　国際協力の意義 …………………………………………………… 245
国际合作意义　The Significance of International Cooperation

VIII　36年略年譜 ……………………………………………………… 258
36年简略年谱　Chronological record of my 36 years

おわりに 266
结束语　Epilogue

凡　例

- 本書は小島康誉著『新疆での世界的文化遺産保護研究事業と国際協力の意義』（佛教大学宗教文化ミュージアム2013）および小島康誉編『Kizil, Niya, and Dandanoilik』（英文・東方出版2016）をベースに後発事項などを加え、筆者が多くの方々のご尽力ご協力をえて、中国・新疆ウイグル自治区で行ってきた世界的文化遺産保護研究・人材育成・関連活動の写真と資料による活動記録である。

  そのため略している部分もあり、上記書籍や下記報告書も合わせてご覧いただきたい。写真は必ずしも当該年に記載していない。海外読者の便を考慮し部分的に中・英文も付した。

- 中訳は周培彦氏、英訳は高田和行氏に尽力いただいた。感謝いたします。

- 人名については必要に応じて当時の役職を記した。どのような立場の人が関わったかを記録として残すためである。敬称は略した。調査隊員の役職については調査組織で記した。中国人名表記については便宜的に相当する日本漢字を用いた。ウイグル族名表記は中国での表記にしたがい、名と姓（父名）の間に半角中グロいりで記した。地名の日本語表記については一般的なものを記し、必要に応じて中国語でも記した

- 紙幅の都合上、写真撮影者は各所に記入していない。大半は筆者撮影である。一部に寺尾恭久・堀尾寶・北野博之・浅岡俊夫・杉本和樹・佐藤右文・奥山大石・乾哲也・安藤佳香・本多廣賢・松田奈月・孫躍新・周培彦・劉暁慶・李軍・劉国瑞・伊弟利斯・阿不都熱蘇勒・張玉忠・于志勇・甘偉・胡平・楊新才・趙新利各氏や新疆ウイグル自治区人民政府・新疆ウイグル自治区文化庁・新疆ウイグル自治区文物局・新疆ウイグル自治区档案局・新疆大学・佛教大学・日中共同ニヤ遺跡学術調査隊・日中共同ダンダンウイリク遺跡学術調査隊・NHK・天津テレビ撮影分を含んでいる。感謝いたします。

- 日中両国の新聞記事も転載させていただいた。感謝いたします。なお一部は時間経過で変色している。

- 日中友好キジル千仏洞修復保存協力会「募金パンフレット」（1987）・「贈呈最終報告」（1989）・佛教大学内ニヤ遺跡学術研究機構編『シルクロード・ニヤ遺跡の謎』（東方出版2002）・日中共同ニヤ遺跡学術調査隊『日中共同ニヤ遺跡学術調査報告書』（法蔵館1996・中村印刷1999・真陽社2007）・日中共同ダンダンウイリク遺跡学術調査隊『日中共同ダンダンウイリク遺跡学術調査報告書』（真陽社2007・文物出版社2009）・各シンポジウム発表要旨などからも転載させていただいた。感謝いたします。

Ⅰ 中国・新疆ウィグル自治区

（どこに）

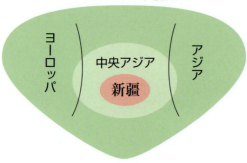

新疆はユーラシア大陸の中心
新疆是欧亚大陆中心
Xinjiang is situated in the heart of the Eurasian Continent

新疆は中国西北部に所在
新疆位于中国西北部
Xinjiang is located in the northwest of China

（どんな）

新疆の中心都市ウルムチ
新疆的中心城市乌鲁木齐
Urumqi, the central city of Xinjiang

タクラマカン沙漠
塔克拉玛干沙漠
Taklamakan Desert

天山山脈
天山山脉
Tianshan Mountains

新疆の主要都市
新疆的主要城市
Major cities in Xinjiang

016

（歴史・面積・民族・人口・産業）

新疆ウイグル自治区は1955年10月1日に成立した。東西南北の文明文化が行きかったいわゆる「シルクロード」の中央に位置し、モンゴル・ロシア・カザフスタン・キルギスタン・タジキスタン・アフガニスタン・パキスタン・インドと国境を接し、国境線は約5600kmにおよぶ。地政学的に古来より重要な一帯であり、古には東西交通の要衝の地であり、19世紀から20世紀にかけては欧米で「グレイトゲーム」と称された領土争奪を目的とした探検・諜報戦が展開された。現代では「一帯一路」のひとつの中心として大きな意味を持っている。

面積は約166万km²、中国の約六分の一、日本の約4.4倍。アルタイ・天山・崑崙の三大山脈がジュンガル盆地とタクラマカン沙漠をはさむかのように聳えている。5000〜7000m級の峰々は万年雪や氷河におおわれ、バインブルクなどの草原には高山植物が咲き乱れ、羊・牛・馬・山羊などが放牧されている。

新疆を理解するキーワードは、シルクロード・多民族・資源・一帯一路の4点であろう。多くの文明文化が行きかい楼蘭・キジル・ニヤに代表される世界的文化遺産が各地に点在している。文明文化を運んだのは人々であり、ウイグル・漢・カザフ・回・モンゴル・キルギス・シボ・タジク・満州・タタール・ウズベク・ダフール・ロシア各族を中心に47民族、約2500万人が協力しあって生活している。

石油・天然ガス・石炭・レアメタルなどが大量に埋蔵されていて、開発が始まっている。タクラマカン沙漠はかつて「死亡の海」と言われていたが、いまでは「希望の海」に変わった。中心都市ウルムチには高層ビルが林立し、近隣諸国との経済活動は活況を呈している。日本企業の進出も始まっている。

新疆が広く日本で知られるようになったのは1980〜81年放送されたNHKと中国中央テレビ共同取材番組「シルクロード」によって、神秘の扉が開かれたことによる。

2009年7月、ウルムチで騒乱が発生し、9月には大規模デモが行われ、これらの大量報道により世界から注目を集めた。2010年、張春賢中国共産党中央政治局委員・新疆ウイグル自治区委員会書記（現全人代副委員長）時代に中国政府による大規模な全面的支援が開始され、後任の陳全国中国共産党中央政治局委員・新疆ウイグル自治区委員会書記により更に強化され、歴史的大発展期を迎えている。騒乱で減少していた投資や観光客なども戻っている。

改革開放40年をへて中国の経済発展は目覚しく、新疆でも投資と観光ブームで各地からのビジネス関係者や観光客があふれている。今後さらに歴史的変化をとげるであろう。

历史 面积 民族 人口 产业

新疆维吾尔自治区成立于1955年10月1日。位于东西文明文化交汇的"丝绸之路"正中，与蒙古、俄罗斯、哈萨克斯坦、吉尔吉斯斯坦、塔吉克斯坦、阿富汗、巴基斯坦、印度接壤，国境线长达5600公里，自古以来就是地缘政治学领域的重要地带，古代还是东西交通要塞，19世纪至20世纪，欧美展开了以掠夺领土为目的探险和谍报战，史称"大博弈"。即使是当代，作为"一带一路"的中心之一，也具有重要的意义。

面积约166万平方公里，大约占中国的六分之一，约为日本的4.4倍。阿尔泰山、天山和昆仑山将准格尔盆地和塔克拉玛干盆地围在中间，高耸入云。5000〜7000米高的各个山峰被常年积雪和冰河覆盖、巴音布鲁克草原上高山植被丰富，放牧着羊、牛、马及山羊。

理解新疆的关键词有四个：丝绸之路、多民族、资源、一带一路。各种文明文化在此交融，分布着以楼兰、克孜尔、尼雅为代表的世界性文化遗产。传播文明文化的是人，以维族、汉族、哈萨克族、回族、蒙古族、吉尔吉斯族、锡伯族、塔吉克族、满族、塔塔尔族、乌孜别克族、达斡尔族、俄罗斯族为主的47个民族，约2500万人口在此生活、相互扶持。

这里埋藏着石油、天然气、煤炭、稀有金属等大量资源，正在进行开发。塔克拉玛干沙漠过去被称为"死亡之海"，现在已经变成了"希望之海"，中心城市乌鲁木齐高楼林立，与周边邻国的经济交往活跃，日本企业也开始进入。

新疆在日本为人所知是因为1980〜81年NHK与中国中央电视台合拍节目"丝绸之路"的播出，由此敞开了其神秘之门。

2009年7月，乌鲁木齐发生暴乱，9月发生大规模游行，这些报道引起了全世界的关注。2010年，中国共产党中央政治局委员张春贤任新疆维吾尔自治区委员会书记（现任全国人大副委员长）时期，新疆获得中国政府大规模的全面支持，后来接

任的中国共产党中央政治局委员·新疆维吾尔自治区委员会书记陈全国时期，支持政策进一步强化，新疆迎来了历史性的发展时期。暴乱减少、投资及游客逐步恢复。

经过40年的改革开放，中国的经济发展显著，新疆也借投资旅游热潮，到处都是来自各地的商界人士和游客，今后定会进一步呈现历史性的变化。

History, Area, Races, Population, and Industry

The Xinjiang Uyghur Autonomous Region was established on October 1, 1955. It is located in the center of the Silk Road where cultures from the north, the south, the east and the west have interacted. It has borders with Mongol, Russia, Kazakhstan, Kyrgyzstan, Tajikistan, Afghanistan, Pakistan and India, stretching about 5,600 km. This Region has been seen as a geopolitically important area and a strategic point between East and West. Thus, information warfare called "the Great Game" was developed among the Western nations aimed at territory grabbing for the period between the end of the 19th century and the beginning of the 20th century. Currently, it holds great political significance as one of contact points from the Chinese side in the light of "One Belt, One Road."

The Region has an area about 1.66 million square kilometers, occupies around one sixth of China and is approximately 4.4 times larger than Japan. Three great mountains of Altai, Tianshan, and Kunlun surround the Dzungaria Basin and the Taklamakan Desert. The peaks of those mountains reaching as high as 5,000 to 7,000 meters are covered with eternal snows and the glaciers. The grassland like Bayinbuluke is filled with blooming alpine plants, where sheep, cows, horses, and goats are pastured.

The four key words to understand Xinjiang can be described as: the Silk Road, a multiethnic community, natural resources, and "One Belt, One Road." This is where a whole variety of cultures have been interacting and world-class cultural heritages represented by Loulan, Kizil, and Niya are found all around. Those who have brought in civilizations and cultures are such people as Uyghur, Han, Kazakh, Hui, Mongol, Kirgiz, Xibe, Tajik, Manchu, Tartar, Uzbek, Daur, Russian, and others, in total 47 ethnics with the population of approximately 25 million. They are working together for their daily lives.

Vast natural resources like petroleum, natural gas, coal, rare metals, and water lie here and their development has just started. Whereas the Taklamakan Desert used to be called "the death sea," at present it has turned out to be "the hope sea." Urumqi, or the central city, is bristled with high-rise buildings and enjoys booming transactions with neighboring nations. Japanese firms' advancement is going on now, as well.

That Xinjiang became widely known in Japan was when lots of mysteries were unwrapped by the pool coverage program The Silk Road released jointly by NHK (Japan Broadcasting Corporation) and China Central Television which had been broadcast from 1980 through 1981.

As intensively reported in the media, the Uyghur insurrection in Urumqi in July 2009 followed by a large-scale demonstration in September attracted worldwide attention. In the era of Zhang Chunxian who assumed the positions of the Chinese Communist Party (hereinafter called CCP) Central Committee Member and Secretary of the CCP in charge of Xinjiang in 2010, currently being the Vice-Chairman of the National People's Congress (hereinafter called NPC), Chinese Government's massive and all-out support started. As his successor Chen Quanguo who is the CCP Central Committee Member and Secretary of the CCP in charge of Xinjiang has boosted this support further, Xinjiang is undergoing historically great development. Investors and tourists once having extremely decreased due to the unrests are beginning to return.

In 40 years after its reform and door-opening policies, China has remarkably developed in economic terms. Xinjiang, as well, is flooded with business people and tourists from everywhere thanks to the boom of investors and tourists. It will surely undergo a historical change from now on.

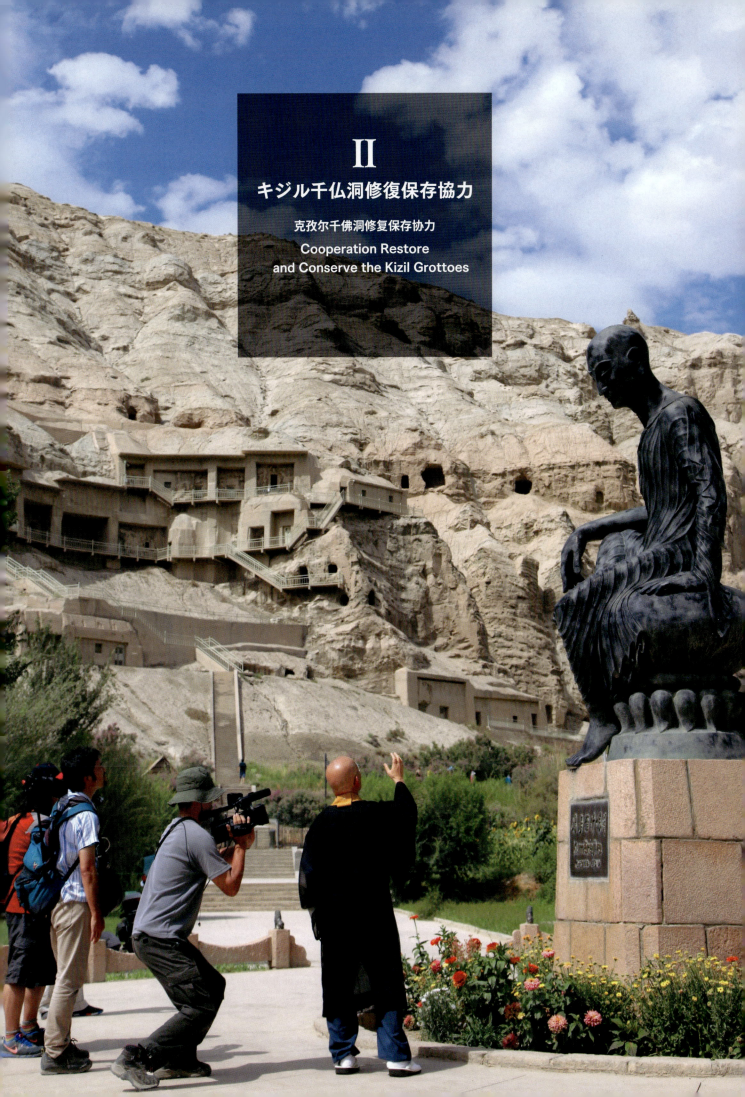

II
キジル千仏洞修復保存協力
克孜尔千佛洞修复保存协力
Cooperation Restore and Conserve the Kizil Grottoes

II キジル千仏洞修復保存協力

1982
新疆初訪問

1982年6月、筆者は宝石買付に新疆を訪れるも高品質品は無く、工芸品公司の案内で交河故城など参観。大雨のため道路通行止めとなり、貨物列車に緊急乗車しウルムチへ帰った。豊富な文化財と温かい人情に魅せられ、その後も度々訪問しプレミアム・アンティークカーペット・玉などを買い付けた。

1982年6月，笔者为采购宝石来到新疆，但是没有找到高品质的宝石，却在工艺品公司的带领下参观了交河故城等地。大雨造成道路不通，紧急改乘货车返回乌鲁木齐。丰富的文化遗产和温暖的人情深深地感染了我，之后多次访问新疆，还购买了优质古丝毯、玉等。

Although I visited Xinjiang to source jewelries in June 1982, there were no quality gems available there. Instead, I went on a sightseeing tour of Ancient City of Jiao River with a staff member of the craftwork bureau as a guide. On my way back, the road was closed due to heavy rain, so that we could not help but take a freight train to go back to Urumqi. Having been attracted to people's humble, warm heart as well as abundant cultural assets, I more often than not visited there to buy premium antique rugs, gemstones, and so on.

交河故城参観後、貨物列車で戻る／参观交河故城后乘货车返回／Return by freight train after visiting Ancient City of Jiao River

1986
キジル千仏洞初参観・個人寄付

1986年5月、筆者は工芸品公司の案内でキジル千仏洞を参観した。盛春寿新疆文化庁処員（後に新疆文物局長）らが同行した。敦煌・雲崗・龍門とならぶ中国四大石窟である。およそ3～8世紀に造営された。クチャ（庫車）西方約70kmの北緯41度47分・東経82度31分一帯の断崖約3kmに約300の石窟が穿たれている。海抜は1100m前後である。荒れ果てた石窟に膨大の壁画、「人類共通の文化遺産だ」と直感した。貧しい中でも細々と保護活動する人たち。この二つの感動が案内してくれた王世田職員の冗談「10万人民元出してくれたら小島さん専用窟を造ってあげる」に「窟は要らないが、10万元は出す、保護に使って」と即答。協議書を交わし、新疆政府の許可を得たのち振り込んだ。

1986年5月，笔者在工艺品公司的带领下参观了克孜尔千佛洞，新疆文化厅处员盛春寿（后任新疆文物局长）与我同行。该石窟与敦煌、云冈、龙门并称中国四大石窟。建于公元3世纪至8世纪，在库车以西70公里、位于北纬41度47分、东经82度31分的断崖中约3公里中穿凿了约300个石窟，海拔在1100米左右。在破败的石窟内存留着大量的壁画，直觉告诉我"这是人类共同的文化遗产"；在艰苦环境下坚持不懈进行保护的人们，这两点深深地打动了我，面对带我来的王世田的玩笑"你如果出10万人民币，就建一座小岛专用窟"，我即刻回答"我不要石窟，我出10万人民币用于保护"。签署协议书，获得新疆政府许可后马上就汇款了。

In May 1986, I visited the Kizil grottoes with a staff member of the craftwork bureau as a guide. Member of the Xinjiang Cultural Agency Sheng Chunshou who later became the Director of the Xinjiang Cultural Assets Bureau accompanied us. It is one of the four great Chinese grottoes, including Dunhuang, Yungang, and Longmen having been built around the third through the eighth century, which is located about 70 km west of Kuqa in the area of 41 degrees 47 minutes northern latitude and 82 degrees 31 minutes eastern longitude at a height of approximately 1,110 m above sea level. It has about 300 grottoes bored into the cliff stretching about 3 km. A huge number of murals depicted within the deserted grottoes stimulated my instinct enough to tell me that this could be a common cultural heritage of mankind. And I saw the people there slowly yet diligently engaged in conservation activities. Having been moved emotionally by these two scenes, when Wang Shitian, the staff member, made a joke to me, "If Mr. Kojima kindly offers CNY 100,000, we will make a practice cave exclusively for you." I instantly responded, "All right, I don't need my practice cave, but will offer that amount." We mutually signed the memorandum of understanding and I remitted that amount after receiving the authorization of the Xinjiang Government.

1986年 谷西区全景／1986年 谷西区全景／The full view of the west valley area in 1986

キジル千仏洞略位置図
克孜尔千佛洞简略位置图／Brief map of the Kizil grottoes

石窟分布図／石窟分布图／The distribution chart of the grottoes

1986年 危険な梯子と痛々しい第38窟／1986年 危险的梯子和令人心痛的第38窟／The risky ladders and the pitiful 38th grotto in 1986

合掌する筆者／笔者合掌／Joining my hands in prayer　　協議書／协议书　　領収書／收据／Receipt
　　　　　　　　　　　　　　　　　　　　　The agreement of understanding

当時はキジルや天池さえ特別許可を必要とした
当时连克孜尔和天池都需要特别许可
The special authorization being required even to visit Kizil and Tianchi in those days

梯子２番目が筆者／梯子上的第二人是笔者／Joining my hands in prayer

1987
１億円贈呈調印

　その後も訪れ中国政府が2000万人民元で修復すると聞き、それなら日本で浄財を募り修復保存費用１億円を寄付すると提案、数度の交渉を経て、1987年５月20日新疆ウイグル自治区の最高指導者・王恩茂中国政治協商会議全国委員会副主席（前新疆書記）列席をえて、新疆迎賓館で王成文新疆文化庁書記と調印した。

之后再次访问时听说中国政府要斥资2000万人民币进行修复，于是我提议在日本募捐1亿日元用于修复保护，经过数次交涉，1987年5月20日，在新疆维吾尔自治区最高领导人、全国政协副主席王恩茂（前新疆书记）的列席下，在新疆宾馆与新疆文化厅王成书记签署协议书。

Upon my visit later, I heard that the Chinese Government had put up CNY 20 million to conduct restoration of the Kizil grottoes and then I offered to contribute another JPY 100 million for restoration and conservation by launching a fund-raising campaign across Japan. After several negotiations, we finally could welcome the Head of Xinjiang and Vice-Chairman of the National Committee of the Chinese People's Political Consultative Conference Wang Enmao (the former Secretary of Xinjiang) at the signing ceremony at the Xinjiang Guest Palace on May 20, 1987 where Secretary of the Xinjiang Cultural Agency Wang Chengwen and I signed the memorandum of understanding.

人類共通の文化遺産を後世へ

協議書調印式／协议书签字仪式／The signing ceremony of the memorandum of understanding

1億円贈呈協議書／1亿日元捐赠协议／The memorandum of understanding to contribute JPY 100 million

1987
日中友好キジル千仏洞修復保存協力会設立

筆者は塩川正十郎文部大臣の示唆を受けつつ募金母体「日中友好キジル千仏洞修復保存協力会」結成に向けて中山太郎衆議院議員・上村晃史上村工業社長はじめ各界著名人に役員就任をお願いし、1987年11月設立にこぎつけた。専務理事を担当し、事務所は社長を務めていたツルカメコーポレーションに置かせていただいた。協力会役員には平凡社『中国石窟・キジル石窟』3巻セットを贈呈し、理解を深めてもらった。

笔者经文部大臣盐川正十郎的示意，着手成立募捐主体"日中友好克孜尔千佛洞修复保存协力会"，邀请众议院议员中山太郎、上村工业社长上村晃史等各界名流担任重要职务，1987年11月成功设立。笔者担任专务理事，将事务所设在时任社长的鹤龟公司内。向协力会各位要员赠送了平凡社出版的《中国石窟 克孜尔石窟》三卷套，以加深他们的理解。

Having been inspired by then Education Minister Masajuro Shiokawa, I asked Taro Nakayama, a Lower House Member, Koshi Uemura, the President of C. Uyemura & Co., Ltd. and many other grand people from various fields to assume the board members of "The Japan-China Friendship Association to Restore and Conserve the Kizil Grottoes" and established it in November 1987. I was in charge of the representative director and set up the secretariat at Tsurukame Corporation where I used to serve as the president. I presented the board members Chinese Grottoes and the Kizil Grottoes in three volumes published by Heibonsha to deepen their understanding.

以下は募金勧誘用パンフレット
以下是募捐用的宣传册
The following are leaflets to solicit for a contribution

ご喜捨のお願い

謹啓　時下、益々ご清祥の御事とお慶び申し上げます。さて、日本と中国は古来より友好往来を重ね、我が国は隣国中国より、漢字、製紙術、律令国家制度、書道、仏教、建築など、いくたの文明文化を学んでまいりました。一時、不幸の期間もありましたが、今日再び、両国の友好は高まっております。

ご高承の如く、釈尊により、インドで興りました仏教は西域を通り、中国へ伝わり、朝鮮半島、日本へと伝来し、日本文化の根幹をなしてまいりました。

中国新疆ウイグル自治区はかつて西域仏教の栄えた地域で、高名な玄奘三蔵や、鳩摩羅什三蔵が活躍した処でありますが、11世紀以降のイスラム教の侵入等により、仏教はほぼ全滅すると共に、数多くの仏教寺院等は、その時の破壊と自然崩壊、そして今世紀初頭の日本をはじめ諸外国の中央アジア探険ブームの中で、いくつかの文化財が持ち去られるなどにより廃墟となりました。

その中でも最大の仏教遺跡がキジル千仏洞であります。ウィガン河の北岸約2キロにわたって、大小さまざまな石窟が堀られ、現在236の石窟が保存されておりますが、その荒廃ぶりは目をおおうものがあり、当時のままを残す美しい石窟もありますが、その大半はわずか形のみ残るもの、壁画がわずかに残るものなど殆どの御仏はお痛わしい限りであります。

この度、中国が巨費を投じて、修復保存を5年計画で行う事となり、日本隊も文化財を持ち出したという過去の経緯もあり、人類の文化遺産を後世に伝うべく「日中友好キジル千仏洞修復保存協力会」を結成し、皆様方よりのご喜捨をお願いする運びとなりました。

中国側も本会の活動を高く評価しております。どうか、私共の意のある処をおくみとり頂きまして、格別のご配慮を頂けます様お願い申し上げます。

末筆ながら、貴方様の益々のご活躍を祈念いたしております。　合掌

日中友好キジル千仏洞修復保存協力会　名誉顧問　**中山太郎**
（日中友好議員連盟理事　元自治大臣）

会　長　**上村晃史**
（上村工業社長　中国東北工学院講師）

かつて10mを越える大立仏があった第47窟

歓迎のことば

克孜尔千佛洞是中国四大石窟之一，已有一千七百多年的历史。长期以来，虽然风雨剥蚀，但至今仍保存了二百多座石窟，一万多平米壁画。这些精美的壁画不仅是研究佛学、佛教艺术，特别是印度佛教史的珍贵资料，还是研究历史学、考古学、民族学、美术史、古语言文字学等许多学科的难得的综合资料。

克孜尔千佛洞在中国新疆的拜城县境内，虽然地处偏远，但它的艺术和研究价值却早为世界学者所重视。幕名去克孜尔千佛洞参观的各国的学者、艺术家和旅游者络绎不绝，其中日本朋友最多。他们回国后撰写了大量文章，有的还出版了画册。中国古代劳动人民留下的这份珍贵文化遗产，其影响超越了一国范围，扩大到了世界各国。

我国早在三十年前就把克孜尔千佛洞列为国家的重点文物保护单位，并建立了专门保护机构。为加强对石窟壁画和保护技术的研究，前几年成立了"新疆龟兹石窟研究所"。目前正在国家文物局的大力支持下，开展对克孜尔千佛洞的维修工作。

维修石窟壁画，必须用物理的、化学的方法加固巨大而结构松散的山崖，这就需要大量的资金。"日中友好克孜尔千佛洞修复保护协力会"的日本朋友为维修石窟、壁画慷慨捐献资金，这有助于石窟、壁画的加快维修和对这份珍贵文化遗产的保护。在此特表感谢。

一九八七年五月二十日

中国人民政治协商会议全国委员会　副主席　**王恩茂**

第177窟〜184窟

キジル千仏洞は中国四大石窟の一つで、すでに千七百年余を経ています。長年にわたる風雨の侵食が激しい中、今なお二百余りの石窟と一万平米以上の壁画が保存されており、学問各分野にとって得難い遺産です。

キジル千仏洞は新疆の拝城県に位置し、辺境の地にもかかわらず、その芸術性と研究材料としての価値は早くから世界中の学者に注目されていました。この中国古代労働人民が残した貴重な文化遺産については、多くの文献、写真集が出版せられその高い評価は世界各国へ広がっています。わが国は三十年以上前から、キジル千仏洞を国家の重点文物保護単位（日本でいう国宝）とし、専門的な保護機構をつくりさらに新疆亀茲石窟研究所を設立しました。このたび国文物局の方針によりキジル千仏洞修復工事を開始することになりました。

石窟壁画の修復に多額の資金が必要であり「日中友好キジル千仏洞修復保存協力会」の日本の方々からの資金援助は、石窟壁画の早急な修復及び貴重な文化遺産の保護にとって朗報であります。ここに特に感謝の意を表します。（大意）

副会長	五百木 茂 (三菱商事 常務)	小山 勇 (中日新聞 常務)	林 寛子 (扇 千景 参議院議員)	顧問 神田 延祐 (三和銀行 副頭取)
	大岡 昇 (大林組 副社長)	須賀 武 (野村証券 副社長)	松原 哲明 (臨済宗妙心寺派龍源寺 住職)	奈良 久彌 (三菱銀行 副頭取)
	奥住 正道 (奥住マネジメント研究所 所長)	鈴木 允 (東海テレビ放送 会長)	水谷 幸正 (仏教大学 学長)	森田 武 (三井仏 常任監査役)
	川崎 元雄 (甲南大学 元学長)	中島 茂清 (全国中小企業団体中央会 前副会長)	安田 暎胤 (薬師寺 執事長)	
	木村 英一 (大阪市立大学 前学長)	西川 俊男 (ユニー 社長)	横瀬 昌夫 (住友金属鉱山 専務)	専務理事 小島 康誉 (ツルカメコーポレーション 社長)
	栗原 徹 (日本信販 専務)	野崎 辰男 (安田火災海上保険 副社長)	渡辺 信済 (京都大学 名誉教授)	

五十音順・役職は'87年10月現在

人類共通の文化遺産　キジル千仏洞を後世へ

谷西区を望む

　　　　人々はどの様な願いをこめて　この千仏洞を穿ち
　　　　　　　　御仏を描いたのでしょう
　およそ一千年という気も遠くなる長い年月　つくり続けられたキジル千仏洞
　　　考古学　民族学　東西文化交流史　美術史　仏教学など多方面からの
　　　　　本格的研究の待たれる貴重な遺産を後世に伝えよう

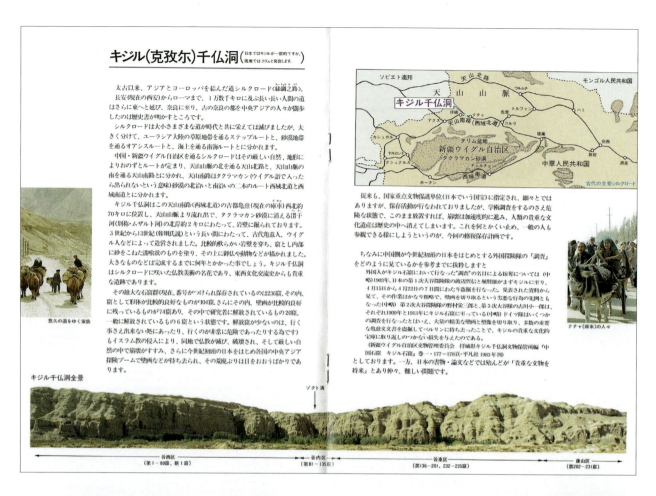

役員社員諸氏と募金活動に奔走

　1987年12月より「人類共通の文化遺産を後世へ」を掲げて募金を開始した。キジル千仏洞は敦煌などと違って殆ど知られていなく、募金は難渋した。役員社員は駆けずり回り、取引先にもお願いした。メディアに報道も依頼した。

　1987年12月掲旗"将人类共同的文化遗产传与后世"开始募捐，克孜尔千佛洞与敦煌不同，基本不为人知，募捐很艰难，公司人员也四处奔波，恳请客户捐款，还请媒体报道。

　In December 1987, we launched the fund-raising campaign under the slogan, "Let's hand down the common cultural heritage of mankind to future generations." But since most people were scarcely familiar with the Kizil grottoes, unlikely Dunhuang, we struggled so hard to raise funds. The board members and staff members were rushing around to ask business partners for the contribution, not to mention the media for broadcasting.

募金勧誘用テレカ・葉書
劝捐用的电话卡、明信片
The telephone card for campaign, the postcard

募金を報じる中日・読売・朝日新聞
中日、读卖、朝日新闻报道募捐
Contribution campaign reported by newspapers like *Chunichi*, *Yomiuri*, and *Asahi*

1988

第一次贈呈

多くの方々のご尽力ご協力により1988年4月28日、新疆人民会堂で黄宝璋新疆副主席列席のもと、トラック等8台2701万円と現金3500万円の計6201万円を贈呈した。松原哲明副会長や筆者ら40名が参加した。その後キジル千仏洞などを参観した。読売新聞が同行取材し8回シリーズで報じた。中間報告を発行した。

经过众多人士的努力和协助，1988年4月28日，在新疆黄宝璋副主席的见证下，在新疆人民会堂捐赠了8台卡车（价值2701万日元）及现金3500万日元，合计6201万日元。松原哲明副会长和笔者等约40人出席了捐赠仪式，之后一起参观克孜尔千佛洞等。读卖新闻随同采访，分8次进行了系列报道。发表了中期报告。

Thanks to tremendous efforts exerted by a number of people, we could donate JPY 62.01 million in total: JPY 35 million in cash and eight vehicles including trucks valued at JPY 27.01 million at Xinjiang People Hall in the presence of Vice-Governor Huang Baozhang on April 28, 1988. 40 people, Vice-Chairman Tetsumyo Matsubara and I included, participated in it. After that, we visited to observe the Kizil grottoes and others. This was covered by Yomiuri Shimbun in eight-part series. We released an interim report.

第一次贈呈を報じるウルムチ晩報・読売新聞
乌鲁木齐晚报、读卖新闻报道了第一次捐赠的情况
The first presentation ceremony reported by *Urumqi Evening News* and *Yomiuri Shimbun*

1989
第二次贈呈

　1989年8月30日、新疆人民会堂で王恩茂副主席列席の下、現金4343万円を贈呈した。松原哲明副会長や筆者ら22名が参加した。その後キジル千仏洞などを参観した。二次にわたり3000をこえる個人や企業からの浄財1億544万円を新疆政府へ寄贈することが出来た。感謝をこめて報告書を寄付者・協力会役員・報道各社へ送った。

　1989年8月30日，在新疆人民会堂捐赠现金4343万日元，王恩茂副主席出席仪式。松原哲明副会长和笔者等22人出席，之后参观克孜尔千佛洞。分两次将3000个以上的个人及企业捐赠的1亿544万日元捐给了新疆政府。为了表示感谢，向捐赠者、协力会骨干、各媒体寄赠了报告书。

On August 30 1989, in the presence of Vice-Chairman Wang Enmao we donated JPY 43.43 million at Xinjiang People Hall. 22 delegates including Vice-Chairman Matsubara and I participated in the ceremony and visited the Kizil grottoes and other ruins afterward. On these two occasions we contributed JPY 105.44 million to the Xinjiang Government. The funds were raised from voluntary contributions from both individuals and companies numbering more than 3,000. I have sent the report of this event with great appreciation to contributors, the board members, and the media.

第二次贈呈を報じる中日新聞と贈呈式
报道第二次捐赠情况的中日新闻及捐赠仪式
Chunichi Shimbun reporting the second presentation and the ceremony

到着した車両／到达的车辆／The arrived vehicles

王恩茂副主席感謝宴（『王恩茂画伝』中央文献出版社2013より）
王恩茂副主席答谢宴《王恩茂画传》摘自中央文献出版社2013）
The gratitude party attended by Vice-Chairman Wang Enmao(sourced from The Album of Wang Enmao published by Central Literature Publishing Co. in 2013)

贈呈報告書（部分）／贈送报告书（部分）／ Presentation report (part)

1988
本格的修復保存工事開始

中国政府の巨費と日本側寄贈資金で1988年修復保存工事が本格的に開始された。飯場・配水塔・下水など基礎的工事から始め、岩盤補強などは蘭州・北京から専門家を招き実験後に行った。

在中国政府投入的巨资及日方捐赠款的支持下，修复保护工程于1988年正式启动。先从食堂、给水塔、下水等基础设施开始施工，针对岩石加固工程，是在邀请兰州、北京方面的专家进行相关实验后开始的。

The full-fledged restoration and conservation work was initiated with a huge amount of expenditure funded by the Chinese Government and the contribution funded by Japan in 1988.

We started with foundation work including a camp, standpipes, and sewage and reinforced cliff rocks after testing materials by inviting specialists from Beijing and Lanzhou.

配水塔・飯場・下水工事／给水塔、食堂、下水工程／Standpipe, a camp, and sewage work

岩盤補強・回廊支柱実験／岩石加固、回廊支柱实验／Reinforcement of cliff rocks, experiment of props for corridor

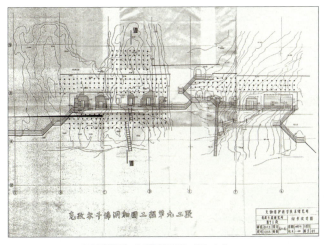

工事設計図／工程设计图／Work design

視察する新疆文化庁長ら／前来视察的新疆文化厅长等
Observed by the Director-General of the Xinjiang Cultural Agency and others

工事中の谷西区／施工中的谷西区／The west valley area on work

修復中の第8窟／修复中的第8窟／The 8th grotto on restoration

修復保存現場を視察する贈呈代表団
视察修复现场的捐赠代表团
The delegates of contributors observing the preservation and restoration work

修復保存現場を視察する贈呈代表団
视察修复现场的捐赠代表团
The delegates of contributors observing the preservation and restoration work

修復前後
修复前后
Before and after restoration

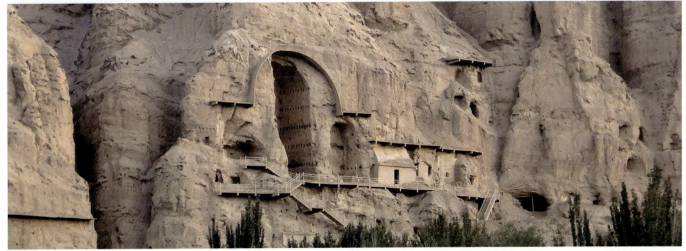

II　キジル千仏洞修復保存協力　035

歓迎を受ける贈呈代表団／受到欢迎的捐赠代表团
A welcome party for the delegates of contributors

呉宝琛所長と／与吴宝琛所长／With Director Wu Baochen

修復資金寄贈記念碑／修复资金捐赠纪念碑
The monument for the contributors of the restoration fund

王恩茂副主席の礼状「…新疆の各族人民は忘れない…」
王恩茂副主席的感谢信"……新疆各族人民不会忘记"
The thank you letter from Vice-Chairman Wang Enmao stating, "Each of our Xinjiang tribes' people can never forget …"

後日、建立された鳩摩羅什三蔵像前で世界平和を願う
几年后，在修建的鸠摩罗什三藏像前祈祷世界和平
At a later date, we prayed for world peace in front of the constructed statue of Rev. Kumarajiva

第17窟／the grottoes numbered 17

第38窟／the grottoes numbered 38

第224窟／the grottoes numbered 224

朝陽に輝く谷西区全景／朝阳映照下的谷西区全景／The full view of the west valley area sparkling in the morning sun

II キジル千仏洞修復保存協力

第188窟／The 188th grotto

第38窟／The 38th grotto

外国探検隊にえぐり取られ痛々しい第224窟／遭外国探险队破坏，惨不忍睹的第224窟／The painful 224th grotto having been gouged by foreign expedition parties

1991
フジテレビ キジル千仏洞紹介番組放映

　1991年3月、筆者が仲介した東海テレビ制作キジル千仏洞紹介番組「新シルクロード考・砂漠に降りた飛天たち」がフジテレビ系列で全国放送された。

　1991年3月，笔者促成东海电视台拍摄制作的克孜尔千佛洞专题节目在富士电视台面向全国播出。

　I helped Tokai Television Broadcast to film the introduction program of the Kizil grottoes which was broadcast nationwide by the Fuji TV network in March 1991.

1994
鳩摩羅什三蔵生誕1650周年記念シンポジウム

　1994年9月、キジル千仏洞で新疆文化庁主催「鳩摩羅什生誕1650周年記念国際シンポジウム」が開催された。鳩摩羅什三蔵像も建立された。筆者は文化参観団と参加し祝辞を述べた。2001年6月にはキジル修復保存協力などが評価され、新疆政府により「小島氏来訪20周年記念大会」が開催された。

　1994年9月，在克孜尔千佛洞召开有新疆文化厅主办的"纪念鸠摩罗什诞辰1650周年国际研讨会"，建鸠摩罗什三藏像，笔者与文化参观团一起参加并致辞。

　In September 1994, The International Symposium in Commemoration of 1,650th Anniversary of the Birth of Kumarajiva was held at the Kizil grottoes under the sponsorship of the Xinjiang Cultural Agency. The statue of Rev. Kumarajiva was reared. I participated in this symposium along with the Cultural Sightseeing Group and made a congratulatory address. In June 2001, the 20th anniversary of Mr. Kojima's visit to Xinjiang was held because my cooperation to conserve the Kizil grottoes and others had been highly evaluated by the Xinjiang Government.

鳩摩羅什三蔵像除幕（中央は新疆文化庁長）と記念撮影／鳩摩罗什三藏像揭幕（中间是新疆文化厅长）及合影／The unveiling ceremony of the statute of Rev. Kumarjiva and the ceremonial photo (Standing at the center is the Director-General of the Xinjiang Cultural Agency)

2007

平山郁夫氏に世界遺産相談

2007年3月、盛春寿新疆文物局長・筆者らはユネスコ親善大使（文化財保護担当）平山郁夫宅で、「シルクロード」世界遺産申請について複数国では調整困難との示唆をえた。

2007年3月，新疆文物局盛春寿局长及笔者等人在世界教科文组织亲善大使（负责文化遗产保护）平山郁夫宅邸获知"丝绸之路"的多国联合申遗，存在协调困难问题。

In March 2007, Director of the Xinjiang Cultural Heritage Administration Bureau Sheng Chunshou and I paid a courtesy call on UNESCO Goodwill Ambassador Ikuo Hirayama (in charge of cultural assets' conservation) at home and received a valuable suggestion as to the application of the Silk Road for a World Heritage Site. According to him, adjusting among multiple nations is quite tough.

2010

新疆亀茲研究院成立25周年記念大会

2010年8月、キジル千仏洞などを管理する亀茲研究院は成立25周年記念大会を開催した。筆者は「キジル1986・我が出発点－中国文化遺産保護研究を使命として」をPPTで講演した。修復前・募金活動・工事の写真を初めて見た参加者の大きな感動が会場にあふれた。盛春寿局長が「新疆の力が十分でなかった時代は小島氏の資金が重要であった、経済的実力の出来た現在は『人に尽くす小島精神』こそ重要である。小島氏より25周年を記念して職員通勤用バスが寄贈される」と発表があり、大きな拍手がおこった。

2010年8月，在管理克孜尔千佛洞的龟兹研究院召开成立25周年纪念大会。笔者通过PPT发表题为"克孜尔 1986 我的出发地—以保护研究中国文化遗产为使命"的演讲。第一次看到修复前、募捐活动、工程照片的与会者的感慨气氛充满整个会场。盛春寿局长说"在新疆能力不足时，小岛先生的资金十分重要，而在我们有了经济实力的今天'尽心为人的小岛精神'才是最重要的，小岛先生要捐赠员工班车用来庆祝25周年"，刚一宣布，就赢得了热烈的掌声。

In August 2010, the 25th anniversary of the Kuqa Research Academy which administers the Kizil grottoes and others was held. I delivered a lecture via PPT with the title of "Kizil in 1986 and My Starting Point — With a Lifelong Mission for Conservation and Research of Chinese Cultural Heritages." Those who saw the photographs for the first time, such as before restoration, the fund-raising campaign and restoration construction, were extremely thrilled with them. Bureau Director Sheng said, "Mr. Kojima's funds had saved us enormously when Xinjiang was lacking financial resources. Now that we have become better off economically, we must learn from Mr. Kojima's spirit of dedication to people." When the announcement that I would donate commuting buses for academy's staffers commemorating the 25th anniversary was made, the audiences exploded with applause.

記念大会と寄贈したバス／纪念大会及捐赠的大巴车／The anniversary and the donated bus

2011
新疆文物局修復資金記念碑改築

　2011年9月、新疆政府により「小島氏新疆来訪30周年記念活動」が開催され、その一環で老朽化した修復資金寄贈記念碑が改築された。居合わせたドイツ研究チームも参加した。

　2011年9月，新疆政府召开"小岛康誉来新疆30周年纪念活动"，作为重要一环，改建了已经老化的修复资金捐赠纪念碑，正好在场的德国研究团队也参加了。

　In September 2011, the Xinjiang Government sponsored the 30th anniversary of Mr. Yasutaka Kojima's visit to Xinjiang. As a part of its celebrations, the monument for the contributors of the restoration fund which had been deteriorated with age was renovated. The German scholars who had happened to be there also participated in this ceremony.

改築された記念碑と代表団／改建后的纪念碑和代表团／The renovated monument and the delegation

2014
協力開始して28年後に世界遺産

2014年6月22日、カタール・ドーハで開催されていた世界遺産委員会生中継をパソコンで見続けていた。キジル千仏洞は「シルクロード：長安－天山回廊の交易路網」33構成資産のひとつとして「世界文化遺産」に登録された。中国の長年努力の結果である。28年間待ち望んだ瞬間、妻と万歳と叫んだ。盛春寿新疆文物局長へ祝電を送った。後日、佛教大学四条センター「世界遺産登録記念講座」で経過などを講演した。

2014年6月22日，笔者通过电脑观看了在卡塔尔多哈召开的世界遗产委员会实况转播。克孜尔千佛洞作为"丝绸之路：长安-天山廊道的路网"33个遗产之一成功登录为"世界文化遗产"，这是中国常年努力的结果。在翘首以盼28年才迎来的瞬间，我和妻子同时高呼万岁，向盛春寿局长发去贺电，以后，在佛教大学四条中心的"世界遗产登录纪念讲座"上介绍了经过。

On June 22, 2014, I kept watching the live coverage of the World Heritage Committee held in Doha, Qatar, on a PC. The Kizil grottoes was officially registered as one of the 33 heritages comprising "Silk Roads: the Routes Network of Chang'an–Tianshan Corridor." China's long time efforts have produced this brilliant result. Having been waiting for 28 years, my wife and I called out "Hurrah" together. I sent a congratulatory message to Bureau Director of the Xinjiang Cultural Assets Sheng Chunshou. At a later date, I lectured about its proceeding under the title of "The Lecture to Commemorate the Registration as the World Heritage" at the Shijo Center of Bukkyo University.

世界遺産委員会Web生中継を撮影、その写真を使ったPPT画面
拍下世界遗产委员网络直播画面，使用了该图片的PPT画面
Shooting the live coverage of the World Heritage Committee website, and the PPT slide using the screenshots

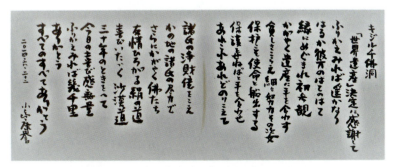

世界遺産決定に感謝即興詩／感恩申遗成功，即兴赋诗
The commemorative improvisation when being decided as the World Heritage

シルクロード 世界遺産決定

（2014年（平成26年）6月23日（月曜日）読売新聞）

【ドーハ＝槙野健】カタールで開かれている国連教育・科学・文化機関（ユネスコ）の世界遺産委員会は22日、中国とカザフスタン、キルギスが推薦した「シルクロード」を世界文化遺産に登録することを決めた。

シルクロードは、古代に中国の絹を西へ運んだ交易路。今回の登録は、中国・洛陽から「天山回廊」と呼ばれるルートを経てカザフスタン南東部のコストべ遺跡に至る総延長約8700㌔の通商路網に沿った3か国計33か所の遺跡を構成要素とする。唐僧・玄奘が経典を収めたとされる大雁塔（中国・西安）や極彩色の仏教壁画が残るキジル石窟寺院（同・新疆ウイグル自治区）などが含まれる。2008～12年、暫定リストに順次登録された。

21日に登録が決まった「富岡製糸場と絹産業遺産群」（群馬県）などとともに、ユネスコの諮問機関が登録するよう勧告していた。

▽関連記事4面▽

決定を報じる読売新聞／读卖新闻报道审议结果／Yomiuri Shimbun reporting the decision

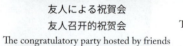

友人による祝賀会
友人召开的祝贺会
The congratulatory party hosted by friends

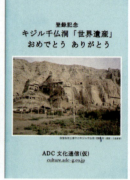

記念誌／纪念杂志
The commemorative booklet

キジルとともに世界遺産となった新疆の遺跡

交河故城・スバシ故城・北庭故城・クズルガハ烽火台・高昌故城を2014年11月再訪し職員諸氏を慰労した。

2014年11月再次访问与克孜尔一同成为世界文化遗产的新疆遗址交河故城、苏巴什故城、北庭故城、克孜尔尕哈烽燧、高昌故城，慰问了那里的工作人员。

I revisited the ruins in Xinjiang registered as the World Heritage, including Ancient City of Jiao River, the Subashi Buddhist Temple Ruins, Ancient City of Beiting, the Kizilgaha Beacon, and Ancient City of Gaochang in November 2014 to express my appreciation to site staffers.

クズルガハ烽火台はチャールターグ山南麓の台地に所在。漢王朝が天山南麓の道沿いに設けた警備用軍事施設。／克孜尔尕哈烽燧／Kizilgaha Beacon

北庭故城はジムサール中心地より北十二キロに所在。後漢の金満城から発展、唐代には北庭都護府などが置かれた。／北庭故城／Ancient City of Beiting

高昌故城はトルファンの東三十キロに所在。唐代には天山南麓の重要な政治・経済・文化の中心であった。／高昌故城／Ancient City of Gaochang

（左頁㊨）スバシ故城はクチャ東北二十三キロに所在。晋唐時代には亀茲仏教の中心であった。大唐西域記にも登場する。／苏巴什故城／Subashi Buddhist Temple Ruins
（左頁㊧）交河故城はトルファンの西十キロに所在。唐代には安西都護府が置かれた。西域の交通の要衝であった。／交河故城／Ancient City of Jiao River

Ⅱ　キジル千仏洞修復保存協力　049

2015
『新疆世界文化遺産図鑑』出版

　2015年10月1日、新疆ウイグル自治区は成立60周年を迎えた。筆者は祝意をこめて王衛東新疆文物局長とキジル千仏洞・交河故城・スバシ故城・北庭故城・クズルガハ烽火台・高昌故城の写真集を出版し、新疆各機関へ贈呈した。翌年4月に日本語版を出版した。

　2015年10月1日，新疆维吾尔自治区成立60周年，为表示祝贺，我与新疆文物局王卫东局长合作出版克孜尔千佛洞、交河故城、苏巴什故城、北庭故城、克孜尔尕哈烽燧、高昌故城摄影集并赠送个新疆各个部门。翌年4月出版日文版。

　On October 1, 2015, the Xinjiang Uyghur Autonomous Region celebrated the 60th anniversary of its foundation. I published a photo collection of the Kizil grottoes, Ancient City of Jiao River, the Subashi Buddhist Temple Ruins, Ancient City of Beiting, the Kizilgaha Beacon, Ancient City of Gaochang and presented it in a congratulatory manner to Bureau Chief of the Xinjiang Cultural Assets Wang Weidong and various organizations in Xinjiang. The Japanese version of it was published in April the following year.

オールカラー写真集／全彩色摄影集／The full-color photo collection

2016
フジテレビ「天山を往く－シルクロード物語」放映

2016年2月、筆者が仲介し出演もしたアジアドキュメンタリーセンター（永野浩史社長）制作キジル千仏洞と天山氷河紹介番組がフジテレビ系列で全国放送された。ADC 文化通信 Webで「シルクロード国献男子30年」「国献男子ほんわか日記」を開始した。

2016年2月，笔者斡旋拍摄并出演由亚洲纪录片中心制作的，介绍克孜尔千佛洞和天山冰河的节目经富士电视台在日本全国播出。开始在ADC文化通信网站连载"丝绸之路国献男子30年""国献男子暖心日记"。

The program featuring the Kizil grottoes and the Tianshan glacier that I appeared on as well as helped Asia Documentary Center to produce was broadcast nationwide by the Fuji TV network in February 2016. I launched An International Dedicator on the Silk Road for 30 Years and The Mellow Diary of an International Dedicator on ADC website.

フジテレビ放映画面から／取自富士电视台播放画面／From the screenshot of Fuji TV

2016
30周年記念行事

2016年9月、新疆文物局と亀茲研究院がキジル千仏洞で「小島康誉とキジル石窟－小島康誉氏新疆文化文物事業投身30周年記念座談会」と「同写真展」を開催した。筆者はPPTで「キジルのおかげで30年」と題してキジル修復保存協力以来の各種活動を紹介した。天津テレビが同行取材した。職員の飲料水は塩分が多く健康を害しているので、浄化設備を贈った。

2016年9月，新疆文物局和龟兹研究院在克孜尔千佛洞召开"小岛康誉与克孜尔千佛洞—小岛康誉投身新疆文化文物事业30周年纪念座谈会"和图片展。笔者通过PPT以"因克孜尔结缘 30年"为题介绍了克孜尔修复保存协力以来的各种实践活动。天津电视台随同采访。由于当地员工的饮用水内盐分较多有害健康，就赠送了净水设备。

In September 2016, the Xinjiang Assets Bureau and the Kuqa Research Academy held the round-table talk show to commemorate the 30th anniversary of devotion for cultural assets in Xinjiang, along with the photo exhibition. I delivered a lecture via PPT under the title of "Thanks to Kizil for 30 Long Years Now" showing a whole variety of activities for restoration and preservation of the Kizil grottoes. Tianjin TV covered this event accompanying me. I presented clarification equipment as some of site staff members impair their health due to drinking water being high in salt.

座談会参加者／座談会参会者／The participants in the round-table talk show

記念写真展／纪念图片展／The exhibition of memorial photos

塩分を含んだ水／含盐水／Water high in salt

飲料水浄化装置／饮用水净化设备／The water-purifying device for drinking

2017
NHK「シルクロード・壁画の道をゆく」放映

　2017年10月、筆者が仲介し出演もしたキジル千仏洞・ダンダンウイリク遺跡・敦煌莫高窟・東京芸術大学クローン展の番組がNHKで放送された。有森也実が旅人役とナレーターを務めた。2018年1月と5月に再放送された。また30分版も放映されるなど人気を博した。中島木祖也エグゼクティブ・プロデューサーは「新シルクロード」でもダンダンウイリク遺跡調査を同行取材した。

　2017年10月，笔者促成并出演的克孜尔千佛洞、丹丹乌里克遗址、敦煌莫高窟、东京艺术大学克隆展节目在NHK播出，2018年1月和5月重播，还播出了30分钟版，获得好评。

　In October 2017, I assisted NHK to cover The Exhibition of Clone Arts sponsored by Tokyo University of the Arts featuring the Kizil grottoes, the Dandanoilik ruins, and the Dunhuang Mogao Grottoes. The program was broadcast on NHK in which I myself appeared. Then, it was broadcast in January and May 2018 again. It gained in popularity so much that it was once again broadcast with the 30-minute edition.

後山区212窟へ向かう筆者らを前方から撮影／从正前方拍摄前往后山区212窟的笔者一行
Shooting me and others from the front as heading for the 212th grotto in the Rear Mountain area

新疆文物局許可をえて、ドイツ隊が殆どの壁画を持ち出した212窟を撮影、これらの写真などを活用して東京芸術大学特別展「素心伝心」が2017年9月に開催された

获得新疆文物局的许可，拍摄了被德国队取走大部分壁画的212窟，使用这些照片于2017年9月举办了东京艺术大学特别展"素心传心"

With authorization of the Xinjiang Cultural Assets Bureau, we shot the 212th grotto most of whose murals had been exported by the German team. These photos were used for the special exhibition sponsored by Tokyo University of the Arts under the title of Sosin/Densin (Artistic heart-to-heart). It was held in September 2017

2018
天津テレビ「大愛無疆」放映

　2018年1月、中国・天津テレビ「泊客中国」が筆者特集3番組「大愛無疆」・「五星出東方利中国」・「西域蒙娜麗莎」を放映した。「大愛無疆」でキジル千仏洞修復保存協力が取り上げられた。中国中央テレビのWeb「央視網」でも放映されている。「泊客中国」は中国で活躍する外国人にスポットをあてた長寿番組。

　2018年1月，中国天津电视台"泊客中国"分3集播出了介绍笔者的专题节目，分别为"大爱无疆"、"五星出东方利中国"、"西域蒙娜丽莎"，"大爱无疆"中介绍了克孜尔千佛洞修复保存协力活动，该节目同时在中国中央电视台的网络平台"央视网"播出。

In January 2018, Tianjin TV's program, China Right Here featured me through a series of three parts titled: No Boundaries for Love of Humanity; Five Stars Appearing in the East Bring Good Fortune to China; and The Mona Lisa in the Western Regions. Cooperation in restoring and conserving the Kizil grottoes was highlighted in No Boundaries for Love of Humanity. China Central TV also broadcast it on its website China Network Television.

「募金は（現在の）1億人民元余相当に達した」と報じる「泊客中国」（Web放映を撮影）　ドローン映像でキジル千仏洞の位置状況が分かりやすい

"泊客中国"报道："募捐金额相当于现在的1亿人民币"（摄于网络播放）　无人机摄影可以清晰地看出克孜尔千佛洞的位置

"The funds raised have reached to the value equivalent to CNY 100 million or more" being reported by China Right Here (screenshot)　Shooting via a drone makes it easier to figure out the location of the Kizil grottoes

2018
安藤佳香教授キジル壁画研究再開へ

　2018年10月、安藤佳香佛教大学教授が新疆文物局と佛教大学内ニヤ遺跡学術研究機構の協力をえて、亀茲研究院と協議書を交わし、2007年実施済み現地共同研究を再開予定である。

　2018年10月，佛教大学安藤佳香教授获得新疆文物局与佛教大学内尼雅遗址学术研究机构的协助，与龟兹研究院签署协议书，打算重新开始2007年实施过的实地共同研究。

　In October 2018, Bukkyo University Professor Yoshika Ando signed the memorandum of understanding with the Kuqa Research Academy backed by the Xinjiang Cultural Assets Bureau and the Academic Research Organization for the Niya Ruins, Bukkyo University and resume the local joint-research which had once completed in 2007.

（修復保存は延々と）

　自然との闘いは延々と続く。天津テレビ写真からも分かるように、天山山脈の浸透水などで進む崩落を防ぐ工事は断続的に行われている。（谷東区で2017年7月撮影）

　与自然的抗争持续不断。如天津电视台的照片所示，防止天山山脉渗透水导致塌落的工程断续进行中。（2017年7月摄于谷东区）

　Struggle for survival in nature never ends. As shown in the images of Tianjin TV, people are intermittently engaged in work to prevent rock from sliding due to seepage water originated in Tianshan Mountains. (Shooting at the east valley area in July 2017)

谷内区の石窟群
谷区内的石窟群
The grottoes inside the valley area

III
日中共同ニヤ遺跡学術調査

中日共同尼雅遗址学术考察
The Japan-China Joint Scholarly
Research of The Niya Ruins

III 日中共同ニヤ遺跡学術調査

（きっかけ）

　1986年からのキジル千仏洞修復保存協力時に、韓翔新疆文化庁文物処長が「新疆には三大著名遺跡がある。楼蘭・キジル・ニヤだ。楼蘭は基本調査終了、キジルは中国政府の巨費と日本の資金協力で修復中、ニヤ遺跡は大規模だが本格的調査は未実施」と発言。筆者は即座に共同調査を提案。世界的文化遺産は保護研究しなければならないと考えていたからである。韓処長はすぐに同意したものの、キジル千仏洞修復資金協力と同様にこの時も許可をえるのは容易ではなかった。

　ニヤ（尼雅）遺跡はタクラマカン沙漠南縁・ミンフゥン（民豊）から約100km北上した一帯に残る前1世紀から5世紀頃まで栄えた古代都市で、『漢書』など記載の西域36国のひとつ「精絶国」である。規模は東西約7km・南北約25km（周辺を含む）と広大で、北緯37度58分34秒・東経82度43分15秒に位置する仏塔を中心に、寺院・住居・生産工房・墓地・果樹園・城壁など約220ヵ所の遺構と数10ヵ所の遺物散布地、さらには河床・大量の枯樹林などが残存している。海抜は1200m前後。沙漠に残存する世界最大の木造都市遺跡である。

在1986年开始协助克孜尔千佛洞修复的过程中，韩翔新疆文化厅处长告诉我"新疆有三大著名遗址，分别为楼兰、克孜尔、尼雅，楼兰考察已基本完成，克孜尔在中国政府的巨资及日方援助下正在修复中，只有尼雅遗址规模宏大却没有实施正规考察"。我当即提议开展共同调查，因为我觉得对世界性文化遗产的保护研究刻不容缓，韩处长也即刻表示赞同，但是和克孜尔千佛洞的修复资金一样，获得许可不是件容易的事情，

尼雅遗址位于塔克拉玛干沙漠南缘的小城民丰以北100公里处，

フランス人工衛星画像／法国人造卫星图像／The French satellite image

スタイン1931年ニヤ遺跡第四次探検収集の「精絶王」木簡の写真（大英図書館蔵）
1931年斯坦因第四次在尼雅遗址探险时收集"精绝王"木简的照片（大英图书馆藏）
The picture of the wooden strip of Jing Jue Guo which is one of the Stein's collection at the 4th exploration of the Niya ruins in 1931 (owned by the British Library)

是兴盛于公元前一世纪至公元五世纪的古代都市，是《汉书》所记载的西域三十六国之一的「精绝国」。其规模宏大，（包括周边地区）东西约7公里，南北约25公里，以位于北纬37度58分34秒，东经82度43分15秒的佛塔为中心，散落着寺院、住宅、手工作坊、墓地、果园、城墙等220处遗迹以及数十处文物散落地，同时还残存着河床和大量枯树林。海拔在1200米左右，是全世界残存在沙漠中的规模最大的木结构遗址城市。

When being engaged in restoring and conserving of the Kizil grottoes, which started in 1986, Manager of the Assets Section of the Xinjiang Cultural Agency Han Xiang once said, "We have three of the most famous ruins in Xinjiang. They are Loulan, Kizil and Niya. Loulan's basic research has been completed, Kizil's restoration is going on now with Chinese Government's huge expenditure along with Japanese financial assistance, but the Niya ruins has yet to be fully researched despite of its huge scale. When I heard this, I instantaneously proposed a collaborative investigation. Because I have believed that we must conserve and research world-class cultural heritages in Xinjiang. Though Manager Han agreed at once, it was not an easy task to get the approval again as mentioned at the time of financial assistance for the Kizil grottoes.

The ruins of Niya was an ancient city, which was located approximately 100 km north of a small city called Minfeng at the south edge of the Taklamakan Desert, having flourished during the age from the 1st century BC through around the 5th century AD. They are called Jing Jue Guo among 36 kingdoms in the Western Regions as referred to in Book of Han. The relics sprawl over such a wide area as stretching roughly 7 km from east to west and 25 km

ニヤ遺跡略位置図
尼雅遗址简略位置图／Brief map of the Niya ruins

from north to south (including the surrounding area). Centering around the Buddhist stupa situated at 37 degrees 58 minutes 34 seconds northern latitude and 82 degrees 43 minutes 15 seconds eastern longitude, there lie about 220 relics, including temples, dwellings, production facilities, graveyards, orchards, and a castle wall, dozens of places with survived remains, and more such as riverbed and huge amounts of decayed woods. The sea level in the vicinity is more or less 1,200 m. It is the remains of the largest wooden state-city still surviving today.

周辺民の案内で到達し、「ニヤ遺跡」と命名したのは、ハンガリー生まれで後にイギリスに帰化したオーレル・スタイン、1901年1月のこと。06・13・31年にも調査をおこない、大量の文物を持ち出し、当時としては卓越した研究をおこない、詳細な報告書で発表した。大谷探検隊の橘瑞超も1909年に進入を試みたが、暑さのためか日程上か遺跡には到達していない。1959年には新疆博物館隊が調査を行い、遺跡北部で墓地を発掘した。これらの調査により二千年を経て今日まで住居の柱などがそのまま残存するタクラマカン沙漠で最大かつ重要な遺跡として注目を集め、一躍有名になったが、大沙漠の奥深くに位置するなどの理由から体系的に調査されることはなく、本格的調査が待たれていた。

匈牙利出生的英国人奥莱尔·斯坦因于1901年1月在周边居民的带领下到达并命名为"尼雅遗址"，他在06、13和31年再次考察这里，带走了大量文物，研究水平在当时可谓卓越，并发表了详细的调查报告书。

日本大谷探险队的橘瑞超在1909年曾经试图进入遗址，但是由于酷暑或是行程问题未能到达。1959年新疆博物馆队进行考察，发掘了遗址北部墓地。经过上述调查，沙漠中沉睡了两千年之久依然完整保留着住宅支柱的塔克拉玛干沙漠中最大且最重要的遗迹引起了人们的关注，瞬间扬名，但是由于地处大漠深处等原因一直没有进行系统的调查，正规调查函待进行。

The person who reached this ruin with the help of inhabitants and named it as the Niya ruins in January 1901 was Sir Mark Aurel Stein born in Hungary and later naturalized in England. He also researched the Niya ruins in 1906, 1913, and 1931 and exported huge amounts of antiquities. His research was then-excellent and released in detailed reports. While Zuicho Tachibana, a member of the second Otani exploration team of Japan, attempted to advance to the Niya ruins in 1909, he failed to reach there probably because of heat wave or demanding itinerary. The Xinjiang Museum conducted research there in 1959 and excavated a graveyard in the northern part of the ruins. This research gathered lots of attention on the ruins and made it famous, yet being located deep inside the great desert might have hindered efforts to take on a systematic research and have long waited for a full-fledged research.

スタイン発掘現場N26と新疆博物館隊／斯坦因发掘现场N26及新疆博物馆队／The Stein's excavated site N26 and the Xinjiang Museum's team

1988

第一次調査（予備調査）

　1988年7月、日本の文化遺産保護姿勢を理解してもらうために韓翔処長らを招聘、ニヤ遺跡やダンダンウイリク遺跡などをふくむ西域南道の遺跡群調査覚書を韓処長と交わした。1988年10月29日から11月16日、「日中共同ニヤ遺跡学術調査」（佛教大学内ニヤ遺跡学術研究機構・新疆ウイグル自治区文物局〈97年3月までは新疆文化庁文物処〉主催、文部科学省助成、国家文物局批准）を敢行した。日本側は筆者や堀尾實通訳など3名、中国側は韓処長を隊長に、王経奎・伊弟利斯・阿不都熱蘇勒・盛春寿など、サポート隊ふくめて日中計14名。隊員一覧は140〜142頁記載。

　民豊から中古トラックと四輪駆動車で干上がったニヤ河跡や林の中を北上。トラックはすぐに故障、四輪駆動車だけで前進するも車輪が砂にとられて頻繁にスタック、途中の小オアシスまでの約90kmに12時間を要した。中方隊員が牛や羊の糞の浮いた汚水を錆びついたタンクに汲んでいるので、ラクダ用の水かと聞くと、人間用だとの答え。唖然とした。

　1988年7月，为了加深了解日本保护文化遗产的态度，我邀请韩翔处长等访日，并与韩处长签订了尼雅遗址等西域南道遗址群考察意向书。1988年10月29日至11月16日，"中日共同尼雅遗址学术考调查"（佛教大学内尼雅遗址学术研究机构、新疆维吾尔自治区文物局〈97年3月前是新疆文化厅文物处〉主办、文部科学省资助、国家文物局批准）正式启动，日方有笔者和翻译堀尾宝等3人，中方队长为韩处长，队员有王经奎、伊弟利斯·阿不都热苏勒、盛春寿等，包括后勤队中日双方共计14人。队员名单在140-142页有详细记载。

　我们从民丰乘坐旧卡车和四轮驱动车沿干涸的尼雅河遗址、穿过树林北上。卡车很快就出现了故障，剩下的四轮驱动车在前行过程中不断被沙子绊住车轮，频繁抛锚，前往中途小绿洲的90公里路程竟然花了12个小时。看到中方队员将漂浮着牛羊粪便的污水吸入锈迹斑的水桶里，"是给骆驼喝的吗？""人喝的"，我们目瞪口呆。

　In July 1988, I invited a party headed by Manager of the Xinjiang Cultural Agency Han Xiang in order to have them understand our nation's basic policy toward conservation of cultural assets. Manager Han Xiang and I signed the memorandum of agreement regarding research of the ruins, including the Niya ruins, the Dandanoilik ruins, and the area around the Western Regions' Southern Route. The Japan-China joint scholarly research of the Niya ruins (hosted by the Academic Research Organization for the Niya Ruins, Bukkyo University and the Xinjiang Cultural Heritage Administration Bureau <the Assets Section of the Xinjiang Cultural Agency until March 1997>, subsidized by the Japanese Education and Science Ministry and ratified by SACH Chinese) was conducted from October 29 through November 16, 1988 by three Japanese members: Mr. Takara Horio, an interpreter, and I, and Chinese members: Wang Jingkui, Yidilisi Abuduresule, and Sheng Chunshou, headed by Wang Jingkui, 14 people in total, including assistants. The list of members is referred to on pages 140–142.

　From Minfeng, we headed north in the woods and along the dried-out Niya river trail by four- wheel drive vehicles and used trucks. The truck broke down soon and the vehicles were frequently mired in the sand. It took 12 hours to reach a small oasis about 90 km away. I happened to come across Chinese stuff putting water in a rusty tank where cows' and sheep's dung floating on. I asked if it was for camels. They answered it was for humans. I just got stunned.

90kmに12時間／约90公里耗时12小时／12-hour drive for about 90 km

調査覚書／调查意向书／The memorandum of agreement for research

Ⅲ　日中共同ニヤ遺跡学術調査　059

糞の浮く汚水を煮沸して飲む
将飘着粪便的污水煮沸并饮用
Drink dung-floating contaminated water after boiling it

ラクダに装備を積み込む
把装备放到骆驼身上
Loading devices on a camel

　ウイグル族の民家にゴロ寝し、翌日ラクダに装備を積み、その上に乗って遺跡へ。頼りとしたのは、スタイン報告書記載の略図と1980年中国中央テレビとNHKの「シルクロード」取材班を案内した伊弟利斯隊員やラクダ使いの記憶だけだった。安全のために政府から派遣された通信士のモールス信号は「現在地不明だが全員無事」。GPSもまだなく、紅柳堆の間を「右だ、左だ」とラクダで3日かけて11月6日早朝に仏塔到達。ここに歴史的調査の幕が開いた。この時の感激は今も忘れられない。

ラクダで遺跡を目指す／乗骆驼找寻遗址／Heading for the ruins on a camel

在维族老乡家合衣睡下，第二天先将装备放在骆驼背上，人坐在装备上，继续向遗址前进。可以参考的只有斯坦因报告书里的简图以及1980年为CCTV、NHK"丝绸之路"摄制组作向导的伊弟利斯研究员和驼工的记忆。处于安全考虑政府派遣的通信士发回的摩尔斯信号也只是"所在地不明但全体平安"。当时还没有GPS，在红柳沙堆中喊着"向右""向左"，骑着骆驼行进三天后，终于于11月6日早上到达了佛塔。在这里掀开了具有历史意义的考察新篇章，当时的感慨与激动令我至今难忘。

Shaking down in a Uyghur house and loading devices on camels next day on which we boarded to head for the ruins. What we relied on were only a simple chart depicted in the Stein's report and memories of a research staff member, Yidilisi Abuduresule and a camel master who had guided the Silk Road TV crews of China Central and NHK in 1980. The message sent by a radio operator who had been dispatched for our safety by the Government: "Though we cannot orient ourselves geographically, we are all safe." Without GPS yet, in the early morning on June 6, we finally found our way to a stupa taking three days on camels saying "right or left" along the bank of Tamarix. Epoch-making research started right at this very moment. I still can't forget the sensation I felt then.

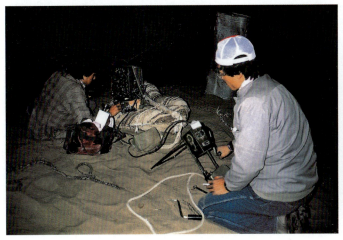

モールス信号で無事を連絡
用摩尔斯信号报平安
Sending a message via Morse code to inform of our survival

ああ疲れた
太累了
Utterly exhausted

遺跡南部は立ち枯れ胡楊と紅柳堆が連続し前進は容易でない
遗址南部枯掉的胡杨和红柳包连绵不断，行进困难
Series of dried-up poplar trees and Tamarix hindered us to advance

画期的調査の幕開けとなった1988年隊（部分）
开启划时代考察之幕的1988年队（部分队员）
The 1988 team (part) initiated an epoch-making research

仏塔に額づく筆者
笔者祭拜佛塔
I bowed down to the Buddha pagoda for prayer

　第一次調査はわずか2日だったが、遺跡中心部を観察し、概要を把握、地表散布遺物の収集を開始し、日中双方とも調査の必要性を確認。筆者は以降の調査覚書（日中両文・以下同様）を買買提祖農・買買提艾力新疆文化庁長と交わした。中国側許可をえて借用してきた遺物数点を水谷幸正佛教大学長・高橋弘次同事務局長へ示すと、「仏教遺跡である、共同研究を是非やろう」との方針が示された。調査を本格化させるにあたり良いキャッチフレーズはないかと考え、火山灰に埋もれたポンペイが街ごと残存していることにちなみ、砂に埋もれたポンペイと捉えて、「シルクロードのポンペイ」・「幻の古代都市」と称した。今では方々で使われている。

　第一次调查仅仅进行了两天，观察了遗址中心区域、掌握了概要、开始收集地表散落文物、中日双方都确认了调查的必要性。笔者与新疆文化厅厅长买买提祖农·买买提艾力厅长交换了今后的调查意向书（日中两种文字 以下同）。佛教大学水谷幸正校长和高桥弘次事务局长看到我征得中方同意借来的几件小小文物后，表示"这是佛教遗址，一定要共同研究"。 我们觉得纪念正规调查的启动，需要一个好的口号，联想到被火山灰埋没的庞贝古城完整地保存了下来，取沙埋庞贝之意，命名为"丝绸之路的庞贝""梦幻般的古代都市"，这个名称至今被各方使用。

The first research took just two days, though, we walked around the center of the ruins for observation so as to come to grips with an outline and began collecting antiquities scattered around in pieces on the ground. We, Japanese and Chinese, found that it was imperative to conduct research. Director General of the Xinjiang Cultural Agency Maimaitizunong Maimaitiaili and I signed the memorandum of agreement (both Japanese and Chinese, the same hereafter) to continue to research further. Once I showed President of Bukkyo University Kosyo Mizutani and Secretary General of Bukkyo University Koji Takahashi several antiquities borrowed with permission from the Chinese side, they immediately set a policy of conducting research, saying, "These are Buddhist ruins. We should collaborate to research with Chinese by all means." Thinking over any good catch-phrase to start a full-scale process of this research, we came up with "Pompeii on Silk Road" and "The Mysterious Ancient City" realizing that the whole city of Pompeii having survived even once buried under volcano ashes like buried Pompeii. Now, those phrases are used all over the place.

点在する遺構（92B9・スタインN3）
分散的遗迹（92B9・斯坦因N3）
The scattered ruins (92B9: Stein N3)

韓翔中方隊長
中方韩队长
Chinese Leader Han Xiang

テープレコーダーに記録する盛隊員
作录音记录的盛队员
Staff member Sheng recording on a tape recorder

調査覚書／调查意向书／The memorandum of agreement for research

1990

第二次調査（予備調査）

　1990年10月27日〜11月17日、井ノ口泰淳・真田康道・李肖・劉文鎖らも加わり、サポート隊あわせて計16名で第二次調査を実施した。世界でも例をみない大沙漠での調査方法を検討した。住居址模式図作成を開始、トラックによるルート開発をおこなった。以降調査覚書を買買提祖農庁長と交わした。

　1990年10月27日至11月17日，包括后勤在内的16名队员实施第二次调查。我们探讨了世界上尚无先例的大漠调查方法。开始制作住居遗址模式图、尝试卡车开拓线路。与买买提祖农厅长交换了今后的调查意向书。

During the period from October 27 through November 17, 1990, we conducted the second research with the total of 16 members, including assistants and examined on how we could conduct research on a vast desert, which would be unparalleled by others. We started with creation of pattern diagrams of dwelling sites, along with opening a road for truck transportation. Director-General Maimaitizunong and I signed the memorandum of agreement to subsequently proceed with research.

1990年隊（部分）
1990年队（部分队员）
The team 1990 (part)

1991年以降調査覚書（日文版）／1991年以后的調査意向书（日文版）
The memorandum of agreement for research in 1991 and beyond (Japanese version)

1991

第三次調査（予備調査）

　1991年10月12日〜11月6日、長澤和俊・高橋照彦・王炳華・于志勇・阿合買提・熱西提・張鉄男らが加わり、サポート隊・中国石油報・東海テレビ取材班ふくめ計21名で第三次調査を実施した。一般的でなかったGPSをいち早く導入し遺跡位置の登録による分布調査を開始し、沙漠車も実験的に導入。遺跡管理人を増員するなど保護強化も開始した。

　1991年10月12日至11月6日，包括后勤队、中国石油报、东海电视台采访组在内的合计21人，进行了第三次调查，使用当时尚不十分普遍的GPS进行分布调查、登记遗址位置，还实验性地投入沙漠车。增加遗址管理人员、强化保护措施。

During the period from October 12 through November 6, 1991, we conducted the third research with the total of 21 members, including assistants and reporters of Chine Petroleum Daily and Tokai TV. We were not the last to adopt the GPS then being unfamiliar to start a distributional research through registering the location of a ruin. We introduced a vehicle for desert-use on an experimental basis and also increased the number of staff members administering the ruins to start reinforcing conservation.

1991年隊（部分）／1991年队（部分队员）／The team 1991 (part)

> **GPS**（グローバル・ポジショニング・システム）
> アメリカ軍の測位衛星30数基中の4基以上から信号を受信し位置を特定する全地球測位システム。中国の「北斗」は2011年末より試験運用開始。日本の「みちびき」は18年11月運用開始予定。

1992
文部省科研費助成開始・第四次調査

三次にわたる予備調査が評価され、1992年4月14日、国家文物局より正式許可書を取得した。4月28日、克尤木・巴吾東新疆副主席列席のもと、筆者と買買提祖農庁長は総合調査を目的とした協議書に調印した。日本政府の評価をいただき文部省（現文部科学省）の科学研究費助成（研究代表：真田康道）が開始された。調査は10月13日〜11月11日、蓮池利隆・孫躍新・沙比提・阿合買提らが加わり、サポート隊・取材班ふくめ計27名で実施した。建築学的調査も開始し、カローシュティー木簡など地表散布遺物採集、ニヤ遺跡西方水系も調査した。

1992年隊（部分）／1992年队（部分队员）／The team 1992 (part)

　三次预备调查获得肯定，1992年4月14日取得国家文物局的正式许可书。4月28日，在新疆政府克尤木・巴吾东副主席的列席下，笔者与买买提祖农厅长签署了以综合考察为目的的协议书。获得日本政府的好评，文部省开始资助科学研究费。10月13日至11月11日，包括后勤队、采访组在内的合计27人实施调查，开始进行建筑学调查，收集地表散落的佉卢文木简等文物，对尼雅西方水系的调查也同时开始。

As the performances of these three preliminary researches were highly valued, we could receive the official certificate of approval from SACH Chinese on April 14, 1992. Director-General Maimaitizunong and I, on behalf of China and Japan, respectively, signed a memorandum of understanding in order to conduct comprehensive research of the Niya ruins in the presence of Vice-Governor of Xinjiang Keyoumu Bawudong on April 28. Having been highly evaluated by the Japanese Government, the subsidy of the Education Ministry for scientific research was commenced. The research was conducted from October 13 through November 11 by 27 members in total, including assistants and reporters. Architectural research was also launched, along with collecting antiquities scattered in pieces on the ground, such as Kharosthi wooden strips, as well as water system survey in the western part of the Niya ruins.

調印を祝して／祝贺签字／In celebration of the signing

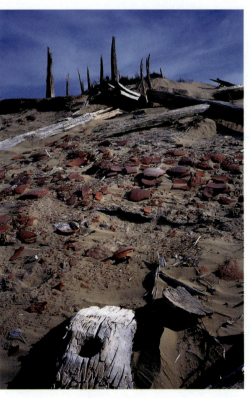

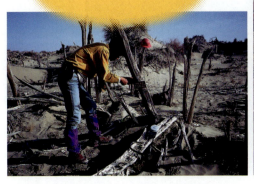

倒柱上が初期のGPS受信機／倒柱上是早期的GPS
The initial GPS placed on the top of a pole

大量の陶片／大量陶片／A huge volume of pottery shards

Ⅲ　日中共同ニヤ遺跡学術調査　065

国家文物局

(92)文物字第288号

关于同意与日本学者合作考察尼雅遗址的批复

新疆自治区文化厅：

你厅新文文字(1992)21号"关于同日本学者合作考察尼雅遗址的再次报告"收悉。经研究，同意你厅与日本学者合作考察尼雅遗址。考察过程中，请严格遵守《中华人民共和国考古涉外工作管理办法》和规定。

此复。

协议书

新疆的老朋友、日本国小岛康誉先生(以下简称B方)一行，在1988、1990、1991年三次参观尼雅遗址的基础上，于1992年4月25日至29日应新疆文化厅(以下简称A方)邀请访问了新疆。在新疆访问期间，双方为合作考察尼雅遗址进行了再次会谈，达成协议如下：

一、考察名称：中日共同尼雅遗迹学术考察
二、考察内容：A，调查遗迹分布范围；
　　　　　　　B，测绘部分遗迹平面图、照像、文字记录；
　　　　　　　C，采集地面文物并进行研究；
　　　　　　　D，研究尼雅遗址已出土的馆藏文物。
三、考察时间：从1992至1993年，进行为期一个月的实际考察。
四、考察队的组建：中方队长韩翔，学术指导王炳华；日方队长小岛康誉，学术指导井ノ口泰淳，其他队员双方均等。
五、经费：中日双方人员考察所需装备与费用由B方负担。考察结束后，B方将于1992年与1993年分两次付给A方协助费及文物保护费共两千五百万日元。
六、考察时所采集的文物，都由A方所有。考察中所获得的资料(包括测图、文字记录、文物照片)由双方共享。双方共同发表考察报告。

为整理考察资料实进行馆藏文物的研究，B方学者留在乌鲁木齐短期停留时间，A方将提供办公场地。
七、凡考察可以继续使用的团体装备由A方负责保管。
八、A方负责准备考察用的交通工具，费用由B方支付。A方应提前制订计划予与B方商量。
九、考察期间，B方人员的人身保险，由B方自行办理；A方人员的人身保险由A方自行办理。双方人员的安全各自负责。
十、此项考察活动已经中华人民共和国国家文物局于1992年4月14日批准。
十一、考察结束后，双方如认为需要在尼雅遗址合作进行考古发掘，须报国家文物局批准。
十二、本协议用中、日两种文字打印、签署，内容相同，具有同等效力。

A方代表　　　　　　B方代表

1992年4月28日

国家文物局許可証／国家文物局许可证
The approval certificate of SACH Chinese

1992年以降調査覚書（中文版）／1992年以后的调查协议书（中文版）
The memorandum of agreement for researches in 1992 and beyond (Chinese version)

1992年調査などを報じる中日新聞／中日新闻报道1992年调查等／*Chunichi Shimbun* reporting the research in 1992

1993
第五次調査

　1993年度からは調査の本格化にともない、規模を拡大し、現地調査期間も長期化させた。 10月8日〜11月27日、米田文孝・古川雅英・貝殻徹・劉宇生・景愛・劉樹人らを加え、サポート隊・東海テレビ取材班ふくめ計56人で実施した。分布調査・住居址模式図作成を継続、大型住居址92B4測量や地質学調査も開始し、遺跡北方の探査もおこなった。中国側の許可をえて分析試料を日本へ持ち帰り研究を開始。沙漠車の本格導入で遺跡へ比較的スムースに到着できるようになったが、遺跡保護のため現地到着後はラクダを併用した。新疆政府からは当初より全面的支持と協力をえていたが、この年より鉄木尓・達瓦買提新疆主席が調査の名誉主席（名誉副主席：吾甫尓・阿不都拉新疆副主席・顧問：季羨林北京大学教授ら）に就任いただいた。また全人代環境資源保護委員会が新華社・中央テレビ・中国石油報からなる取材班を派遣し、これ以降ニヤ調査は中国内外で大きく報道されるようになった。

　随着调查的逐步正规化，1993年开始扩大规模、延长实地考察时间。10月8日至11月27日，包括后勤队、东海电视台采访组在内的合计56人实施调查。继续进行分布调查、制作住居遗址模式图、针对大型住居遗址92B4开展测量及地质学调查、还探查了遗址北方。征得中方许可，将分析材料带回日本进行研究。由于正式引入了沙漠车，我们可以比较顺利地到达遗址，但是为了保护遗址，到达现场后，还要使用骆驼。新疆政府一直就给予了全面的支持和协助，从这一年开始，铁木尓・达瓦买提主席出任考察名誉主席。而且，全国人大资源环境保护委员会还派出了由新华社、中央电视台、中国石油报等组成的采访组，从那以后，尼雅考察开始在海内外被大量报道。

　As research being made fully-fledged from the 1993 research on, the scale of the joint expedition expanded to 56 members in total including assistants and reporters of Tokai TV, and the period of research work was also prolonged as from October 8 through November 27. We continued to conduct distributional research, create pattern diagrams of a dwelling site, launched measuring the large-scale dwelling site of 92B4 and geometrical research, and made a survey on the northern part of the ruins. With the permission of the Chinese side, we brought back analysis samples to study in Japan. We fully adopted vehicles for desert-use, which enabled us to reach the ruins more easily than ever before. After arrival, however, we used camels on site in order to not impair the ruins. While fully supported by the Xinjiang Government from the initial stage, we were fortunate enough to have Governor of Xinjiang Tiemuer Dawamaiti assume the position of the Honorary Chairman from this year on. The Environmental Resources Conservation Committee of the NPC dispatched a reporting team comprising Xinhua, Central Television, and China Petroleum Daily. From then on, the Niya ruins research was widely reported within and without China.

苦戦する沙漠車を眺めるラクダ隊
观望沙漠车奋战的骆驼队
The camel team watching the struggling desert vehicle

新華社・中国中央テレビ・石油報取材班
新华社、中央电视台、石油报采访组
The news crews from Xinhua, Central Television, and *China Petroleum Daily*

1993年隊（部分）／1993年队（部分队员）／The team 1993 (part)

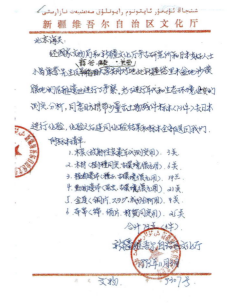

分析用資料持出許可書／分析用资料带出许可书
Removal permit of analyzing materials

92A8（スタインN26）

92A5（スタインN7）

93A4	93A5 (スタインN17)		
92A23E	93A18 (スタインN1)	96A7	93A1 (スタインN22)
92A1 (スタインN9)	93A13	91NG (スタインN34)	

Ⅲ 日中共同ニヤ遺跡学術調査　073

遺構部分／遗迹部分／A part of a ruin

遺構部分／遗迹部分／A part of a ruin

1994

国家文物局 発掘許可

　1994年1月29日、中国と外国との共同調査として最大規模のニヤ調査を全面的支持してきた国家文物局は調査実績を評価し、張徳勤局長名で発掘許可を発出した。国家文物局令による外国隊への発掘許可第1号である。待望の許可であり、李東輝新疆副主席列席のもと、同日、筆者と解耀華新疆文化庁書記は94〜96年分協議書に調印した。調査の本格化・長期化に対応すべく、日本側は同年4月、海部俊樹元首相・張局長を名誉会長、塩川正十郎衆議院議員らを顧問、水谷幸正学長（のちに中井真孝学長、福原隆善学長、安藤佳香教授へ順次交代）と筆者を代表として、佛教大学に「中国新疆ニヤ遺跡学術研究機構」（略称：佛教大学内ニヤ遺跡学術研究機構）を設立した。

　1994年1月29日，一直全面支持中外共同调查中最大规模的尼雅调查的国家文物局高度评价调查成果，张德勤局长签名下发发掘许可。这是国家文物发给外国考察队的第1号发掘许可，是盼望已久的许可。在新疆政府李东辉副主席的列席下，当天笔者与新疆文化厅解耀华书记签署了94年至96年协议书。为了对应调查的正规化和长期化，日本方面也于同年4月在佛教大学成立了以原首相海部俊树、张德勤局长为名誉会长、众议院议员盐川正十郎为顾问、水谷幸正校长（后依次为中井真孝校长、福原隆善校长、安藤佳香教授）和笔者为代表的"中国新疆尼雅遗址学术研究机构"（略称：佛教大学内尼雅遗址学术研究机构）。

In recognition of the outstanding performances as mentioned above, SACH Chinese which had fully endorsed the Niya ruins' research issued the excavation approval under the name of Director Zhang Deqin on January 29, 1994. This was the first excavation approval ever issued for a foreign explorer by SACH Chinese. This was the certificate we were long waiting for. Secretary of the Xinjiang Cultural Agency Xie Yaohua and I signed the three-year memorandum of understanding from 1994 through 1996, in the presence of Vice-Governor of Xinjiang Li Donghui on the same day. In order to implement full-fledged and long-term research, we have established the Academic Research Organization for the Niya Ruins in Xinjiang China, or briefly the Academic Research Organization of the Niya Ruins, Bukkyo University, with ex-Prime Minister Toshiki Kaifu and Director of SACH Chinese Zhang Deqin as Honorary Chairmen, then-Lower House member Masajuro Shiokawa as a Special Adviser, and Bukkyo University President Kosyo Mizutani (followed by Shinkou Nakai, Ryuzen Fukuhara, and then Yoshika Ando) and I as a representative in April 1994.

発掘許可証抄訳

　貴方がニヤ遺跡調査を完成させるときに、私は喜んで貴方に通知する。貴方が提出した新疆文物考古部門と調査を継続し発掘する申請は既に中国政府関係部門が批准した。（中略）ニヤおよび新疆地区は我国文物考古の重点区域のひとつであるが、沙漠地帯で自然条件は困難であり、屋外調査・発掘・生活は大変困難である。貴方は長年新疆考古学研究と文物保護活動で大変大きな貢献をした。私は国家文物局を代表して貴方と同僚たちに敬意を表し、中日合作考古調査・発掘活動が更に大きな成果をあげるよう祈る。

The excerpt from the excavation certificate

　Upon the completion of the Niya ruins research, it is my great pleasure to notify you that the relevant division of the Chinese Government has ratified your application to continually research and excavate in collaboration with the Xinjiang Archaeological Institute. (snip) The Xinjiang District, including Niya, is one of the most important archaeological cultural assets in our country, yet as it lies in the desert, the harshness of nature has made outdoor research, excavation and lives so difficult. You have made such a supreme contribution to research of the Xinjiang archaeology and antiquities conservation over the years. On behalf of SACH Chinese, I would like to express you and your fellow staff my sincere respect and pray for the further success of China-Japan collaborative archaeological research and excavation work.

中日合作尼雅考察协议书

新疆维吾尔自治区文化厅（以下简称A方）与日本友好人士小岛康誉先生（以下简称B方）共同合作对中国新疆地处塔克拉玛干沙漠腹地的尼雅遗址在1988、1990、1991连续三次参观的基础上，于1992、1993年经国家文物局批准进行了正式考察，取得了初步的成果。中日双方考察队员在对遗址进行普查的基础上，又经过重点复查，弄清了部分遗址分布状况，发现了许多新的遗址和墓群，制作了遗址分布图，采集了许多文物，开始了地理环境的考察，并对N₂遗址进行了正式的详细测绘。前面的工作尽管取得了许多成果，但对尼雅遗址的研究来说，还只是初步的基础工作，有许多研究课题等待着去做。为此，B方于1993年10月16日至11月27日应A方邀请访问了新疆。在访问期间，双方对今后继续合作考察与研究尼雅遗址进行了再次会谈，达成协议如下：

一、考察名称：中日共同尼雅遗址学术考察。
二、考察内容：A、调查遗址分布范围。
　　　　　　　B、进行个别墓地和遗址的清理发掘。
　　　　　　　（此项工作必须事前单项申请国家文物局批准后进行）。
　　　　　　　C、测绘部分遗址平面图、照相、文字记录。
　　　　　　　D、采集文物、标本并进行研究。
　　　　　　　E、研究尼雅遗址已出土的馆藏文物。
三、考察时间：从１９９４年至１９９６年进行为期三个月左右的实际考察。（每年一个月左右）
四、考察队的组建：中方队　长：韩　翔
　　　　　　　　　中方学术队长：王炳华
　　　　　　　　　日方队　长：小岛康誉
　　　　　　　　　日方学术队长：井ノ口泰淳
中日双方队员数量均等。
五、经费：中日双方人员考察所需装备及费用由B方负担。
六、协力项目：A、１９９４年B方向A方无偿提供三台GPS。
　　　　　　　B、B方将于１９９４年至１９９６年分三次付给A方协助费及文物养护费共贰仟万日元。（其中一部分将按中方意愿，用物资装备支付）
　　　　　　　C、调查结束后，B方向A方无偿移交全部由B方购置的调查设备及仪器。（大约价值两千五佰万日元）
七、考察期间，凡是可以多次使用的装备由B方负责保管。
八、A方负责确保考察需用的交通工具，费用由B方支付，但A方必须提前制订预算并与B方商量。
九、考察中采集的文物归A方所有。考察中获得的资料（包括测图、文字记录、文物照片）由双方共享。双方共同撰写考察报告，用中、日两种文字同时发表。在共同的考察报告正式发表前，双方考察队员不得以个人名义发表有关尼雅考察的论文。为整理考察资料或进行馆藏文物研究，日方学者如需在乌鲁木齐短期停留时，A方将提供办公场地。
十、考察期间，双方人员的人身保险各自办理，双方人员的安全各自负责。
十一、此次活动暂时计划三年，即从１９９４年至１９９６年，如需延长，另订协议。
十二、考察结束后，双方协商，将在日本和中国举行尼雅学术考察研讨会；在日本举办尼雅遗址文物展览会。
十三、本意向书用中日两种文字打印、签名，内容相同，具有同等效力。本协议自签订之日起正式生效。

A方代表　　　　　　B方代表

1994.4.29

1994～96年調査協議書（中文版）
1994至1996年调查协议书（中文版）
The memorandum of understanding for research from 1994 through 1996 (Chinese version)

日中間最大規模の調査を推進するために佛教大学内ニヤ遺跡学術研究機構を設立。他大学などの研究者招聘の窓口ともなった
为推进日中间最大规模调查，在佛教大学内设立尼雅遗址学术研究机构，同时也是邀请其他大学研究人员的窗口
The Academic Research Organization for the Niya Ruins, Bukkyo University was established to help foster the largest-ever research between Japan and China whereby serving a gateway to inviting researchers from other universities

全人代環境資源保護委員会 ニヤ調査写真展

1994年5月、北京図書館でニヤ調査写真展「ニヤ:沙漠に消えた古代王国」が開催された。筆者や李希光新華社記者が曲格平全人代環境資源委員会主任・ノーベル賞受賞の李政道などにニヤ調査を説明した。6月には中央テレビがニヤ調査の30分番組を全国放送した。

1994年5月，在北京图书馆举办题为"尼雅：消失在沙漠的古代王国"尼雅考察摄影展。笔者和新华社记者李希光向全国人大环境资源委员会曲格平主任、诺贝尔奖获得者李政道先生介绍了尼雅考察。6月，中央电视台播放了30分钟的尼雅考察节目。

In May 1994, a photo exhibition titled Niya: An Ancient Kingdom Disappeared in a Desert was held at the Beijing Library where Xinhua reporter Li Xiguan and I made the presentations on the Niya ruins' research for Chief of the Environmental Resources Conservation Committee of the NPC, and Nobel Laureate Li Zhengdao and others. Central Television broadcast nationwide on the research of the Niya ruins for half an hour in June.

1994
第六次調査

1994年9月、筆者と王炳華新疆文物考古研究所長は94年度調査発掘詳細協議書に調印した。9月25日〜11月5日、田辺昭三・伊東隆夫・浅岡俊夫・吉崎伸・高妻洋成・米川仁一・李文瑛・李季・楊林・王邦維・楊逸疇・王守春らも加わり、サポート隊ふくめて計56名で実施。発掘・木質調査・関連都市住居調査も開始した。

1994年9月，笔者和新疆文物考古研究所王炳华所长在94年度调查发掘细节协议书上签字。9月25日至11月5日，包括后勤队在内的56名人员实施调查，发掘、木质调查、相关城市住居调查也同时展开。

In September 1994, Director of the Xinjiang Archaeological Institute Wang Binghua and I signed a detailed memorandum of understanding on excavation in 1994. During the period of September 25 through November 5, the field research was conducted with the total of 56 members including assistants. Excavation and the researches of wood and relevant urban dwellings started.

1994年隊（部分）／1994年队（部分队员）／The team 1994 (part)　　　　　　　　東京新聞／东京新闻／Tokyo Shimbun

1995

フジテレビ「風砂の蜃気楼－日中共同ニヤ遺跡調査」放映

1995年5月、東海テレビ91〜93年調査取材番組「風砂の蜃気楼－日中共同ニヤ遺跡調査」がフジテレビ系列で全国放送された。同月、ニヤ遺跡写真集『夢幻尼雅』出版、王丙乾全人代副委員長と会見しニヤ調査の報告を行い、日本国公使や張徳勤国家文物局長らも出席し、全人代環境資源委員会栄誉賞が授与された。

1995年5月，东海电视台在富士电视系列面向全国播出了91年至93年随同采访录制的节目。同月，尼雅遗址摄影集《梦幻尼雅》出版，拜会全国人大副委员长王丙乾、汇报尼雅考察的情况，日本公使和国家文物局张德勤局长出席，接受全国人大环境资源委员会的奖项。

In May 1995, the research from 1991 through 1993 covered by Tokai Television was televised nationwide by the Fuji TV network. In the same month, the photo collection, Dreamy Niya, was published. I met with Vice-Chairman of the NPC Wang Bingqian to report the research of the Niya ruins. In the meanwhile I was presented the Honor Award of the Environmental Resources' Committee of the NPC in the presence of the Japanese Minister and Director of SACH Chinese Zhang Deqin.

『夢幻尼雅』人民日報／《梦幻尼雅》人民日报／Dreamy Niya by People's Daily　　　東海TV番組ハガキ／东海电视节目明信片／The postcard of a Tokai TV program

1995
第七次調査

　1995年8月、筆者と買買提祖農庁長は95年度発掘詳細協議書に調印した。調査は9月28日〜11月5日、新たに中島皆夫・杉本和樹・岳峰・任式楠・孟凡人・斉東方・楊晶・李軍らを加えサポート隊と新疆日報記者ふくめて計56名で実施した。より高精度GPSを導入し分布調査精度の向上をはかった。墓地発掘。92B4精査発掘。93A35測量発掘。カパクアスカン村測量。小学校へ学用品などを贈呈。現地調査以外に新疆文物考古研究所で収集済み遺物の研究を日本側も開始し、本年は井ノ口泰淳・高橋照彦・蓮池利隆らがカローシュティー木簡などの研究と写真撮影を行った。

　1995年8月，笔者与买买提祖农厅长签署95年度发掘细节协议书，调查于9月28日至11月5日进行，包括后勤队和新疆日报记者，合计56人。使用精度更高的GPS，提高了分布调查的精准程度。发掘墓地、发掘并精查92B4、测量发掘93A35、测量卡巴克阿斯坎村。向小学校赠送学习用品等。除实地考察外，日方还在新疆考古研究所对收集的文物开始进行研究，本年度拍摄并研究了佉卢文木简。

　The detailed memorandum of understanding for the excavation and research in 1995 was signed between Director-General Maimaitizunong and me in August 1995. During the period of September 28 through November 5, the field research was conducted with 56 members in total, including assistants and reporters of *Xinjiang Daily*. The research involved introducing the higher precision GPS to improve the accuracy of distributional research: the discovery of a graveyard; the detailed excavation of 92B4; making a survey on 93A35 to excavate; making a survey on the Kapakeasican village; donation of school supplies to elementary schools. The Japanese team started to research collected antiquities at the Xinjiang Archaeological Institute besides researches on site; the study and the photo shootings of Kharosthi wooden strips.

1995年隊（部分）／1995年队（部分队员）／The team 1995 (part)

調査開始して7年後に大発見 「五星出東方利中国」発掘

　1995年10月12日、露出している木棺の一部を発見、中国側学術隊長の王炳華新疆文物考古研究所所長指揮のもと測量と発掘をおこなった。14日開棺。わずかに開いた隙間から覗き込んだ于志勇が叫んだ。「わぁすごい、王 侯 合 昏 千 秋 萬 歳・・・まだある」と文字を読み上げた。居合わせた日中双方全員が「万歳！」と拳を突き上げた。「五星出東方利中国」をふくむ王族墓地であった。保護のため発掘、6棺を取り上げた。その夜のベースキャンプは異常な興奮に包まれた。

　中国側隊長の岳峰新疆文化庁処長につづいて乾杯を促された筆者は「1988年、日中共同ニヤ調査を開始して以来、今日が最良の日だ、日中双方全員の共同努力のおかげだ、乾杯！」と普段は飲まない白酒を何杯も一気飲みした。また筆者は新疆ウイグル自治区成立40周年記念式典に出席し、ホータン地区貧困脱出工程資金・ホータン博物館建設資金を贈呈した。

　1995年10月12日，发现了裸露在外的部分木棺，在中方队长新疆文物考古所王炳华所长的指挥下，实施测量和发掘，14日开棺，从细微的缝隙处窥视的于志勇喊道"太棒了！王 侯 合 昏 千 秋 万 岁……还有"，在场的双方队员举拳高呼"万岁"。是藏有"五星出东方利中国"的王族墓地，我们进行了保护性发掘，取出6棺。当天晚上，宿营地被异常兴奋的气氛包围着。

　中方队长岳峰发言后我举杯祝酒"自1988年开始中日尼雅考察以来，今天是最美好的日子，这是中日双方共同努力的结果，干杯！"将平时几乎不喝的白酒一饮而尽。同年，笔者还出席了新疆维吾尔自治区成立40周年纪念仪式、向和田地区捐赠脱贫工程资金以及和田博物馆建设资金。

　On October 12 1995, an exposed wooden coffin was discovered. Under the instruction of Director of the Xinjiang Archaeological Institute Wang Binghua who served as the Chinese scholarly team Leader, we proceeded with survey and excavation. On October 14, the time came to open up the coffin. Yu Zhiyong peered through the slightly opened coffin and cried out, "Wow, it's wonderful!" and read out letters, "*Wang Hou He Hum Qian Qiu Wang Sui* (Best wishes for the King's marriage) and there's something more." All members both of the Japanese and the Chinese teams present there raised their fists yelling, "Hurrah!" It was the royal graveyard where the silk brocade "Five stars appearing in the east bring good fortune to China" was

王墓発掘現場／王族墓地发掘现场／The excavation site of the king's grave

included. We excavated in order to conserve and lifted six coffins out. We were filled with an unnatural excitement that night.

Following Chinese Leader Yue Feng, I was urged to make a toasting speech and said, "Today is the best day for us since we launched the Japan-China joint research of the Niya ruins in 1988. All of the members of both the Japanese and the Chinese teams have endeavored to make this dream come true. Cheers!" I drank down baijiu which I rarely drink, again and again. Meanwhile, I attended the 40th anniversary of the Xinjiang Uyghur Autonomous Region and donated fund for the escape-from-poverty scheme of the Hotan Prefecture and for the construction of the Hotan Museum, as well.

開棺調査

11月6日から12日、現地調査に引き続き、岳峰・王炳華・李軍・沙比提・阿合買提・于志勇・張鉄男・劉玉生・田辺昭三・吉崎伸・孫躍新・杉本和樹・佐藤右文や筆者らが発掘した6棺の開棺調査を新疆文物考古研究所で国家文物局派遣の王軍処長・王亜蓉研究員とともに行い、男女合葬ミイラをはじめ、「王侯合昏千秋萬歳宜子孫」・「五星出東方利中国」錦など貴重遺物多数を検出した。閻振堂国家文物局副局長・宿白北京大学教授・厳文明同教授・徐苹芳中国社会科学院研究員らが視察に訪れた。

11月6日至12日，继续进行实地调查，与国家文物局派来的王军处长和王亚蓉研究员一起在新疆考古研究所对发掘的6个木棺进行开棺调查，发现了男女合葬木乃伊以及"王侯合昏千秋万岁宜子孙"、"五星出东方利中国"织锦等许多珍贵文物。国家文物局闫振堂副局长、北京大学宿白教授、严文明教授、中国社会科学院徐苹芳研究员也前来视察。

On November 6 through 12, continuing research on site, we studied each of the six excavated coffins at the Xinjiang Archaeological Institute together with Chief Wang Jun and Researcher Wang Yarong who were dispatched by SACH Chinese. Besides a couple-mummy burial, we found lots of valuable antiquities such as silk brocades embroidered with the words, "Best wishes for the King's marriage" and "Five stars appearing in the east bring good fortune to China." Vice-Director of SACH Chinese Yan Zhentang, Professors of Peking University Su Bay and Yan Wending, a researcher at the Chinese Social Science Institute Xu Pingfang, and others visited us for observation.

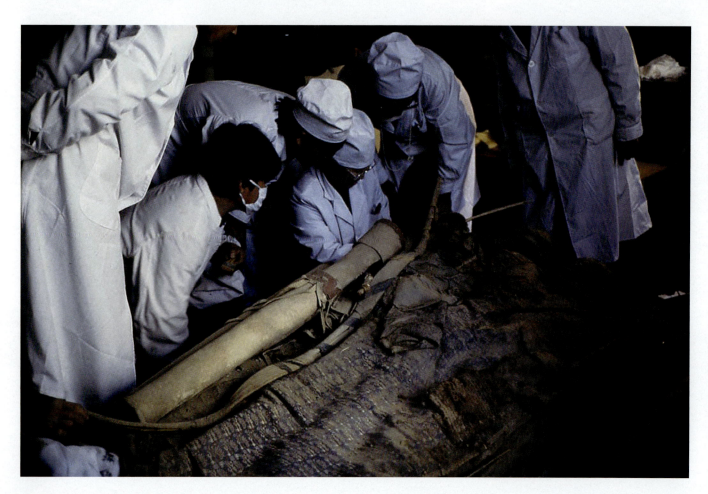

95MN1号墓地M3棺調査 細心の注意をはらって／謹慎小心地調査95MN1号墓地M3棺
Researching the coffin M3 in the #95MN1 graveyard with great care

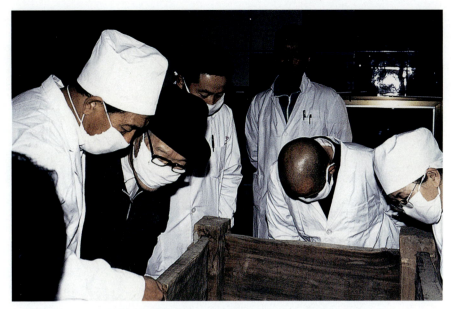

1959年ニヤ遺跡を調査した李遇春（左2）も開棺調査を参観
1959年曾调查过尼雅遗址的李遇春（左2）也参观了开棺调查
Li Yuchun (2nd from left) who had researched the Niya ruins in 1959 observed research at the coffin-opening site

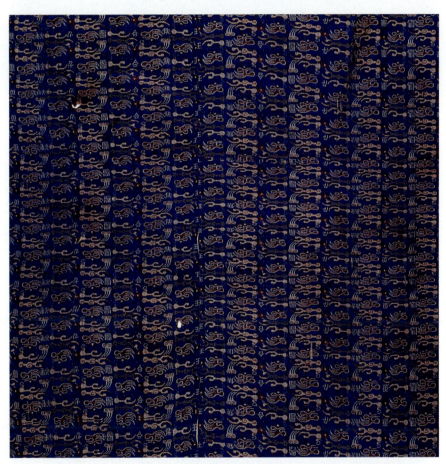

二人を覆っていた「王侯合昏千秋萬歳宜子孫」錦（部分）　82・83・89・114頁ご参照
二人身上覆盖着的"王侯合婚千秋万岁宜子孙"织锦（部分）　请参考82・83・89・114页
The silk brocade covering them embroidered as "Best wishes for the King's marriage" (part)
Refer to page 82・83・89・114

⇦左の男性は身長174cm、右の女性は身長162cm、精絶国王と后と推測されている
　左側的男性身高174CM，右側的女性身长162CM，推测是精绝国王和王后
　A man on the left is 174 cm tall and a woman on the right is 162 cm tall. They are presumed to be the king and the queen of Jing Jue Guo

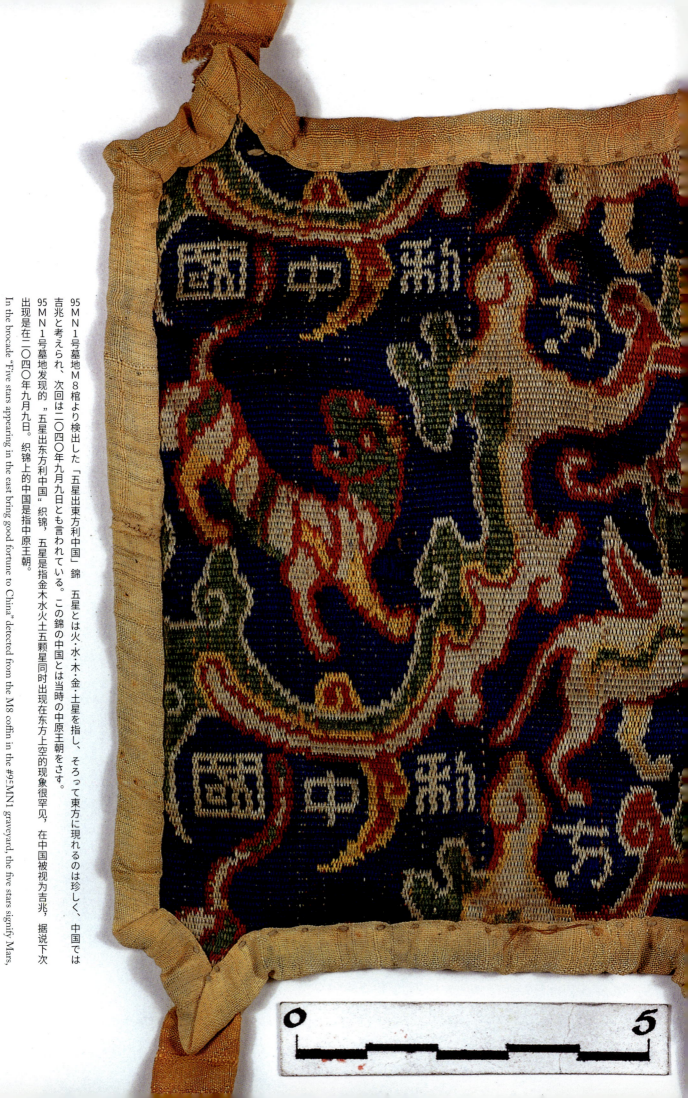

95MN1号墓地M8棺より検出した「五星出東方利中国」錦 五星とは火・水・木・金・土星を指し、そろって東方に現れるのは珍しく、中国では吉兆と考えられ、次回は二〇四〇年九月九日とも言われている。この錦の中国とは当時の中原王朝をさす。

95MN1号墓地发现的"五星出东方利中国"织锦,五星是指金木水火土五颗星同时出现在东方上空的现象很罕见,在中国被视为吉兆,据说下次出现是在二〇四〇年九月九日。织锦上的中国是指中原王朝。

In the brocade "Five stars appearing in the east bring good fortune to China" detected from the M8 coffin in the #95MN1 graveyard, the five stars signify Mars, Mercury, Jupiter, Venus, and Saturn which rarely appear in the east and if they should appear, it is thought to be a fortunate omen. For your reference, the next appearing date is said to be on September 9, 2040. Zhong Guo, or Central Kingdom, embroidered in the silk brocade indicates the Central Plains Dynasty.

国家文物局・新疆文化庁「王墓発掘」発表

1995年12月、北京で95年調査での王侯貴族墓地の発見・発掘に関する記者発表が行われ、張徳勤局長・吾甫尔・阿不都拉新疆副主席・宿白北京大学教授・厳文明同教授・王中俊新疆文化庁書記・岳峰・王炳華・田辺昭三・真田康道・孫躍新・筆者らが出席した。内外で大きく報道された。

1995年12月，在北京召开了关于95年调查发现、发掘王族墓地的记者招待会，张德勤局长、新疆政府吾甫尔·阿不都拉副主席、北京大学宿白教授、严文明教授、新疆文化厅王中俊书记、岳峰、王炳华、田边昭三、真田康道、孙跃新、笔者等人出席发布会。国内外有大量报道。

In December 1995, the discovery and the excavation of the royal graveyard in the 1995 research were announced at a press conference in Beijing with attendance of Director Zhang Deqin, Vice-Governor of Xinjiang Wufuer Abudula, Pekin University professors Su Bai and Yan Wenming, Secretary of the Xinjiang Cultural Agency Wang Zhongjun, Yue Feng, Wang Binghua, Shouzou Tanabe, Kodo Sanada, Sun Yuexin, and me. This discovery was widely reported within and without China.

大発見と報じる人民日報・新疆日報／报道重大发现的人民日报、新疆日报

Both *People's Daily* and *Xinjiang Daily* reporting this as a great discovery

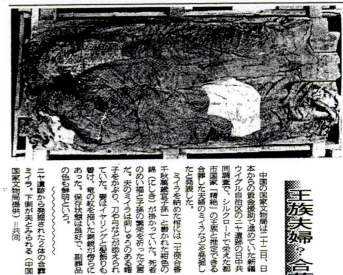

日本経済新聞　1995年（平成7年）12月23日

王族夫婦？合葬ミイラ　中国ニヤ遺跡

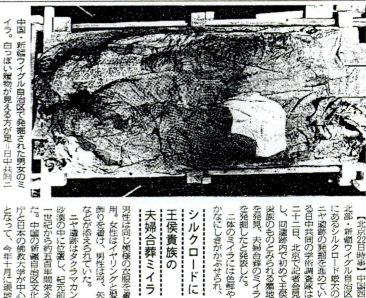

毎日新聞　1995年（平成7年）12月23日

シルクロードに王侯貴族の夫婦合葬ミイラ

王族ミイラ発見と報じる日本経済新聞・毎日新聞
报道发现王族干尸的日本经济新闻、每日新闻
Nihonkeizai Shimbun and *Mainichi Shimbun* describing this as the discovery of royal mammy

王墓測量・発掘状況
王族墓地測量及发掘情况
Survey and excavating scene of the king's graveyard

1996
ニヤ調査「1995年中国十大考古新発見」に

1996年2月、ニヤ調査は国家文物局・中国文物報により「1995年中国十大考古新発見」に選ばれた。

　1996年2月，尼雅调查被国家文物局、中国文物报评为"1995年中国十大考古新发现"

In February 1996, the Niya ruins' research was selected as the 10 great archaeological new discoveries in 1995 by SACH Chinese and *Chinese Cultural Resources News*.

1996
報告書（第一巻）出版

　1996年4月、日中双方は88〜93年度調査の成果を井ノ口泰淳・真田康道・長澤和俊・米田文孝・伊東隆夫・浅岡俊夫・周培彦・古川雅英・貝柄徹・高橋照彦・高妻洋成・蓮池利隆・韓翔・岳峰・盛春寿・王炳華・于志勇ら隊員諸氏の尽力と文部省科学研究費補助研究成果公開促進費をえて『日中／中日共同ニヤ遺跡学術調査報告書』第一巻（日中両文）として刊行した。成果の早期公開の原則にそうものである。

　遵循尽早公开研究成果的原则，1996年4月，在中日双方队员的共同努力级文部省科学研究费辅助研究成果公开促进费的支持下，将88年至93年的调查成果总结出版了《日中/中日共同尼雅遗址学术调查报告书》第一卷（日中文）。

In April 1996, both of the Japanese and the Chinese teams published research results from 1988 through 1993, titled, The Report of *Japan-China/China-Japan Joint Scholarly Research of the Niya Ruins Vol. 1* (both in Japanese and Chinese) thanks to tremendous efforts made by staff members, as well as the Grant-in-Aid for Publication of Scientific Research Results funded by the Educational Ministry. This publication is based on the principle of the earliest possible release of results.

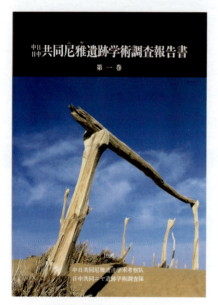

報告書／报告书／The report

報告書刊行を報じる読売新聞
报道报告书出版的读卖新闻
Yomiuri Shimbun reporting the publication of the report

第2章　調査成果

91NL:14，夹砂灰陶，领部有刻划的波状线纹。尖圆唇，高领，侈口（图一 9）。
91NT:7，夹砂面红陶，轮制，圆唇，领较高（图一 10）。
91NT:6，夹砂面灰面，外表皮泛灰绿色。方唇，唇外有沿，侈口，领较高，鼓肩（图一 11）。
91NL:15，夹砂面黄棕色，轮制，圆唇，侈口，领较高（图一 12）。
91NO:2，微夹砂素面红陶，轮制，尖圆唇，唇外起沿，侈口，高领（图一 13）。
91NA:6，微夹砂素面红陶，轮制，方唇微侈口，领较窄，鼓肩（图一 14）。
91NL:16，夹砂陶，轮制，领部有两道凸棱纹，方唇，折沿，直口，领较高，鼓肩（图一 15）。
91NP:7，夹砂面灰陶，轮制。尖圆唇，沿不明显，高领，侈口，鼓肩（图一 16）。
91NA:7，夹砂红陶，轮制，肩领部有一处刻划的符号。方唇，微起沿，侈，口高领，鼓肩，腹。文书在该罐旁（图一 17）。
91NP:4，夹砂面红陶，轮制。尖圆唇，微侈口（图一 18）。
91ND:2，夹砂面红陶，轮制。方唇，微起沿。微侈口，高领，鼓肩（图一 19）。
91NN:4，夹砂面红陶，轮制。圆唇，唇外微起沿，侈口，微束领，高领，鼓肩，腹（图一 20）。
91NO:11，夹砂面素面红陶，轮制。方唇，微侈口，高领（图一 22）。
91NT:8，夹砂面素面红陶，轮制，方唇，侈口，高领（图一 23）。

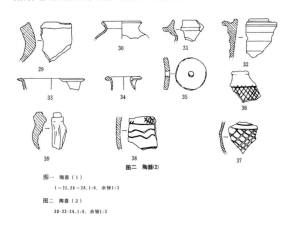

図一　陶器（1）
1〜22，26〜28，1:6，余皆1:3

図二　陶器（2）
30・33・34，1:6，余皆1:3

— 57 —

6　ニヤ遺跡出土のカローシュティー文字資料の研究(1)

91NS9 矩形本体【図版43（下）】
本体表（149㎜×62㎜）

図13　91NS9木簡本体表

【本文】
1) saṃvatsara[ga] 2 masa 4 …… maharajasa rajatirajasa
2) mahaṃtasa jeyaṃtasa dharmiasa mahanuava raja toṃgraka devaputrasa
3) asti chunaṃmi peta aṿanaṃmi kilme …… bhiti bhradu
4) aṅgiya nama te buma vikridati tasuca cateyasa putra catiasa
5) maṣe bumas misiye milimi yena bhiṣapayati aṃña bahi
6) [mi] ṣiyasa …… bhiṣapayati khi 4 1 esa buma ……
7) asa aṅgiyasa vikrida krida catiasa ni środa muli ……
8) ha vaṃnaga kaṣa ma [ka] jaha vaṃnaga hasta 10 2 tatra ……
9) tasuca cateyasa kitsatsa piteyasa so ……
10) ṣadavida tsag ……

【和訳】
(1)大王、王中の王、(2)偉大なるジェーヤンタ、法を知る偉大なる、トングラカ天子の治世、2年4月の時、(3)ペータ・アヴァナの土地・・・二番目の兄 (4)アンギヤという名の者、その土地を売りに出した。タスチャ職チャテーヤの子供チャティアサは、(5)月に、ミリマの種を作付けができる耕地を他の多くの (6)耕地の・・・5キィの種を作付けできる・・・その土地が (7)アンギヤの売りに出された・・・チャティアサの代価・・・ (8)柔らかいヴァンナガ12ハスタが、そこで・・・ (9)タスチャ職チャテーヤ、キツアツア職ピテーヤの・・・ (10)シャダヴィダ職の・・・

〈91NS9〉notes
saṃvatsaraga ＜ saṃvatsare
saṃvatsare: 87; 90; 98; 110; 116; 120-1; 155; 169; 180; 187; 193; 195; 222; 298; 318; 321; 331; 419-20; 436; 488; 506; 527; 574; 583; 592; 676; Rapson index. p. 376
saṃvatsara, m. (rarely n.) a full year, a year (having 12 [TS.] or 13 [VS.] months or

— 324 —

6　1991〜93年分布調査の成果

測る。部屋dと同じく、北側が不明である。西壁の南西隅には、開口部がある。部屋内部には、土器（紅陶）の細片が多量に散布しており、角杯も確認できた。部屋fの東側外部には垣があり、そのさらに外側にも垣が一部確認できる。垣と垣の間にも、土器片が散布しており、その地点では他に鞍形のすり石も露出していた。

部屋bより空閑地をおいて東に位置する部屋gは、南北が4.1mで、東西が残存部で2.6mを測る。部屋bよりは北東に2.8m隔たる。部屋g内部は動物の糞が大量に堆積しているため、家畜小屋と見て間違いない。南壁西隅には、開口部がある。区画hは、垣で囲まれた空間で、建物ではない。家畜小屋gとの間隔は、3.1mを測る。hの北壁西隅には、幅80cmの開口部を確認できる。部屋bとの間にL字形に垣があり、hと接する部分に開口部を設ける。

部屋a・c南西側には、建物と平行する形で垣を確認できる。部屋の南西隅部分からはもう一つの垣が延びており、先の垣と合わせて通路状をなし、南側に伸びて途中で西に折れる。

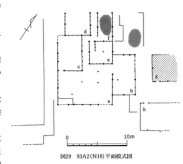

図29　93A2(N18)平面模式図

93A3（図30、図43-V3、図版19）

区画aは、東西が5.7m、南北が6.8mで、垣で囲続されている。内部は獣糞と藁類が堆積しており、家畜を飼養していたものとみられる。この北側にも区画や通路があり、区画内では同様に獣糞などが厚く堆積する。規模としては、東西が3.8mと2.5mの二つの区画とその間の0.8m幅の南北通路で、いずれも北側の状況は不明ながら2.4m程度は確認できる。区画aの南東隅からは、8m程度の長さで南方向に垣が伸び、そこで西に垣が折れて続いていく。南

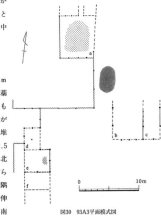

図30　93A3平面模式図

— 136 —

TABLE OF CONTENTS

Chapter 1　Location of the Site and Details of the Research
  1. Site Location and its Surrounding Environment ……………………3
  2. Beginning and Development of the Research ……………………16

Chapter 2　Research Results
  1. Research Outline ……………………37
  2. Research Record of 1988 (by *Sheng Chun Shou*) ……………………41
  3. Research Record of 1990 (by *Liu Wen Xiao*) ……………………48
  4. Research Record of 1991 (by *Liu Wen Xiao*) ……………………52
  5. Archeological Research of a site north of the Niya Site in 1993 (by *Zhang Tie Nan, Yu Zhi Yong*) ……………………73
  6. Distribution Research Results from 1991 to 1993 (by *Sanada Yasumichi, Takahasi Teruhiko*) ……………………82
  7. Measurement Research of "N2" Dwellings Site in 1993 (by *Takahasi Teruhiko*) ……………………165
  8. Topographical Survey around the Stupa (by *Furukawa Masahide, Kaigara Toru*) ……………………169

Chapter 3　Natural Scientific Research and Analysis
  1. Wood Type Identification of Lumber Collected in 1993 (by *Itoh Takao*) ……………………179
  2. Deterioration State of Lumber Collected from Dwellings Site "N2" (by *Kohdzuma Yohsei*) ……………………182
  3. Chemical Analysis of Collected Materials Related to Bronze and Glass (by *Saito Thutomu*) ……………………187

Chapter 4　Study
  1. Review and New Results of Niya Archeological Research (by *Wang Bing Hua*) ……………………193
  2. Outline and Housing Structure of Niya Site "N3" (by *Shabiti Ahmat*) ……………………212

— 406 —

1996
第八次調査

　1996年8月には海部俊樹名誉会長・水谷幸正佛教大学学長・中井真孝同事務局長・筆者らが王楽泉中共新疆委員会書記・阿不来提・阿不都熱西提新疆主席・張柏国家文物局副局長らに共同調査への一層の支援と97年佛教大学で開催予定のシンポジウム・文物展への協力を要請し、同意をえた。同月、96年度調査の詳細協議書を筆者と王中俊新疆文化庁書記が交わした。遺物研究と写真撮影は伊東隆夫・高橋照彦・高妻洋成・坂本和子らが前年検出の王族ミイラ・織物中心に行った。10月2日〜11月6日、吉田恵二・田中清美・内田賢二・近藤知子・伊斯拉斐尓・玉蘇甫らも加わり、サポート隊あわせて計58名で現地調査を実施した。大型GPSを導入し地形図作成を開始。住居址・生産工房址の測量を開始。仏教寺院発掘し壁画検出。北方調査で遺構・遺物発見。遺跡南端地区にサークル状土塁を発見した。

　1996年8月，海部俊树名誉会长、佛教大学水谷幸正校长和中井真孝事务局长及笔者等拜会中共新疆委员会王乐泉书记、新疆政府阿不来提・阿不都热西提主席、国家文物局张柏副局长，寻求对共同调查的进一步支持并希望积极协助计划97年在佛教大学召开的国际研讨会和文物展，获得了同意。当月，笔者与新疆文化厅王中俊书记签署96年度调查细节协议书。围绕以上年度发现的王族干尸、织锦进行文物研究、举办摄影展。10月2日至11月6日，包括后勤队在内的58名队员实施实地考察。导入大型GPS开始制作地形图，开始测量住居遗址和生产工坊遗址。发掘佛教寺院并发现壁画。在北方调查时发现遗迹、文物。遗址南端发现圆形状土坡。

In August 1996, Honorary Chairman Toshiki Kaifu, Bukkyo University Chairman Kosyo Mizutani, Secretary General Shinkou Nakai and I visited Secretary of the Xinjiang Committee of the CCP Wang Lequan, Governor of Xinjiang Abulaiti Abudurexiti and Vice-Director of SACH Chinese Zheng Bai to ask to further support the joint research, as well as to cooperate for the symposium and the cultural assets exhibition slated at Bukkyo University in 1997. We received their acceptance. In the same month, Secretary of the Xinjiang Cultural Agency Wang Zhongjun and I signed the detailed memorandum of understanding on the 1996 research. The research and the photo shootings of antiquities were focused on the royal coffin and the fabrics. The field research was conducted with 58 members in total, including assistants, from October 2 through November 6. We started creating topographic maps employing the large GPS. We also started making a survey on dwelling sites and surrounding remains of production facilities along with excavating Buddhist temples to detect murals. We discovered ruins and relics in the north investigation. A circle-structured mount was discovered in the southern district.

各種機器を活用して測量／运用各种器械进行测量／Survey employing various devices

1996年隊（部分）／1996年队（部分队员）／The team 1996 (part)

93A35（スタインN5）FS 発掘後の仏寺遺構 中央の穴はスタイン？発掘跡／发掘后的佛寺遗址／The relic of a Buddhist temple after excavation

93A35 発掘現場と検出壁画／发掘现场及发现的壁画／The excavation site and the murals detected

96MNBCF1 ニヤ遺跡北約40kmで発見した約3000年前の遺構と遺物の数々／在尼雅遺址以北約40公里处发现大约3000年前遗迹和多件文物
Relics and remains estimated to be aged about 3,000 years in the area about 40 km north of the Niya ruins

岳峰中方二代隊長と
与第二任中方队长岳峰
Together with the second Leader of the Chinese team Yue Feng

Ⅲ 日中共同ニヤ遺跡学術調査　095

南方城址と橋状遺構／南方城址和桥状遗迹／The south-castle remain and the bridge-shaped relic

炎天下での発掘
炎炎烈日下进行发掘
Excavation under the blazing sun

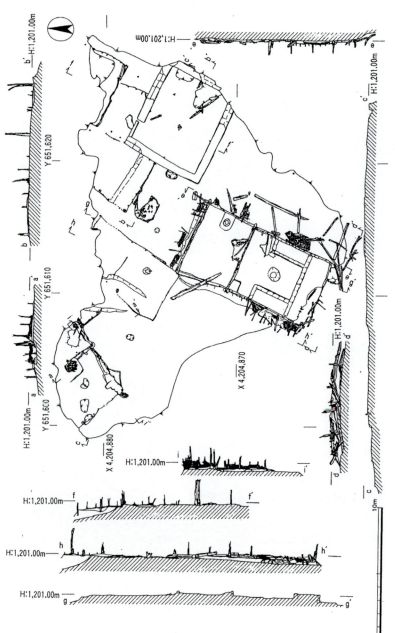

92B4は19の住居がサークル状に所在する大型遺構、その1・2号住居の測量図面　現状変更と景観破壊の恐れのある「発掘」でなく、遺構を覆っている砂を除き、旧地表面を出す「清掃」に留めた
92B4是19个住居遗址构成的环状大型遗址，其中1・2号住居的测量图　没有进行可能改变现状、破坏景观的"发掘"，只是进行"清扫"：即去除覆盖遗迹的沙子，将旧地表露出
92B4 is the large-scale relic where 19 houses stand in a circle, the survey drawing of its 1st and 2nd houses, keeping it to so called "Cleaning" by which sand covering relics is removed rather than "Excavation" which might alter the status quo and ruin the scenery

1・2号住居の発掘後と発掘前／1・2号住居发掘后和发掘后前／The 1st and the 2nd houses before and after excavation

109頁ご参照
请参照109页
Refer to page 109

Ⅲ　日中共同ニヤ遺跡学術調査　　097

1996

国務院 ニヤ遺跡「全国重点文物保護単位」指定

　1996年11月、中国国務院はニヤ遺跡全体を「全国重点文物保護単位」に格上げ指定した。12月、佛教大学内ニヤ遺跡学術研究機構はこれまでの調査成果を記者発表、日本側二代学術隊長の田辺昭三は「五星」錦について「埋葬された男女が結婚したとき、中国王朝から贈られたものでは」などとコメントした。

　1996年11月，中国国务院将尼雅遗址整体认定为"全国重点文物保护单位"。12月，佛教大学内尼雅遗址学术研究机构举行记者招待会，发布以往的调查成果，第二任日方队长田边昭三指出"五星"织锦应该是"埋葬在内的男女结婚时，中原王朝赠送给他们的"。

　In November 1996, the whole Niya ruins site was upgraded to be designated as the conservation unit of the national significant relics by the State Council. In December, the Academic Research Organization for the Niya Ruins, Bukkyo University, held a press conference about the results of the prior research, Second Leader of the Japanese scholarly team Shouzou Tanabe referred to the silk brocade (Five stars) as a present from the Chinese Dynasty when a buried couple were married.

ニヤ機構発表を報じる読売・産経・中日・京都新聞
报道了尼雅研究机构发布会的读卖、产经、中日、京都新闻
The newspapers, such as *Yomiuri*, *Sankei*, *Chunichi*, and *Kyoto*, reporting the press release from the Niya Organization

1997
「日中共同ニヤ遺跡シンポジウム・文物展」開催

　1997年3月、新疆政府の決定により新疆文化庁より文物処が分離され、文物行政管理全般を掌握する新疆ウイグル自治区文物局が成立した。同月、中井真孝・筆者は艾尔肯・米吉提新疆文物局副局長と文物展協議書に調印した。また克尤木・巴吾東中共新疆委員会副書記、米吉提・納斯尔新疆副主席列席のもと、筆者と岳峰局長が97年以降の詳細協議書に調印した。9月、佛教大学新図書館開館記念「日中共同ニヤ遺跡学術研究国際シンポジウム・出土文物展」を開催、海部俊樹名誉会長・張宝智中国大使館文化参事官・水谷幸正・高橋弘次・中井真孝・杉本憲司佛大教授・買買提祖農庁長・宋新潮国家文物局処長・徐苹芳・林梅村・樋口康隆橿原考古学研究所所長・赤松明彦九州大学教授ほか日中双方隊員の長澤和俊・田辺昭三・井上正・真田康道・伊東隆夫・孫躍新・蓮池利隆・岳峰・王炳華・孟凡人・沙比提・阿合買提・于志勇・張鉄男・筆者らが挨拶や発表を行い、のべ約500人が参加した。

　9月から12月まで、中国歴史博物館で「全国近年考古新発見精品展」が開催され、日中隊検出の「五星出東方利中国」錦や「王侯合昏千秋萬歳宜子孫」錦なども出陳された。

　1997年3月，新疆政府决定将文物处从新疆文化厅分离出来，成立全盘负责文物行政管理的新疆维吾尔自治区文物局。同月，中井真孝和笔者与新疆文物局艾尔肯・米吉提副局长签署文物展协议书。在克尤木・巴吾东副书记、米吉提・纳斯尔副主席的列席下，笔者与岳峰局长签署97年以后细节协议书。9月，召开佛教大学新图书馆开馆纪念"中日共同尼雅学术研究国际研讨会、文物展"，合计约500人参会，非常多人观展。

　In March 1997, the decision by the Xinjiang Government to separate the Assets Section from the Xinjiang Cultural Agency resulted in establishing the Xinjiang Cultural Assets Bureau to manage the whole field of relic administration. In the same month, the memorandum of understanding for the antiquities exhibition was concluded between Vice-Director of the Xinjiang Cultural Administration Bureau Aierken Mijiti and Shinkou Nakai, along with me. Yue Feng and I signed the detailed memorandum of agreement after 1997 in the presence of Vice-Secretary of the Xinjiang Committee of the CCP Keyoumu Bawudong and Vice-Governor of Xinjiang Mijiti Nasie. In September, the symposium on the Japan-China joint scholarly research of the Niya ruins and the unearthed antiquities exhibition were held at Bukkyo University to commemorate the establishment of its new library. Approximately 500 people in total attended the ceremony.

　The Exhibition of Recent Archaeological Discoveries in China was held at the National Museum of Chinese History from September through December and the silk brocades such as "Five stars appearing in the east bring good fortune to China" and "Best wishes for the King's marriage," detected both by the Japanese and the Chinese teams were also exhibited.

文物展協議書調印
文物展协议书签字
The signing of the memorandum of understanding
for the antiquities exhibition

ニヤ調査を大きく報じる『人民中国』『News week』（日本版）
大幅报道尼雅考察的『人民中国』『News week』（日文版）／*People's Daily* and *Newsweek* (Japanese version) widely reporting the Niya research

シンポジウム会場
研讨会会场
The symposium venue

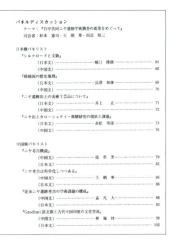
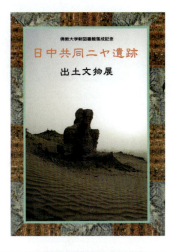

要旨・図録（部分）／概要・图录（部分）／The summary paper and the pictorial record (part)

Ⅲ　日中共同ニヤ遺跡学術調査　101

文化

日中共同ニヤ遺跡学術調査の意義

みずたに・こうしょう氏 学歴、専門は大乗仏教思想。一九二八年三重県生れ。龍谷大学大学院修了。龍谷大学名誉教授、仏教大学教授（共著）、『四トルキスタンの仏教』（訳著）など多数。

水谷 幸正

小生の弟子として僧りょになっていたので、私がニヤの久しぶりの業績だ。このたびの学術調査は、その反省と教訓の上に立って行っていい。日中共同事業をベースに、ニヤ遺跡調査研究が二十一世紀の大事業になるであろう。

西域に残る多くの遺跡のは、かつて多くの外国探検隊によって、その文物が持ち出された。その心に深い傷痕を残している。二十二日から京都市北区紫野花ノ坊町、佛教大学紫野キャンパス恵光館瞭原考古学研究所長らが中国の研究者とパネルディスカッションを行う。

学術研究機構代表

西域 〝幻の古代都市〟精絶国
鮮やかに浮かぶ貴族の生活

ニヤは、紀元前一〜後四世紀にかけて栄えた西域南道に位置する「精絶（せいぜつ）国」の遺跡であり、「幻の古代都市」と呼ばれている。これほどの規模で本格的未調査の遺跡は世界のみ込まれている。

イタリアのポンペイ遺構になぞらえて「シルクロードのポンペイ」、あるいは「幻の古代都市」と呼ばれるようになった。

調査は井ノ口泰淳（龍谷大学名誉教授）学術隊長、真田康道（佛教大学教授）副隊長、田辺昭三（京都造形芸術大学教授）第二次学術隊長、をはじめ、各分野の専門学者の協力を得て、八年前の第一回予備調査以来、昨年まで八回にわたり、各省との深い交流を持っていた名古屋の経済人、小島康誉さんの努力によって保存会が結成され、一九八七年以降、文部省科研費の助成も得て、実地調査を継続しながら、あらゆる困難を克服して、今年も十月より第九回の学術調査を実施することになった。その時、彼は一九九三年までの成果についての「報告書」第一巻として出版した。

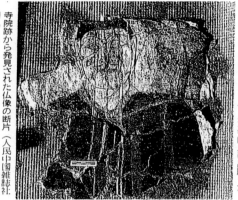

調査の意義・文物展を報じる京都新聞
报道调査的意義、文物展的京都新聞
Kyoto Shimbun reporting significance of the research and the exhibition of antiquities

かつてほどないにしても、「シルクロード」という語感は、多くの日本人に文学的なある種のロマンを抱かせる。タクラマカン砂漠、パミール高原などといえば、いまでも探検的な知的好奇心をそそっている。タクラマカンを含む中国の西北地方（西域ともいう）が現在の新疆ウイグル自治区である。この地域から東へ向かうシルクロードは、インドから中国へ、さらに朝鮮半島から日本へと仏教が伝播（ば）してきたルートでもある。ブッダロードと呼んでもよい。西域は仏教が中国へ東漸してゆくたんなる通過地域ではなく、独自の仏教文化を形成していた。その形あるものの多くが破壊され、あるいは地中に埋もれてしまった。西域仏教事情については、いまだに不明のことがらが多い。

西域（天山北路、天山南路、西域南道）の調査は、十九世紀後半から二十世紀にかけて、ヨーロッパの学者を中心に（日本の大谷探検隊を含む）断続的に行われた。それらの中で特に有名なのが、かのオーレル・スタインである。ニヤだけについていえば、一九〇一年より四回にわたり、仏塔を中心にした住居、墓地、家畜小屋、ブドウ畑などの多くの遺構、さらに河床、大量の樹林など、栄えた〝広大な地域〟だと。そして、「楼蘭（ろうらん）」とともに〝精絶王国〟の都市そのものが大規模に栄えたが、同じくスタインにより有名にされた。戦後、ニヤ遺跡の発掘調査を中国調査隊がしているが、本格的な調査研究は最近まで実施されないままであった。

でも数少ないという。西域の仏教遺跡は敦煌をはじめ本格的であるが、三〜十三世紀に遺営された三三三三窟で有名であり、八年前の第一回予備調査以来、仏像菩薩像の断片出土のカローシュティ木簡発見などさまざまとなったのは一九九五年中国十大考古新発見に選ばれ、国家文物局からもこの発掘は「一九」文物保護単位に選ばれたのも宣うべき重要な資料である。中国国家文物局がこの発掘を「一九九五年中国十大考古新発見」に入れ、また遺跡全体が「全国重点文物保護単位」に選ばれたのも宣う（むべ）なるかなである。

今年は日中国交正常化二十五周年にあたる。この記念として、仏教大学新図書館落成記念として、ニヤ学術研究国際シンポジウムおよびニヤ遺跡出土文物展を開催し、日本での初公開として来る九月二十二日から京都市北区紫野花ノ坊町、佛教大学紫野キャンパス恵光館で開かれる。二十二日午前10時の開会式に続き、大学教授らの基調講演、二十三日は日中の調査隊員によるシンポジウムと出土文物展。二十四日は研究発表の後、午後から樋口隆康原考古学研究所長らが中国の研究者とパネルディスカッションを行う。

出土文物展は二十八日まで。

生活用具などが驚異的な状態で残存していること、多くのカローシュティ木簡出土、仏像菩薩像の断片発見などがある。学者たちを興奮させたのは、墳墓の発掘である。王国の支配階級者のものと推定され、死体は乾燥しきっており、身につけた服装や副葬品も極めて保存状態がよく、織物、玉（ぎょく）、金属のイヤリング、ガラス玉のネックレス、銅鏡、漆箱入りのくし、化粧品、ヤ遺跡出土文物展を開催しよう、これまでの成果の一部を披露することにした。もちろん、日本において初めての公開である。私たちの西域への貢献、遺跡文物の保護、環境保全に配慮しつつ、中国政府のご理解ご支援、中国学者の究明のみならず、東西文化交流史上まさに重要な資料である。中国国家文物局がこの発掘を「一九九五年中国十大考古新発見」に入れ、また、遺跡全体が「全国重点文物保護単位」に選ばれたのも宣う（むべ）なるかなである。

田辺昭三京都造形芸術大学

「王の木簡」など46点
ニヤ遺跡 出土文物展始まる
前一〜後4Cの都市国家
日中共同で調査

日中共同で発掘調査を進めている中国・新疆ウイグル自治区の都市遺跡「ニヤ遺跡」の発掘成果を紹介する「日中共同ニヤ遺跡学術研究出土文物展」が二十二日から、京都市北区の佛教大学・常照ホールで始まり、訪れた市民らは中国の貴重な文化時代の数々を熱心に見入っている。

同大新図書館の落成記念行事の一環。ニヤ遺跡は、紀元前一世紀〜紀元四世紀に栄えた都市国家として「漢書西域伝」には「精絶国」として登場する。仏教やブドウ酒に関する内容の書かれた長方形の木簡や、王の命令書などが一九八八年から九五年までに発見され、九八年ニヤ遺跡周辺の調査に参加し大きな成果を出した。

ニヤ遺跡で発掘調査した出土品などを紹介するニヤ遺跡出土文物展（京都市北区・佛教大常照ホール）

同展では「精絶国」と記された長方形の木簡、カローシュティ文字で王の命令が書かれた楔（くさび）形の木簡、渦巻き文の毛織物ほか、一九九五年に木棺に合葬されているのが発見された男女のミイラの写真パネルも展示されている。二十八日までの午前九時〜午後五時。入場無料。

佛大ホール

ちなみに文物の保険金額は9億8千万円
文物的保险金額为9亿8千万日元
For your reference, insurance amount for cultural assets is worth JPY 980 million

文物展を参観する海部俊樹元首相・高橋弘次学長・張宝智参事官・買買提祖農庁長ら
原首相海部俊树等参观文物展
Ex-Prime Minister Toshiki Kaifu observing the exhibition of antiquities

1997
第九次調査

　1997年8月と9月、田辺昭三・吉田恵二・吉崎伸・高橋照彦・杉本和樹・真田康道・井上正らが新疆文物考古研究所で遺物研究と写真撮影を行った。10月2日～11月5日、石田志朗・張玉忠・柳洪亮・龔国強らを加え、サポート隊あわせて計45名で現地調査を実施した。1997年以降の協議書も調印済みであったが、国家文物局・新疆文物局と数度の打合せの結果、現地調査に一区切りつけ、研究や報告書出版などを継続することで日中双方は合意し、日本側は本年調査終了時に測量機器など全装備を中国側へ贈呈した。国家文物局へ総括報告書を提出した。

　1997年8月和9月，在新疆文物考古研究所进行了文物研究和拍照。10月2日至11月5日，包括后勤队在内的合计45人实施实地考察。尽管签订了1997年以后的协议书，但是经与国家文物局、新疆文物局的多次协商，日中双方决定将实地调查限定于一个区域，继续进行研究及出版报告书等，日方在本年度调查结束后将测量器械等全部装备赠送给了中方。向国家文物局提交了总结报告书。

　In August and September 1997, the study of remains and the photo shootings were carried out at the Xinjiang Archaeological Institute. The field research was conducted from October 2 through November 5 with 45 members in total, including assistants. While the memorandum of understanding from 1997 on had already been signed, we decided to terminate field research for the moment after a series of discussions with SACH Chinese and the Xinjiang Cultural Assets Bureau. Both Japanese and Chinese sides agreed to focus on research and publications of reports. The Japanese team presented all the equipment, such as survey instruments, when research was terminated in 1997. We have submitted the comprehensive report to SACH Chinese.

1997年隊（部分）／1997年队（部分队员）／The team 1997 (part)

俺も隊員だァ〜／我也是队员啊！／"Hey, I'm part of a team, too!"

1998
上海博物館「シルクロード考古珍品展」開催

　1998年4月から10月まで、上海博物館で「シルクロード考古珍品展」が開催され、本調査隊収集の文物多数が展示され、買買提明・扎克尔新疆副主席・王中俊新疆文化庁書記・岳峰・筆者らが開会式に出席した。約50万人が参観し大きな反響を呼んだ。

　1998年4月至10月底，上海博物馆召开"丝绸之路考古珍品展"，本调查队收集的多件文物参展。约50万人观展，反响强烈。

　From April through October 1998, The Exhibition of Valuable Archaeological Relics on the Silk Road was held at the Shanghai Museum where a number of antiquities collected through our researches were displayed and received great response like gathering approximately 500 thousand visitors.

上海博物館長らと
与上海博物馆长等
With Director of the Shanghai Museum and others

王書記詩／王书记的诗
Poem by Secretary Wang

岳中方隊長論文
中方队长岳峰的论文
Thesis of Chinese Team Leader Yue

104

1999
調査報告会開催

1999年11月には日中双方は佛教大学四条センターで、真田康道・孫躍新・徐華田新疆文化庁書記・劉暁慶新疆政府外事弁公室処長・岳峰・伊弟利斯・阿不都熱蘇勒・于志勇・筆者など約100人が参加し、調査報告会を開催した。

1999年11月，日中双方在佛教大学四条中心召开调查报告会，约100人参会。

In November 1999, both the Japanese and the Chinese teams held a debrief session at the Shijo Center of Bukkyo University with attendance of about 100 people.

国会を参観
参观国会
Observing the Diet

2000
報告書（第二巻）出版

2000年1月には日中双方は97年度調査までの成果を水谷幸正・田辺昭三・真田康道・吉崎伸・岳峰・王炳華ら諸氏の尽力をえて『日中／中日共同ニヤ遺跡学術調査報告書』（第二巻・日中両文）として刊行した。日文・中文・図録の３冊セットである。

2000年1月，中日双方共同努力将97年及以前的调查成果总结成册，出版《日中/中日共同尼雅遗址学术调查报告书》（第二卷日中文）

In January 2000, both the Japanese and the Chinese teams published The Report of Japan-China/China-Japan Joint Scholarly Research of the Niya ruins Vol. 2 (in Japanese and Chinese) which had recorded the results of the researches conducted up until 1997, thanks to great efforts made by various people. It comes with three copies, including the Japanese version, the Chinese version, and the pictorial record.

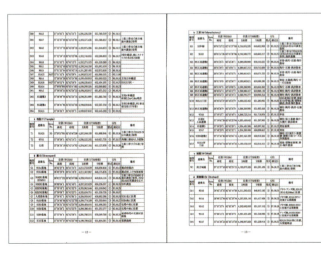
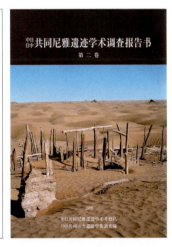

測定値一覧表（部分）など
測定値一覧表（部分）等
List of measurement values and others (part)

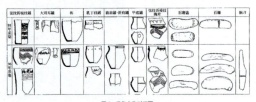
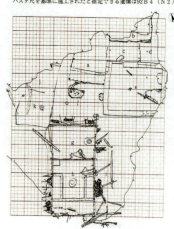

ダンダンウイリク調査ふくめて大沙漠での調査・発掘・保護・研究、そして報告書・シンポジウム……並大抵ではない。諸氏ご尽力の一端を理解したまわれば幸いである。包括丹丹烏里克調査在内、在大漠中進行調査、発掘、保護、研究、還要出版報告書、召開研討会……非比尋常。如能理解各位所付努力、甚感欣慰。

I would be very much obliged should you understand how unprecedented it had been to implement research, excavations and conservation in the extraordinarily vast desert, and then to carry out studies, reports, and symposium, and the case of research at Dandanoilik into the bargain.

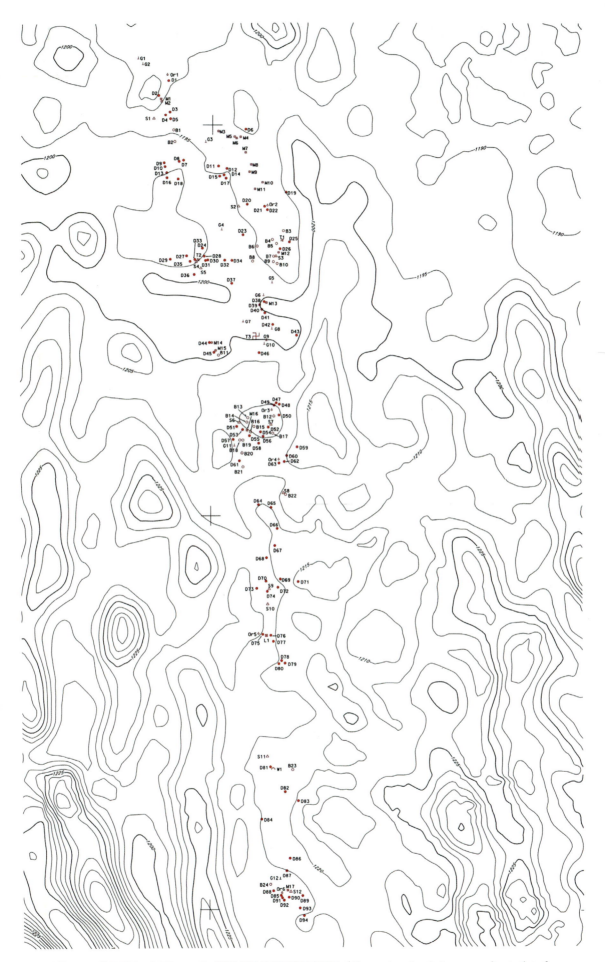

※遺構番号は地図番号で表示している／遺构编号以地图编号来显示／The number of a relic is corresponding to that of a map

$$\Delta T = -\frac{T_{1/2}}{\ln 2}\frac{\Delta \delta}{1+\delta^{14}C/1000} \quad \cdots\cdots(3)$$

ここで、$T_{1/2}$は^{14}Cの半減期（5568yr）。
採集地が地理的に近い試料群の年代の平均値（$Tavg$）はそれらの単純平均を、推定誤差$\Delta Tavg$は誤差伝播から(4)式を用いて算出した。

$$\Delta Tavg = \sqrt{\frac{1}{N-1}\sum_{i=1}^{N}(T_i-\bar{T_i})^2 + \sum_{i=1}^{N}\Delta T_i^2} \quad \cdots\cdots(4)$$

ここにNは試料数。

d 結果と考察

^{14}C年代測定結果を表2・3に示す。年代値は、1556〜2403yBPを示した。試料6010については$\Delta^{14}C$がほぼ0‰となり、核実験が頻繁に行われた1950〜60年代よりやや以前のものと思われる。また、試料6015は、$\delta^{14}C$が-29.5‰と、200〜300年程度前のものと推察されるが、ニヤ遺跡の年代と相当離れているため、炭素同位体のカウント数を十分に得ず、測定を中断した。このため、年代値を計算していない。

遺跡北部、中央部および南部とで年代にあきらかに系統的な差があり、遺跡の南方で年代が新しいことがわかる。遺跡北部、中央部、南部では年代の平均値はそれぞれ2328±156yBP（5019、5024、5026）、1922±134yBP（7001、7004、7009、7043）、南部では異なる発掘地域によって2系統の年代群からなり、それぞれ1562±117yBP（6001、6005、6012）、1684±157yBP（6016、6018、

地点	試料番号	^{14}C年代(yBP)	平均
遺跡北部	5007	1667±147	
	5009b	2196±57	
	5019	2354±46	2373±37
	5024	2361±39	
	5026	2403±93	
遺跡中央部	7001	1857±103	
	7004	1914±94	1922±41
	7009	1951±39	
	7043	1964±75	
遺跡南部	6001	1558±61	
	6005	1556±53	1562±39
	6010	1572±84	
	6012	1697±99	1623±32
	6015	1718±79	1684±51
	6016	1636±82	
	6018	Modern ($\Delta^{14}C$=+3.2±27.7)	
	6023	Recent ($\Delta^{14}C$=-29.5±27.1)	

表2 木材試料の^{14}C年代値一覧

— 386 —

not been found.

3. A second investigation, following on the heels of 1993, examined the distribution of remains in the Taklimakan Desert, located to the north of the Niya site. During this investigation, pottery, bronze swords, stone sickles and gemstones were discovered 40km north of the Niya site. These artefacts and remains predated those found in the Niya ruins, belonging to the Bronze Age. This is of great import in considering the history and environment of the Niya basin.

4. Investigations unearthed a clay castle in the south of the Niya ruins. It was surrounded by two- to three-metre earthen walls in an oval shape, the longest measuring 185m and the shortest 150m. Inside, there were remains of tamarisks, but no identifiable ruins of buildings. To prevent modern-day oil development dwellings located at the south gate were investigated, and those further to the south of that gate. The castle gate had one wooden crossbeam, and showed evidence of having been damaged by fire. The beam style proved similar to Kaladon and Endelay castles, which are in the Keriya Valley basin, and in addition Kharosthi wooden tablets 96A7 were found dating to the 6th year of King Mahili. This ancient castle's discovery filled some gaps in the research of the site of the Niya ruins, as well as providing new data on the site.

5. Investigations carried out at the Niya site utilising the Global Positioning System (hereafter GPS) made a major contribution to confirming the location of the ruins, but the biggest handicap to searching around there was the lack of a map of that area. Therefore, in order to map out the ruins found there, an evaluation was begun using satellite photographs. Furthermore, a network of measurements for the entire Niya site needed to be set down, which required improvements in the detail of investigations still to be solved. It was envisaged that the high quality of GPS would be the key to the solution, but customs clearance delays put back the project until the following year.

1997 Research Report

The area had been under investigation since 1994, but it seemed like it was coming to an end for the time being. Hence the task in 1997 was mainly to fill in the gaps left from the investigations of the previous year. The main research is detailed below.

— 410 —

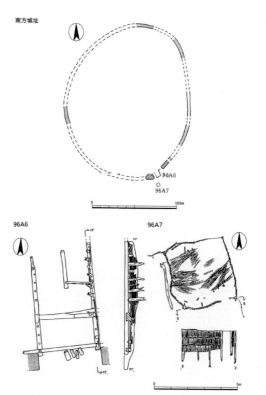

93A9 (N14) 南部作坊遺址的1・2号窯、1号池塘実測図 (1:200)
93A9 (N14) 南方工房址1・2号窯、1号池実測図 (1:200)

南方城址示意図 (1:2000) 96A6 城門、96A7 房址実測図 (1:100)
南方城址模式図 (1:2000) 96A6 城門・96A7 住居実測図 (1:100)

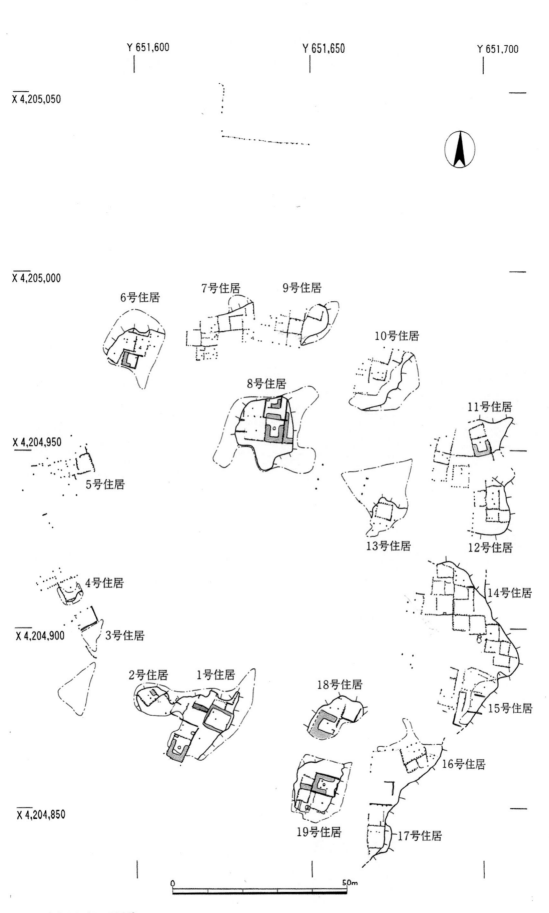

遺迹分布図（1：1000）
遺構配置図（1：1000）

96-97頁ご参照／请参照96-97页／Refer to page 96-97

2000
ウルムチで「国際シンポジウム」開催

　2000年3月、ウルムチの環球ホテルで「中日共同ニヤ遺跡学術調査シンポジウム・報告書（第二巻）発行式」を開催した。買買提明・扎克尔新疆副主席・徐華田新疆文化庁書記・祖農・庫提魯克庁長・尼相・依不拉音新疆政府外事弁公室主任・韓翔・岳峰・王炳華・伊弟利斯・阿不都熱蘇勒・于志勇・張玉忠・楊林・孟凡人・林梅村・李遇春・中国考古学界第一人者の兪偉超中国歴史博物館長・楊志軍国家文物局司長・趙豊中国絲綢博物館副館長・田辺昭三・真田康道・吉崎伸・伊東隆夫・孫躍新・周培彦・井上正・切畑健・筆者ら日中双方約150人が参加した。

　2000年3月，在乌鲁木齐环球酒店召开"中日共同尼雅遗址学术调查研讨会暨报告书（第二卷）发行仪式"，中日双方约150人参加。

　In March 2000, the symposium on Japan-China joint scholarly research of the Niya ruins and the ceremony to celebrate the publication of the report (Vol. 2) were taken place at World Plaza Hotel in Urumqi with attendance of approximately 150 people from Japan and China.

兪偉超館長と／与俞伟超馆长／Together with Director Yu Weichao

シンポジウムを報じる人民日報・新疆日報・新疆経済報（部分）
报道研讨会的人民日报、新疆日版、新疆经济报（部分）
People's Daily, *Xinjiang Daily* and *Xinjiang Economic Daily* reporting the symposium (part)

2001

ニヤ調査「20世紀中国考古大発見100」に

2001年3月、ニヤ遺跡調査は国家文物局・『考古』より「20世紀中国考古大発見100」に選ばれた。4月から02年1月まで林梅村北京大学教授を佛教大学へ招きカローシュティー文書の研究を推進した。

2001年3月，尼雅遗址考察被国家文物局、《考古》杂志选入"20世纪中国百项大考古大发现"。4月至02年1月，邀请北京大学林梅村教授在佛教大学进行佉卢文文书研究。

In March 2001, the Niya research was selected as one of the Chinese 100 greatest discoveries in the 20th century by SACH Chinese and the magazine called Archaeology. From April through January 2002, Peking University Professor Lin Meicun was invited to enhance research of Kharosthi documents at Bukkyo University.

『二十世紀中国百項考古大発見』より（中国社会科学出版社）
摘自《二十世纪中国百项考古大发现》／ *100 Major Archaeological Discoveries in the 20th Century in China*

2002
国家文物局「五星出東方利中国」を「出国展覧禁止文物」指定

2002年1月、「五星出東方利中国」錦が国家文物局により中国の膨大な全文物から「出国展覧禁止文物」64点のひとつに選出された、対外展示による劣化を防ぐためで、いわば「国宝中の国宝」に指定されたともいえる。

2002年1月，"五星出东方利中国"织锦经国家文物局筛选，在中国数目庞大的文物中脱颖而出。成为64件"禁止出国展览文物"之一，目的是为了防止对外展出造成的损害，可以说被指定为了"国宝中的国宝"。

In January 2002, the silk brocade "Five stars appearing in the east bring good fortune to China" was selected by SACH Chinese as one of the 64 prohibited antiquities from being exhibited abroad among Chinese immeasurable antiquities. This is tantamount to be selected as the national treasure among national treasures, as being so valuable as to prevent it from being deteriorated by exhibiting abroad.

2002
NHK「シルクロード・絹と黄金の道展」に出陳

2002年8月～12月、東京国立博物館と大阪歴史博物館で「シルクロード・絹と黄金の道展」が開催され、「王侯合昏千秋萬歳宜子孫」錦など本調査隊検出文物が多数出陳され、大きな反響を呼んだ。東博での開会式には買買提明・扎克尔新疆副主席らが出席し、海部俊樹ニヤ機構名誉会長と会見した。長年ご指導をえた塩川正十郎財務大臣に大阪展を参観いただいた。

2002年8月至12月，东京国立博物馆和大阪历史博物馆举办"丝绸之路：绢与黄金之路展"，"王侯合昏千秋万岁宜子孙"织锦等多件文物参展，引起了极大的反响。新疆政府买买提·提明扎克尔副主席出席东京国立博物馆的开幕仪式，并与尼雅机构名誉会长海部俊树会见。邀请多年予以指导的盐川正十郎财务大臣在大阪参观展览。

From August through December 2002, The Silk Road: the Exhibition of Silk and Gold was held at the Tokyo National Museum and the Osaka Historical Museum where a number of antiquities detected by the research team, such as the silk brocade "Best wishes for the King's marriage." This exhibition received an enthusiastic public response. Vice-Governor of Xinjiang Maimaitiming Zhakeer and others attended the exhibition and talked with Honorary Chairman Toshiki Kaifu at the exhibition in Tokyo. Furthermore, Financial Minister Masajuro Shiokawa who had long offered invaluable support for me kindly visited the exhibition in Osaka.

大阪展参観の塩川大臣
参观大阪展的盐川大臣
Minister Shiokawa visiting the exhibition in Osaka

同展『図録』より転載
摘自该展览"图录"
Reprinted from the exhibition's pictorial record

2002
『シルクロード・ニヤ遺跡の謎』出版

2002年11月、諸氏の玉稿をえてニヤ調査の概要紹介本を出版した。井ノ口泰淳日本側初代学術隊長・田辺昭二二代学術隊長・兪偉超中国歴史博物館長の高論を転載しておく。2005年1月には中国語版を出版した。

2002年11月，获得各位赐稿，出版介绍尼雅考察概要的书籍。2005年1月出版中文版。

In November 2002, We released the introductory book summarizing the Niya research thanks to valuable supports offered by various people. The Chinese version was published in January 2005.

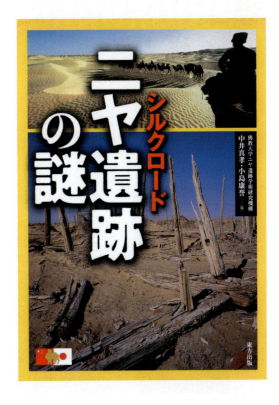

前頁の木簡を開封した状況。

ニヤ遺跡出土のカローシュティー文書

Inokuchi Taijun 井ノ口泰淳

ここに言うカローシュティー文字とはカローシュティー(Kharosthī) 文字と言う意味で、用いられている言語を指しているのではない。カローシュティー文字はもともと西北インドに於いて紀元前三世紀頃より後三世紀頃に至る時代に用いられた文字で、限られた時期・地域でのみ用いられた特殊な文字である。

カローシュティー文字の起源は紀元前四～五世紀、イラン地域で用いられていたアラム文字で、インド・アーリヤ語を書写するように改善したもので、右横書きの文字である。この文字を用いて書写された言語は中期インド・アーリヤ語(プラークリット) 西北インド方言で、現在はガンダーラ語と名付けられている言葉である。

この特殊な文字・言語が西北インドから遠く離れた中国新疆ウイグル自治区のタクラマカン砂漠中の所謂西域南道に於いて用いられていた事を示す物がカローシュティー文書である。西北インドのカローシュティー文字資料は金石碑銘と樺皮写経であるのに対して、西域出土のものは大部分が木簡で、前者は仏教信仰・文化との関係が密接であるが、後者は官庁行政に関連した世俗文書である。

西域のカローシュティー文書の出土地はニヤと楼蘭の両遺跡であり、総数約八〇〇点を数え、その九割以上がニヤ遺跡から発見され、特にN・V・XV遺跡からは二〇〇点近い文書が出土している。これら多数のカローシュティー文書の大部分は既に解読され、その内容も細かく検討されつつある。

ニヤ出土のカローシュティー文書は大半は木簡であり、その形状に従って楔形、矩形、長方形等数種に分かたれ、他に二十数枚の皮革文書も発見されている。記載内容を概括して言えば、いわゆる世俗文書であるが、細分すれば1．王または支配者の布告文、2．命令書、3．証文、4．報告書・返答書等に分かつことが出来るとされている。

ニヤ出土のカローシュティー文書が作成された詳細な時期に就いては諸説あり、おおよそ紀元三世紀半ばより四世紀半ばに至る約百年程の間であろうと考えられるが未だに定説は無い。

また、この文字を用いた西北インドの民族と西域南道の民族との歴史上の関係も、両者間の仏教とその他の文化の類似と差異も、さらに同時に出土した漢文書との関係もまだ十分に明らかにはされていない。

これらの諸問題の解明は今後の研究の進展に委ねられている。

(龍谷大学名誉教授)

「砂漠考古学」のこと

Tanabe Shouzo　田辺昭三

タクラマカン砂漠周辺は、至るところ古代遺跡の宝庫である。シルクロードの幹線が東西にはしり、その道筋には仲介交易によって栄えた都市国家がオアシスを中心に点在し、興亡をくりかえしていた。私たちが調査したニヤ遺跡も、そのような都市国家の一つであった。

「砂漠考古学」とは、たとえばニヤ遺跡のように砂漠の一角に廃墟となって取りのこされ、或いは現在砂漠の砂に埋もれている史跡を通して、歴史を解明しようとする学問である。「砂漠考古学」といっても、考古学を離れて特別な目的をもっているわけではなく、調査の対象を砂漠の文物に限定するだけのことで、調査法、研究法も、またその方法論もすべて考古学一般と同じであり、究極には歴史学の一分科学であるといってよい。

日本の国土に砂漠は存在しない。この自明の事実にもかかわらず、私たちは日本から遙かに遠い中央アジアの砂漠にまで、史跡を求めて日中共同調査を長期にわたって実行した。この調査は、多くの課題をかかえて出発したが、困難をもかえり見ず、なぜ外国にまで進出して砂漠の史跡を調査したのか。いま直ちにその理由を挙げるなら、以下の三点に尽きるだろう。まず、月並みだが日本古代文化の源流はシルクロードにある。正倉院収蔵品をはじめ日本の古代文化とつながるシルクロードの文物は数多い。日本文化の原点を探るためにも、シルクロード研究は不可欠の分野である。次に、砂漠では、一般に遺存し難い木製品や染織品などの有機質遺物が、実に良好な保存状態で発見される場合が多い。いうまでもなく、その主な理由は極度の乾燥状態にある。発見された文物の比較検討、近年著しい進歩を続けている文物の保存科学的研究など、砂漠の文物でしか果せない研究が可能なことも、砂漠調査の重要な理由の一つである。砂漠考古学研究のもう一つの理由は、砂漠に取り囲まれたオアシス都市国家の厳しい自然環境のために、都市国家への文化の移動、流入が単純化され、研究上有利な条件となっている点である。つまり、砂漠を往来する一筋の道を、幾筋もの道で複雑に結ばれた近隣の都市国家間を結んでいるのである。砂漠における文化の移動を軸に文化を考える方が、単純な一筋の道を考えるより、わかり易いことはいうまでもないだろう。

（神戸山手大学教授）

疲れた身体に鞭打って、今日の報告と明日の打ち合わせ。

二代の精絶国王──九五年発見ニヤ一号墓主の身分

Yu Weichao　俞 偉超

十数年間に及ぶニヤ調査の精神、中でも小島康誉氏の大志は尊重する価値がある。『中日・日中共同ニヤ遺跡学術調査報告書』第二巻に収録された研究成果は幅広く、数多くの研究者が研究を深める必要があるが、私は九五年発見ニヤ一号墓地について、出土した銅鏡によって墓地の年代を推測すれば、およそ紀元二世紀後半から三世紀前半まで、即ち漢代末期から魏晋期までと決めることができる。埋葬品から推測することが可能である。一号墓地の主人の身分とその関係に関しても、特にM3の遺体は被っていた「王侯合昏千秋万歳宜子孫」錦およびM8から出土した「五星出東方利中国」と「討南羌」のような古い言葉が多く書かれているが、「王侯合昏（婚）千秋万歳」「延年益寿」「討南羌」錦は、墓の主人は二代にわたる精絶国王と后であることをはっきりと表している。というのは、当時の出土文物には「千秋万歳」「延年益寿」のような古い言葉が多く書かれているが、「王侯合昏（婚）」錦は全くない。当時は階級の厳しい社会であったため、王と后以外の人は使えなかったであろう。即ち、このような文字を織り込んだ錦は流通商品ではなく、宮廷専用のところで作られ、皇帝の命令により王、后に授与される。ニヤで発見されたカローシュティー文書と自称することから、「王侯合昏（婚）」錦は当地の王と后しか使えなかったことが分かる。従って、M3の男女の遺体は王と后であり、M3より下に埋葬されていたM8の遺体は先代の王と后である。

M8から出土した錦を観察しても、都善国が任命した当地の長官すなわち精絶国の王と后しか使えなかったことが分かる。つまり、「五星出東方利中国」と「討南羌」を繋げると、南羌との戦いには必ず勝つ事が出来ると言う意味になるから、これも中原王朝から授与された錦であることが分かる。授与された理由は、おそらく精絶国は「討南羌」の戦いに参加し、大いに貢献したからであろう。

以上をまとめると、九五年発見一号墓地は精絶の王室墓地であり、M3とM8は二代にわたる王と后の墓であり、他の墓は精絶王の親族の墓である。

（前中国歴史博物館館長）

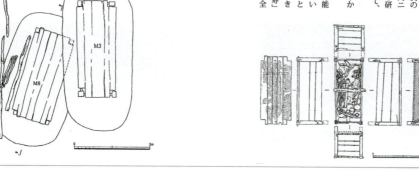

2004
7年ぶりニヤ遺跡へ NHK同行取材

2004年10月、浅岡俊夫・安藤佳香・孫躍新・張玉忠・李軍・筆者らが遺構の変化状況を観察するためニヤ遺跡へ入った。日本側にとって7年ぶり。石油開発にともない沙漠公路から小オアシス（カパクアスカン）まで簡易舗装されていて、驚いた。各遺構に大きな変化はなかったが、若干の盗掘跡が見受けられた。また部分崩壊した仏塔の修復が新疆文物局により進行中であった。遺跡北部で未登録と思われる墓地3ヵ所を登録した。この踏査にはNHK「新シルクロード」取材班が同行取材した。

撮影中のNHK取材班
拍摄中的NHK采访组
NHK reporters on shooting

2004年10月，为观察遗址变化情况进入尼雅，这是日方时隔7年再进尼雅。伴随石油开发，简易沙漠公路已铺设到了卡巴克阿斯坎村，笔者很震惊。各个遗构虽没有大的变化，但是可见一些被盗痕迹。新疆文物局正在修复部分坍塌的佛塔。对尚未登记的遗址北部3处墓地予以登记。NHK"新丝绸之路"摄制组随同采访。

In October 2004, we set foot on the Niya ruins to observe how each remain had undergone changes. It was the first visit in seven years for the Japanese team. I was surprised to see a limited, paved road built for petroleum development which leads to Kapakeasican from Desert Highway. Though there was not much change made in each ruin, we found some looting traces. In the mean time, the restoration of the partially eroded stupa was underway by the initiative of the Xinjiang Cultural Assets Bureau. We registered three tombs in the northern area which were considered to be unregistered. The reporters of NHK also accompanied us for featuring The New Silk Road.

2005
NHK「新シルクロード」放映

2005年、ほぼ一年にわたって、「新シルクロード」が放映され、「タクラマカン西域のモナリザ」でニヤ調査とダンダンウイリク調査が紹介された。また4月から10月、「新シルクロード展」が東京・神戸・岡山で開催され、本調査隊検出の錦やダンダンウイリク隊検出壁画が出陳された。12月から2006年3月まで、香港で「絲路珍宝－新疆文物大展」が開催され本調査隊検出のカローシュティー木簡や錦などが出陳された。06年8月、筆者は官邸を訪れ小泉純一郎首相に調査概要を報告し、「五星出東方利中国」錦の盾を贈呈した。

2005年，"新丝绸之路"节目连续播放将近一年，以"塔克拉玛干西域的蒙娜丽莎"为题，介绍了尼雅考察和丹丹乌里克考察。4月至10月间，在东京、神户、冈山举办"新丝绸之路"展，本调查队出土的织锦及丹丹乌里克队发现的壁画参展。12月至2006年3月，香港举办"新疆文物大展"，本调查队发现的佉卢文木简和织锦等参展。2006年8月，笔者在首相官邸向小泉纯一郎首相汇报调查概要，赠送"五星出东方利中国"织锦的盾形工艺品。

In 2005, The New Silk Road was televised for almost a year. When The Mona Lisa of Taklamakan in the Western Regions was featured, the Niya and the Dandanoilik researches were highlighted. From April through October The New Silk Road Exhibition was held in Tokyo, Kobe, and Okayama where silk brocades and murals detected by the Niya and the Dandanoilik teams, respectively, were displayed. From December through March 2006, The Great Exhibition of the Xinjiang Cultural Assets was taken place in Hong Kong where Kharosthi wooden strips and silk brocades detected by our team were displayed. In August 2006, I visited the Office of the Prime Minister and met Prime Minister Junichiro Koizumi to report the outline of the research and presented him with a silk-brocade shield of "Five stars appearing in the east bring good fortune to China."

ウルムチでの「新シルクロード」プレスリリース
在乌鲁木齐"新丝绸之路"的记者招待会
The press release of The New Silk Road in Urumqi

2007

報告書（第三巻）出版

　2007年10月には日中双方は第二巻以降の研究成果を浅岡俊夫ら諸氏の尽力をえて、『日中／中日共同ニヤ遺跡学術調査報告書』（第三巻・日本語版）としてまとめ、文部科学省オープン・リサーチ・センター整備事業（平成15〜19年度）関連刊行物として刊行した。報告書第一巻〜三巻は計7kgに及ぶ。11月、佛教大学四条センターで「日中共同シルクロード学術研究国際シンポジウム」を開催した。

　2007年10月，在日中双方的共同努力下，将第二巻以后的研究成果汇编成《日中/中日共同尼雅遗址学术调查报告书》（第三卷日文版），作为文部省公开调查中心整备事业关联刊物出版。报告书的一至三卷合计7公斤，11月在佛教大学四条中心召开"日中共同丝绸之路学术研究国际研讨会"。

　In October 2007, the Japan-China joint team summarized the achievements of their research following the 2nd volume, namely The Report of Japan-China Joint Scholarly Research of the Niya Ruins Vol. 3 (Japanese version) thanks to untiring efforts of the people concerned. This report was released as a related publication of the development project of the MEXT's Open Research Center. In November, the international symposium on the Japan-China collaborative scholarly research in the Silk Road was held at the Shijo Center of Bukkyo University.

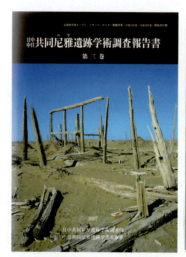

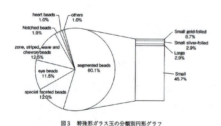

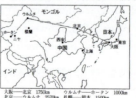

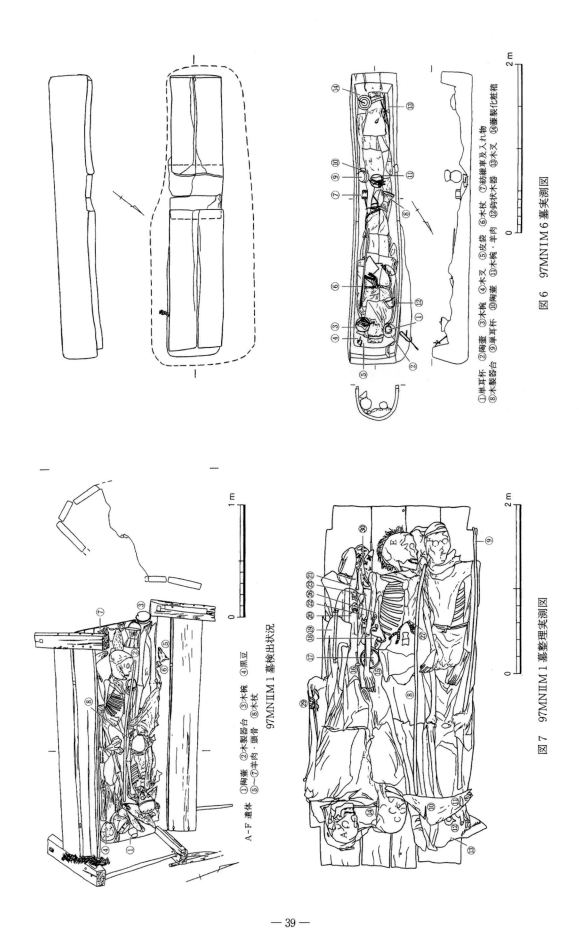

図6 97MNIM6墓実測図
図7 97MNIIM1墓整理実測図

Ⅲ 日中共同ニヤ遺跡学術調査

2009
北京大学と「漢唐西域考古：ニヤ・ダンダンウイリク」国際シンポジウム開催

2009年11月、日中双方は北京大学・中国社会科学院とシンポジウムを北京大学考古文博学院で開催した。山極伸之佛教大学長・中原健二同文学部長・安藤佳香・浅岡俊夫・吉崎伸・岡岩太郎・伊東隆夫・吉田恵二・孫躍新・周培彦・田中清美・市川良文・冨澤千砂子・呉志攀北京大学副書記・童明康国家文物局副局長・孫華北京大学副院長・盛春寿局長・林梅村・栄新江・王子今・巫新華・鉄付徳・王衛東新疆文物考古研究所長・于志勇・張玉忠・張鉄男・李軍・筆者などが約100人参加し、挨拶や発表・討議が熱心に行われ大成功をおさめた。

出席者（部分）
出席者（部分）
The participants (part)

2009年11月，日中双方在北京大学考古文博学院与北京大学、中国社会科学院共同举办研讨会。佛教大学山极伸之校长、北京大学吴志攀副书记、国家文物局童明康副局长、北京大学孙华副院长、盛春寿局长、新疆文物考古研究所王卫东所长等约100人出席会议，大家热烈致辞、积极发言讨论，研讨会圆满成功。

In November 2009, the symposium sponsored by the Japan-China joint team, Peking University and Chinese Academy of Social Sciences was held at School of Archaeology and Museology, Peking University participated by President of Bukkyo University Nobuyuki Yamagiwa, Vice-Secretary of Peking University Wu Zhipan, Vice-Director of SACH Chinese Tong Mingkang, Vice-Director of School of Archaeology and Museology Sun Hua, Bureau Director Sheng Chunshou, Director of the Xinjiang Archaeological Institute Wang Weidong and others. It achieved a great success with the attendance of about 100 researchers of various fields who made addresses, presentations and a vigorous discussion.

呉副学長・山極学長・童副局長・盛局長の挨拶と日程／吴副校长、山极校长、童副局长、盛局长的致辞和日程
Addresses by Vice-President Wu, President Yamagiwa, Vice-Director Tong and Director Sheng, and the schedule

盛局長「新疆は内地に比べて厳しい所。現地調査の条件は厳しく、待遇面の問題もあり、人材の流出も多い。新疆の皆さんは頑張ってほしい。内地の人は応援してほしい」、筆者「日中双方の一流専門家の幅広い発表はたいへん嬉しい。20数年前に新疆で共同調査を始めるのは至難であった。20年余の調査研究保護事業の成果も大きいが、多くの方に研究テーマを提供できたことも大きな成果であり、それは末長く提供し続けるだろう。今後も微力を尽くす」と。

盛局长说道"相比内地，新疆环境恶劣，实地考察条件艰苦，加之待遇问题，造成人才流失严重。希望新疆各位加油，希望内地给与支持"；笔者说道"来自日中双方一流专业人士的发言令人高兴。20多年前在新疆开始共同考察相当困难。20多年来的调查研究保护事业成果巨大，能为众多人士提供研究课题也是重要成果，相信可以长期提供，今后我将继续贡献绵薄之力"。

Bureau Director Sheng once stated, "Xinjiang is a tough place comparing with inlands, or urban areas. The conditions for research on site are far severer and there is a problem with the treatment of people working here into the bargain, which has often entailed outflow of valuable human resources. I want people in Xinjiang to hang in here and people in urban areas to stick up for Xinjiang."

In response to his statement, I said, "I'm very pleased with a whole variety of presentations offered by prominent specialists from both Japan and China. It was almost next to impossible to start a collaborative work in Xinjiang two decades back. The achievements earned by the undertakings over 20 years for research, studies, and conservation were so great, and yet at the same time it was also a great achievement to have been able to release research subjects to a number of people. This should go on much longer. And I will keep hanging in there."

III　日中共同ニヤ遺跡学術調査　119

ニヤ・ダンダンウイリク調査は中国外国協力・学問疎通の模範例と報じる中国文物報
中国文物报：尼雅、丹丹乌里克考察是中外合作、学术沟通的典范
Chinese Cultural Resources News reporting that the Niya and the Dandanoilik researches are a role model for academic collaboration between China and other countries

ワシントンポストも度々報道／华盛顿邮报也多次报道
Reported frequently by *Washington Post*

清華大学写真展
清华大学摄影展／The photo exhibition at Tsinghua University

2011
清華大学と「ガンダーラからニヤ」共催

2011年4月、清華大学創立100周年記念行事で写真展を共催した。

2011年4月，作为清华大学建校100周年纪念活动之一，共同举办摄影展

Cosponsoring the photo exhibition on the occasion of the 100th anniversary of the foundation of Tsinghua University in April 2011.

2012
ウルムチ・ロンドンでのシンポジウムで発表

2012年10月、中国社会科学院考古研究所・新疆文物局がウルムチで「漢代西域考古と漢文化国際シンポジウム」を開催し、約150人が発表した。日本側は伊東隆夫・田中清美・浅岡俊夫・孫躍新・周培彦・筆者が発表した。尖閣諸島国有化直後の緊張状態で日本側一部参加者の取り消しも出た。11月、筆者は大英図書館シンポジウム「ヘディン・スタインの遺産と最近の探検」で「世界的文化遺産保護研究を使命として」を発表した。

2012年10月，中国社会科学院考古研究所、新疆文物局在乌鲁木齐召开"汉代西域考古与汉文化国际研讨会"，约150人发表论文。由于钓鱼岛事件刚刚发生不久，事态紧张，部分日本学者取消参会。11月，笔者在大英图书馆"赫定、斯坦因的遗产及最近的探险"研讨会上作题为"以保护研究世界性文化遗产为使命"的演讲。

In October 2012, the Archaeological Institute of the Chinese Social Science Academy and the Xinjiang Cultural Assets Bureau held the international symposium on the archaeological perspective of the Western Regions in the Han Dynasty and its culture in Urumqi. About 150 people made their presentations. In a highly strained context just after the nationalization of the Senkaku Islands, some of scheduled participants had cancelled their visit. In November, I was invited to make a presentation under the title of "My Life-long Mission for Conservation and Research of World-class Cultural Heritages" at the symposium on Hedin and Stein's Legacy and New Explorations held by the British Library.

緊張時こそ文化交流！／关系紧张时更需要文化交流
At the time of tension, cultural interaction is all the more important!

大英図書館シンポジウム参加者と／大英图书馆研讨会
The symposium organized by the British Library

2013

佛教大学でシンポジウム・写真展開催

歓迎宴（部分）／欢迎宴会（部分）／The welcome party (part)

2013年11月、日中双方は佛教大学宗教文化ミュージアムで「シルクロード新疆での世界的文化遺産保護研究と国際協力」国際シンポジウムと同写真展を開催した。小野田俊蔵佛教大学宗教文化ミュージアム館長が挨拶し、安藤佳香・浅岡俊夫・吉崎伸・張玉忠・焦健・呉勇・田小紅・筆者が発表した。

2013年11月，日中双方在佛教大学宗教文化博物馆同时召开"对丝绸之路新疆的世界性文化遗产的保护研究与国际合作"国际研讨会和摄影展。

In November 2013, the International Symposium, namely The Conservation and Research of World-class Cultural Heritages on the Silk Road in Xinjiang and International Cooperation, and the photo exhibition were held at the Bukkyo University Museum of Religious Culture.

2014

新疆文物「ニヤ遺跡調査特集」発行

2014年9月、新疆文物考古研究所『新疆文物』は「ニヤ遺跡調査特集」号を発行した。多くの文物写真と実測図をふくむ労作である。于志勇中方二代目学術隊長の尽力によるものである。

2014年9月，新疆文物考古研究所《新疆文物》出版"尼雅遗址调查专刊"，是包括文物照片和实测图在内的劳心之作，得益于第二任中方队长于志勇的付出。

In September 2014, the Xinjiang Archaeological Institute published a special issue in its bulletin XinJiang Cultural Relics featuring the research of the Niya ruins that contains a number of photos of cultural assets and survey drawings. It could come out thanks to vigorous exertion by Yu Zhiyong who had served as the second Leader of the Chinese scholarly team.

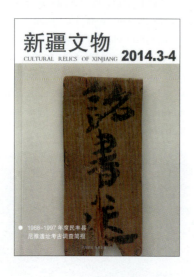

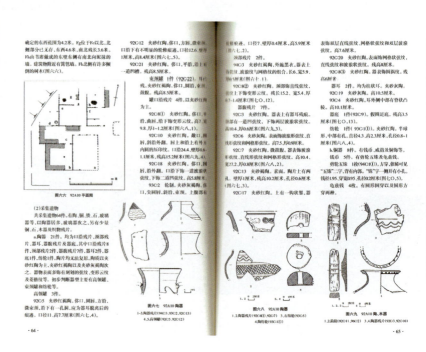

出土品紹介（部分）
出土文物介绍（部分）
Unearthed antiquities (part)

2014
北京大学教授らにニヤ遺跡で調査紹介

2014年12月、北京大学カローシュティー研究会が開催された。筆者は段晴教授や欧米の研究者へニヤ調査をPPTで紹介。カローシュティー木簡写真提供を求められ、新疆側へ連絡をと応じた。その後一行とニヤ遺跡へ入り、王炳華中方初代学術隊長と状況を紹介した。

2014年12月，召开北京大学佉卢文研讨会，笔者用PPT向段晴教授和欧美学者介绍了尼雅考察，学者们希望提供佉卢文木简照片，我回答请你们与新疆方面协调。之后与研究者一行进入尼雅，与中方首任学术队长王炳华一起介绍了概况。

In December 2014, the Kharosthi research meeting was held at Peking University and I introduced the Niya research using PPT to Professor Duan Qing and other Western researchers. As I was requested to provide the photo of Kharosthi wooden strips, I advised them to make contact with the Xinjiang side. Afterwards, we together entered the Niya ruins and I described the current context with Wang Binghua who had served as the first Leader of the Chinese scholarly team.

参観する一行／参观者一行／Visiting party

2015
保護強化小型沙漠車贈呈

2015年10月、筆者は変化状況を撮影するため甘偉新疆文物局主任助理・張化傑和田文物局長らとニヤ遺跡へ入った。世界遺産追加申請の前段階として、仏塔など主要遺構で保護柵工事が進行中であった。広大な遺跡を侵入者から守るのは容易でない。諸氏が奮戦している。保護強化のため保護巡視用の小型沙漠車"POLARIS"を贈呈した。

2015年10月，为拍摄变化情况，笔者进入尼雅遗址。作为追加申请世界遗产的前期工作，正在为佛塔等主要遗迹加设保护围栏。要保护宏大的遗址免受入侵绝非易事，诸君一直在奋战中。赠送了强化保护用的巡视用小型沙漠车。

In October 2015, I entered the Niya ruins to take photos of how it had undergone change. At a stage prior to the additional application to the World Heritage, work of the protection fence for pagodas and main relics was under way. It is not an easy task to safeguard vast relics against intruders. The people concerned are struggling hard. I donated a small-sized desert vehicle, called POLARIS, for use of patrol to enhance protection.

保護柵工事、保護強化を願って／工程保护栅栏，希望保护强化／Protection-fence work in the hope of reinforcing conservation

Ⅲ　日中共同ニヤ遺跡学術調査　123

2017
天津テレビ「五星出東方利中国」撮影

　2017年6月、中国・天津テレビ「泊客中国」クルーと筆者特集番組撮影のためニヤ遺跡へ入った。筆者の遺跡入りは12回目。質問に応じ、タクラマカン沙漠や崑崙山脈にはまだ未発見の遺跡があるだろうと答えた。2018年1月、天津テレビが筆者特集3番組を放映、「五星出東方利中国」でニヤ調査が取り上げられた。

　2017年6月，为拍摄笔者的专题节目，与中国天津电视台"泊客中国"剧组一起进入尼雅遗址，这是我第12次进入遗址。针对提问，我回答到：在塔克拉玛干沙漠和昆崙山脉还有未发现的遗址吧。2018年1月，天津电视台播放了3集有关笔者的专题节目，在"五星出东方利中国"中介绍了尼雅考察。

　In June 2017, I entered the Niya ruins along with the crew members of Tianjin TV program, or China Right Here which featured about me. This was my 12th visit there. In response to the question, I answered that there would be some relics have yet to be discovered in the Taklamakan Desert and the Kunlun Mountains.

　In January 2018, Tianjin TV broadcast the three-part program featuring me. They took up the Niya ruins in its version of Five Stars Appearing in the East Bring Good Fortune to China.

尹暢キャスター・遺跡保護監視員と
与尹畅制片人、遗址保护巡视员
Together with Anchor Yin Chang and a relic-guard watcher

  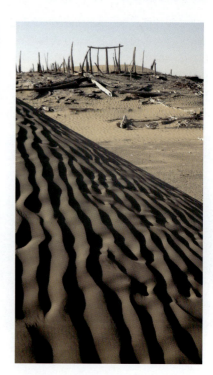

王炳華中方初代学術隊長「一帯一路の交流を示す人類の至宝、小島の組織力が無かったら」、于志勇二代学術隊長「ニヤ調査は最も早く長く最大」、筆者「文化遺産保護は皆の責任」と（Web放映を撮影）

节目中，首任中方学术队长王炳华说："显示了一带一路历史的人类瑰宝，如果没有小岛先生的张罗……"，第二任学术队长于志勇说："尼雅考察时间最早、期间最长、规模最大"，笔者表示"保护文化遗产是共同的责任"（摄于网络播放）

Wang Binghua who served as the first Leader of the Chinese scholarly team saying, "A supreme human treasure as shown in the interactions by "One Belt, One Road" could not be discovered without organizing power of Mr. Kojima"; Yu Zhiyong who served as the second Leader of the Chinese scholarly team saying, "The Niya research is the fastest, the longest, and the largest one"; and me saying, "Conservation of cultural heritages is responsible for all" (Screenshot)

2018
ニヤ遺跡調査30周年記念活動決定

2018年3月、筆者と王衛東新疆文物局長・李軍副局長・于志勇学術隊長らは「ニヤ遺跡調査30周年」にあたり、中国側は『調査図録編』出版・「文物展」開催、日本側はこの『写真・資料集』出版・佛教大学連続市民講座・写真展開催で合意した。

2018年3月，笔者与新疆文物局王卫东局长、李军副局长、于志勇学术队长就"尼雅遗址考察30周年"，达成如下一致意见：中方出版《调查图录编》、举办"文物展"；日方出版该《照片资料活动记录》、在佛教大学举办系列市民讲座和图片展。

In March 2018, on the occasion of the 30th anniversary of the Niya ruins' research, Director of the Xinjiang Cultural Assets Bureau Wang Weidong, Vice Director Li Jun, Leader of the Scholarly team Yu Zhiyong, and I agreed to the following points: Chinese side publishes the pictorial records of the research and holds the cultural assets exhibition, and Japanese side publishes the collection of photos and research materials and organizes the public lecture series at Bukkyo University and a photos exhibition.

新疆文物局で打合せ
在新疆文物局协商／The meeting at the Xinjiang Cultural Assets Bureau

2018
『中国新疆36年国際協力実録』出版、「市民講座」等開催へ

2018年10月、日本側はこの『中国新疆36年国際協力実録』を出版した。11月から19年3月、安藤佳香教授企画により佛教大学四条センターで「シルクロード：美の道・壁画の道」と同写真展を開催予定である。

2018年10月，日方出版了该《中国新疆36年国际合作实录》。11月至19年3月，将在佛教大学四条中心举办安藤佳香教授策划的"丝绸之路：美之路・壁画之路"及图片展。

In October 2018, the Japanese side published the collection of photos and research materials as mentioned above. From November 2018 to March 2019, The Silk Road: the Road with Aesthetic Value, the Road with Murals and the photos exhibition are slated to be held in accordance with a planning by Professor Yoshika Ando.

2018
『調査図録編』出版予定、「ニヤ調査回顧展」開催へ

2018年10月、中国側は『調査図録編』出版予定である。9月から19年2月、新疆博物館で文物展「ニヤ調査回顧展」（仮称）を開催予定である。筆者は会場で「日中ニヤ調査をふりかえって」を講演予定である。

2018年10月、中方计划出版《调查图录编》、9月至19年2月，计划举办"尼雅考察回顾展"（暂定）文物展。

In October 2018, the Chinese side is scheduled to publish the pictorial records of research. From September 2018 to February 2019, the exhibition of cultural assets.

多領域の専門家が協力して

多領域专家合作／Collaboration among specialists from a whole variety of fields

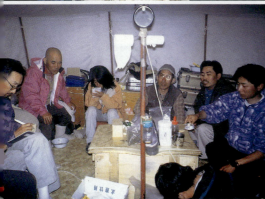

Ⅲ　日中共同ニヤ遺跡学術調査　　127

皆で世界的文化遺産保護研究

共同保护研究世界性文化遗产／Conserving and researching world-class cultural heritages all together

使命感×精神力×体力×協調力

　大沙漠での過酷な約3週間。「世界的文化遺産を保護研究するぞ」といった使命感・強靭な精神力・体力・協調力がないと耐えられない。更には組織力・国際協力力・資金力が必要である。

　在沙漠的恶劣环境中度过大约3周时间。如果没有"坚决保护研究世界性文化遗产"的使命感、坚韧的毅力、体力、协调力是无法忍受的。而且，组织力、国际合作以及资金也是必不可少的。

　Research for about three weeks in the vast desert demands incredible endurance. Without solid mental, physical, and cooperative strength, not to mention a strong sense of mission like "I will conserve and study world-class cultural heritages by all means," it should be unbearable. On top of that, We need organizing power, the capability of international cooperation, and funding capacity.

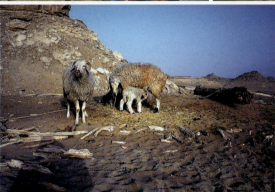

奮闘を伝える各種資料

传达奋斗精神的各种资料／Various materials to tell tremendous efforts

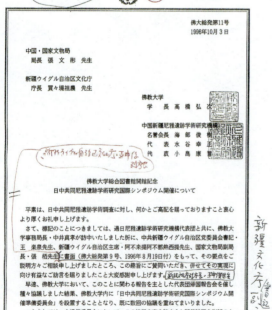

1994年調査

日程　9月27日～11月5日

参加者　中国隊16名　韓翔・王炳華・王経奎・于志勇・アハメティ・張鉄男・
　　　　　　　　　シャビティ・劉玉生・（人冬）文康・李季・楊林・
　　　　　　　　　楊逸嘯・王守春・王邦維・李文瑛・王宗磊・
　　　　日本隊14名　小島・真田・井ノ口・伊東・高橋・小野田・田辺・高妻・
　　　　　　　　　浅岡・吉崎・米川・後藤・市川・蓮池

隊　長：小島・韓翔
考古班：N2発掘　田辺・井ノ口・高橋・浅岡・吉崎・米川・後藤・市川・小野田・
　　　　　　　　李文瑛・王宗磊
　　　　：N37発掘　王炳華・王経奎・于志勇・張鉄男・シャビティ・劉玉生・
　　　　　　　　（人冬）文康・李季・楊林・楊逸嘯・王守春・王邦維
木質班：伊東・高妻・
分布班：真田・アハメティ・コルパン・蓮池
残留班：蓮池・市川

9/27
6:10　仏教大学のバスで仏教大学を出発。
8:15　関西空港着。　9:45　日本隊全員集合完了。11:35　離陸。
12:31　上海空港着。于志勇氏が迎えに来ている。
13:30　通関手続きで問題発生。光波測距儀を中心に梱包を開いて調べを受ける。
　　　通関事務所に承認の印を受けるために于氏が出向いたがなかなか戻らない。
14:50　保証金10万円を支払う。
15:15　承認書が届く。　15:20　国内線に移動。
15:40　輸送料8000元が必要となり、真田先生・于氏・後藤氏の3名で両替に出かけ
　　　る。　16:10　搭乗終了。　16:27　離陸。
18:12　北京空港着。一時間ほどの整備のため着陸。この間を使ってミーティング
　　　を行う。日程・契約書の写し等を配布する。
22:55　ウルムチ空港着。
24:00　華僑賓館に到着。

9/28
9:00　朝食。
10:00　送迎のバスに乗る。　10:30　考古研に到着。
10:45　日中ミーティング。日本隊全員。中国隊側は韓翔氏・王炳華氏・国家文物局
所長・王邦維北京大学教授・楊逸嘯（地理院）・沙毘提氏・李氏・張鉄男・劉玉生・
于志勇等。韓翔氏・王炳華氏挨拶。日本隊挨拶。670万円の引き渡し。
13:25　ミーティング終了。
14:00　昼食。
15:10　記者会見に出席するため人民公堂へ。　16:30　記者会見開始。
17:45　記者会見終了。華僑賓館に戻る。小島・真田・田辺・井ノ口の4名は図書
　　　館の寄付の件で出向く。
19:00　夕食。

9/29
9:00　朝食。
10:00　小島・真田以外の12名は送迎のバスに乗って博物館を参
　　　観する。　14:30　昼食。　14:50　送迎バスで考古研へ向かう。

－ 1 －

15:00　考古研着。真田氏から張鉄男へ365,777元が支払われる。その後考古研所蔵
　　　の文物を参観する。
17:45　華僑賓館に帰着。小休止の後、　18:55　賓館から人民公堂へ向かう。
19:20　会堂着。　19:20　歓迎宴が始まる。
21:25　歓迎宴終了、会堂を出る。　21:50　賓館到着。

9/30
9:00　朝食。昼食までは自由時間。装備の点検等を行う。　12:00　昼食。
13:10　華僑賓館を出て空港へ。16:23　予定より一時間以上遅れて離陸。
17:51　和田空港着。19:05　賓館到着。　19:50　和田文官所で参観。
20:30　夕食。

10/1
8:00　朝食。　9:30　和田賓館を出発、予定より30分遅れである。
12:20　ケリヤ着。ここで昼食。
15:30　民豊招待所着。　16:00　後続トラック隊も到着する。
18:00　燃料等の積み替え。　18:40　装備の確認。
19:30　夕食。　21:15　ミーティング、明日の段取り確認。

10/2
7:30　インスタント・ラーメンの朝食。　8:00　手荷物積み込み。
8:30　民豊招待所出発。1号車ベンツ砂漠車（小島・孫）、2号車タンク車（真田）
　　　3号車トラック（吉崎・高橋）、4号車ベンツ砂漠車（井ノ口・田辺・伊東・
　　　高妻・浅岡）、残り5人は荷台に分乗。
12:10　カバカスカン手前3Km付近で停車。後続の2・3号車を待ちながら昼食。
14:00　全車そろって出発。
15:00　タマジャ・マザール付近で後続隊を待つ。
15:35　2号車がスタック。1号車が牽引に向かう。
15:40　3号車が追いつく。2号車に積んでいた枯れ草がエンジンの熱で燃え始め
　　　る。懸命で消火に当たり、約5～6分で消し止める。
16:00　やっと4台が揃う。　16:20　再出発。それぞれ行けるところまで行って、
　　　残された車を迎えに来ることにする。
17:45　仏塔から21.7Kmの地点でタンク車のエンジンが故障し動かなくなる。積み
　　　荷の水は他の砂漠車でBCまでピストン輸送することになる。
18:10　3台揃って出発。　18:20　3号車スタック。1・4号車は待機する。
18:30　1号車が3号車の牽引に向かう。　19:30　スタック脱出。出発。
19:45　1号車が途中で分かれた場所に引き返す。3台が揃う。
20:00　仏塔から14～5Kmの地点（N:37° 48' 15"、E:82° 46' 49"）で野営。
21:35　インスタント・ラーメンの夕食。

10/3
8:30　インスタント・ラーメンの朝食。テント撤収。
9:05　出発。　9:15　ニヤ遺跡入り口の標示板通過。
9:30　N:37° 49' 40"、E:82° 45' 36"地点で1号車パンク。修理に手間取るが
　　　結局はタイヤ交換。
11:05　N:37° 52' 49"、仏塔から10.6Kmの地点で小休止。ルートの
　　　選択を誤り、スタックを繰り返す。
14:00　GPSを使ってルート探し。　15:00　出発。
16:00　1号車、4号車と続いてスタック。　17:20　3台がやっと揃うが、1号

－ 2 －

1994年 9月 8～10日

合宿日程表

	9月8日（木）	9月9日（金）	9月10日（土）
6:30		起床 洗面等 体操	起床 洗面等 体操
8:00		朝食（8:00～8:30） 研修	朝食（8:00～8:30） 研修<講義>
8:30	JRバス 京都駅11:20発 ゼミナール12:51着	（測量実習 辻先生）	（カローシュティー文字資料 井ノ口先生） （考古学について 田辺先生） 連絡事項
12:00		昼食（12:00～13:00）	昼食（12:00～13:00） JRバス ゼミナール13:10発
	昼食（13:00）		
13:00	研修（13:30） （オリエンテーション 真田先生）	研修 （測量実習 辻先生）	
14:30	研修<講義> （木質科学について 伊東先生）		
17:00		入浴	
17:30	夕食（17:30～18:30）	夕食（17:30～18:30）	
19:00	研修<講義> （測量概論 辻先生）	ミーティング	
21:00	入浴		
22:00	就寝	就寝	

※ 先生方のご都合で日程が変更されることもありますが、ご了承下さい。

The Organization of Resaerch of the Niya Sites

1996

10月11日（金）　晴れ

起床　　8：30
朝食　　9：10　　ＢＣ
昼食　　　各班別
夕食　　19：20　　ＢＣ
就寝　　0：00

全隊の行動　尼雅遺跡滞在
各班にわかれ調査を行う　小島・真田・吉田は北方調査へ

考古調査班（田辺・吉崎・米川・中島・近藤・杉本・小野田・加藤・古手川）
9：10　朝食
　　　撮影用ヤグラの積み込み
10：00　北方調査班ＢＣを出発
10：30　ベースキャンプ発
　　　途中、砂漠車のスタック4回・故障1回
13：40　ようやくN14に到着
14：00　昼食と休息
15：00　N14・N13の現状を観察
16：30　ミーティング
16：45　N14着
17：25　ベースキャンプ着・機材準備
　　　ＢＣの白テント設営、無線機材設置
19：20　夕食
20：00　N14建物配置の略図作成
21：45　ミーティング

ＧＰＳ測量調査班　（内田・市川）
終日考古調査班と同一行動

中国隊Ｎ5調査参加班（田中・稲益）
10：30　N5仏堂を田中氏とクリーニング
13：30　昼食
16：00　作業開始
　　　Ｎ5－15建物の清掃
19：00　作業終了

－ 9 －

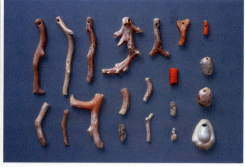

出土品から人々の豊かな生活が浮かび上がってくる
从出土文物可见人们优裕的生活
You can imagine affluent lives of people from excavated artifacts

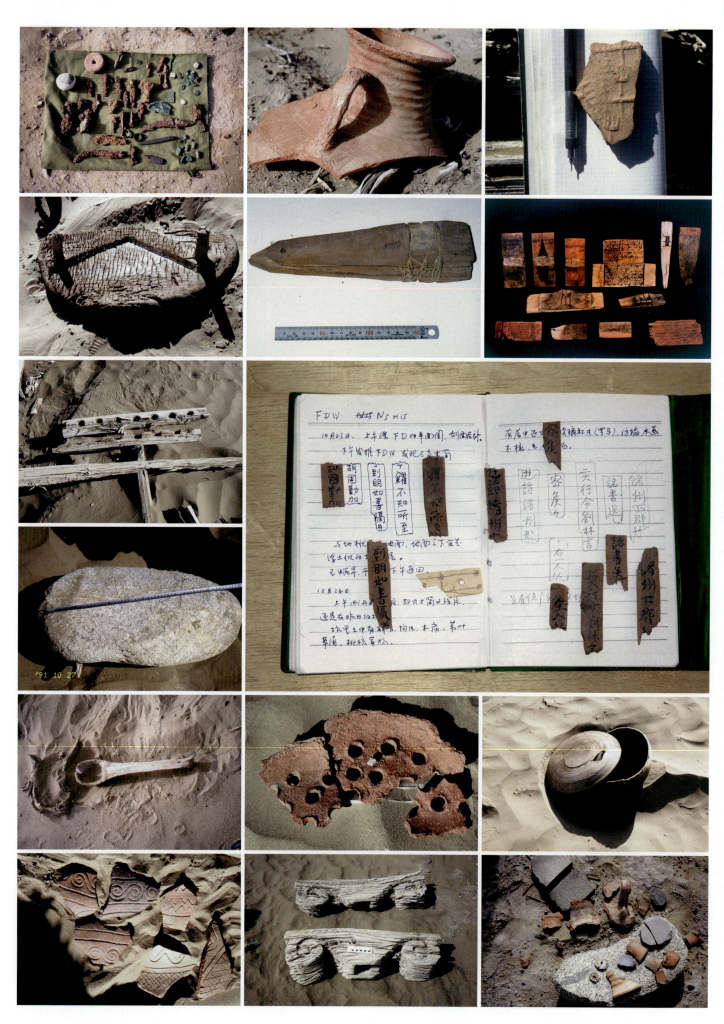

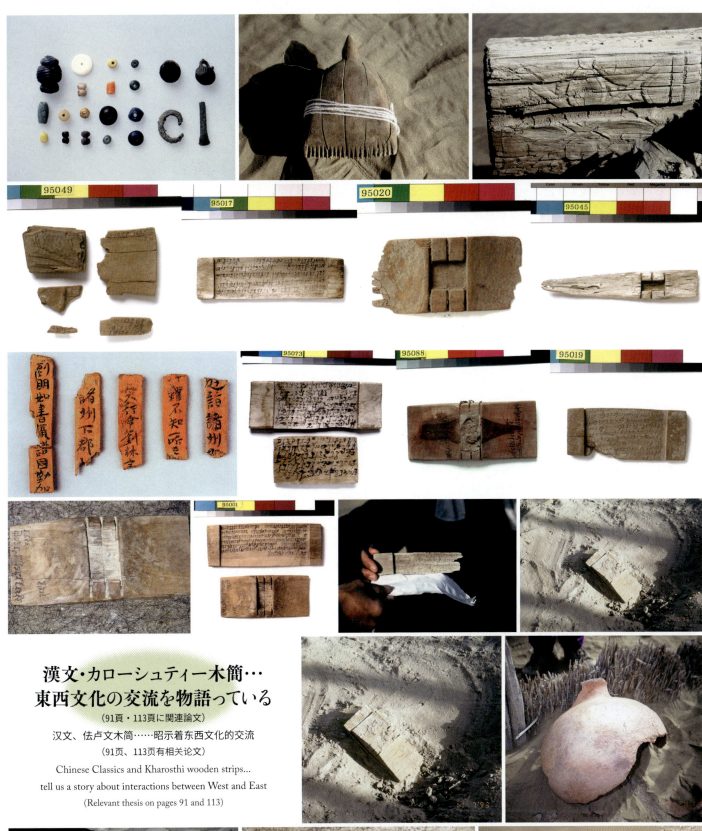

漢文・カローシュティー木簡…
東西文化の交流を物語っている
(91頁・113頁に関連論文)

汉文、佉卢文木简……昭示着东西文化的交流
(91页、113页有相关论文)

Chinese Classics and Kharosthi wooden strips...
tell us a story about interactions between West and East
(Relevant thesis on pages 91 and 113)

Ⅲ 日中共同ニヤ遺跡学術調査 137

（成果概要）

研究領域が多岐にわたることもあり、後述のように多くの機関の研究者が参加した。専門分野は外事管理・文化財管理・国際協力・考古学・仏教学・西域文献学・東西交渉史・建築学・地理学・地質学・木質科学・仏教美術史・染織学・撮影・測量などである。これら多くの方々の努力により、次のような成果をあげることができた。

- 仏塔・寺院・墓地・住居・生産工房・土塁・家畜小屋・果樹園・貯水池・並木・建築部材や遺物散布地など約250ヶ所の遺構を発見し、GPSで経緯度を登録し、遺構分布図を作成した。
- 大型GPSを活用し、周辺地形図を作成、遺跡全容を明らかにした。
- 遺跡北方約40kmに更に古い遺構・遺物を発見し、生活拠点の南下を明らかにした。
- 関連都市の住居を測量調査し、遺跡住居構造を明らかにした。
- いくつかの住居を発掘し、生活状況を明らかにした。
- いくつかの住居群や生産工房を測量調査し、都市構造を明らかにした。
- 寺院を発掘調査し、壁画などを検出し、西域仏教解明の手がかりをえた。
- 王族の墓地を発見発掘し、国宝級遺物多数を検出し、精絶国が当時の中原王朝と政治経済文化面で密接な関係があったことを明らかにした。
- 各種の墓地を発掘し、埋葬方法に新しい知見をえた。
- 住居の柱材などをC14法により測定し、遺跡年代確定の大きな手がかりをえた。
- カローシュティーおよび漢文木簡をふくむ大量の貴重文物を検出し、新しい知見をえた。
- カローシュティーおよび漢文文書を解読し、新しい知見をえた。
- いくつかの動物の化石を検出し、遺跡一帯の地質形成で新しい知見をえた。
- これらの結果、西域36国「精絶国」の全容を明らかにした。

成果概要

因为涉及多个研究领域，如后所述，众多机构的研究者都有参与。专业领域有外事管理、文化遗产管理、国际合作、考古学、佛教学、西域文献学、东西交涉史、建筑学、地理学、地质学、木质科学、佛教美术史、染织学、摄影、测量等，在众多人士的努力下，取得了如下成果。

- 发现佛塔、寺院、墓地、住居、生产作坊、土垒、牲口棚、果树园、贮水池、行道树、建筑构件及文物散落地等250余处遗迹，用GPS记录经纬度，制作了遗迹分布图。
- 使用大型GPS，制作周边地形图，弄清了遗址全貌。
- 在遗址以北约40公里处发现年代更久远的遗迹和文物，显示生活据点有南迁现象。
- 测量调查相关城市的住居，弄明了遗址住居构造。
- 发掘几处住居遗址，弄明了生活状况。
- 测量调查几处住居群和生产作坊，弄了明城市构造。
- 发掘调查寺院遗址，收集壁画，掌握了破解西域佛教的线索。
- 发现并发掘王族墓地，出土多件国家级文物，可以肯定精绝国与当时的中原王朝在政治经济文化方面有着密切的联系。
- 发掘各种墓地，在埋葬方法上获取了新知。
- 通过对住居柱子作C14测定，获得了确定遗址年代的重要线索。
- 发现大量包括佉卢文及汉文木简在内的珍贵文物，获得了新知。
- 解读佉卢文及汉文文件，获得了新知。
- 发现动物的化石，由于遗迹一带的地质形成得到新的知识了。
- 依据上述成果，弄明了西域36国"精绝国"的全貌。

Summary of achievements:

Since the scope of studies extends over a wide range of fields, a number of researchers from various organizations participated in this project as being referred to below. Specialized fields include a liaison function, the management of cultural assets, international cooperation, archaeology, Buddhism, philology of the Western Regions, history of East-West interactions, architectonics, geography, geology, ligneous science, history of Buddhist art, dyeing science, shooting skills, and survey. People in these fields made tireless efforts, which resulted in the following achievements:

- Confirming about 250 relics, such as pagodas, temples, gravesites, dwelling sites, production workshops, earth works, stables, orchards, reservoirs, line of trees, architectural members and sites with dispersed remains followed by registering their latitude-longitude locations via GPS to create the distributional diagram of those relics.
- Creation of the surrounding topological chart using large GPS to clarify the whole picture of the ruins.
- Discoveries of much older relics and remains about 40 km north of

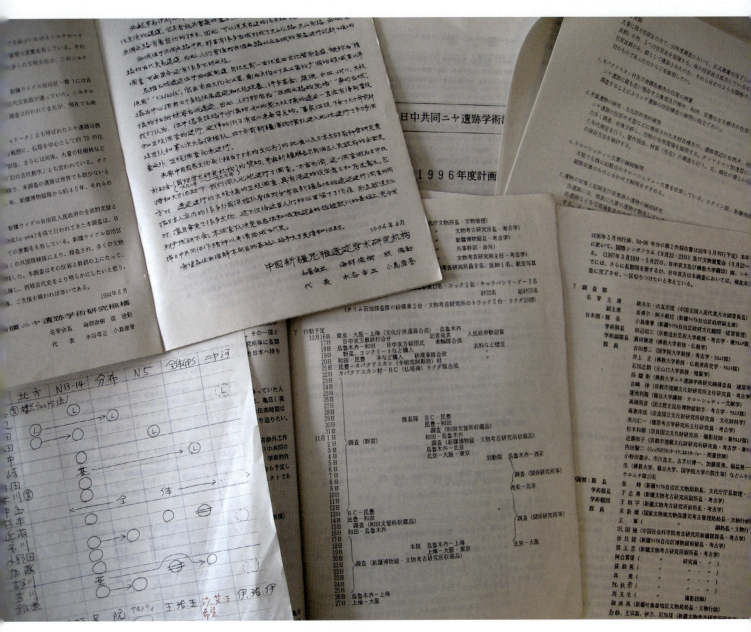

計画書各種（部分）／各种计划书(部分)／The various kinds of plans (part)

the Niya ruins to verify living quarters moving south.
- Making a survey on dwelling sites of relevant cities to identify the structure of ruined residences.
- Excavating some residences to clarify the ways of living.
- Making a survey on some groups of dwelling sites and production facilities to clarify urban structure.
- Excavating to research temples and detecting murals to get a clue to identify Buddhism in the Western Regions.
- Discovery and excavating of the royal graveyard and detecting national-treasure class of many antiquities to clarify a close relationship in terms of politics, economics, and culture between Jing Jue Guo and Chinese Dynasties in those days.
- Excavating various gravesites that offered new insight into burying methods.
- Measuring post materials by means of C14, which gave us a lead to define ruin's age.
- Detecting loads of valuable cultural assets, including Kharosthi and Chinese wood strips to gain new insight.
- Deciphering documents in Kharosthi and in Chinese classics to gain new insight.
- Detecting some fossils that offered us new insight in terms of geological formation in the area of the Niya ruins.
- All these findings add up to clarifying the whole picture of Jing Jue Guo among 36 kingdoms in the Western area.

（調査組織）

　日中共同ニヤ遺跡学術調査隊の調査組織は下記の通りである。参加年度は〈　〉に記入した。役職は報告書に記載された当時のものを使用した。（参加年度順）

中日共同尼雅遺址学術調査队的组织结构如下所示。参加年度计入〈　〉中，职位是出版报告书时所任的职务（以参加年度为顺）
Described as below is the researching organization of the Japan-China joint scholarly research of the Niya ruins. The participated year is put in parentheses. The names of positions are those used at the time. (In order of the year participated)

名誉主席	鉄木尔·達瓦買提（全国人民代表大会副委員長）	
名誉副主席	吾甫尔·阿不都拉（新疆ウイグル自治区副主席）	
顧問	李羲林（北京大学一級教授·学務委員）	
	王中俊（新疆ウイグル自治区文化庁書記·副庁長）	
	買買提祖農·買買提艾力（新疆ウイグル自治区文化庁庁長）	
日本側隊長	小島康誉（佛教大学内ニヤ遺跡学術研究機構代表）〈1988・90・92・93・94・95・96・97〉	
学術隊長	井ノ口泰淳（龍谷大学名誉教授）〈90・91・93・94・95〉	
	田辺昭三（京都造形芸術大学教授）〈94・95・96・97〉	
学術副隊長	真田康道（佛教大学教授）〈90・91・92・93・94・95・96・97〉	
隊員	堀尾　寶（寺尾商会部長）〈88・90〉	
	北野博之（ツルカメコーポレーション社員）〈88〉	
	窪田憲龍（龍谷大学大学院生）〈90・92〉	
	長澤和俊（早稲田大学教授）〈91〉	
	青木　淳（佛教大学大学院生）〈91〉	
	高橋照彦（国立歴史民俗博物館助手）〈91・92・93・94・95・96・97〉	
	緒方正親（龍谷大学大学院生）〈91・92〉	
	猪沢良秀（龍谷大学大学院生）〈91・92・93〉	
	孫　躍新（京都大学共同研究員）〈92・93・94・95・97〉	
	蓮池利隆（龍谷大学講師）〈92・93・94・95・96・97〉	
	米田文孝（関西大学講師）〈93〉	
	古川雅英（科学技術庁技官）〈93〉	
	貝柄　徹（関西外国語大学講師）〈93〉	
	有馬嗣郎（佛教大学大学院生）〈93〉	
	林真理子（関西大学大学院生）〈93〉	
	上杉彰紀（関西大学生）〈93〉	
	亀元佳苗（関西大学生）〈93〉	
	大谷宏治（関西大学生）〈93〉	
	後藤雅彦（国学院大学大学院生）〈94〉	
	伊東隆夫（京都大学木質科学研究所教授）〈94・96〉	
	浅岡俊夫（六甲山麓遺跡調査会研究員）〈94・95〉	
	吉崎　伸（京都市埋蔵文化財研究所主任）〈94・95・96・97〉	
	高妻洋成（奈良国立文化財研究所研究員）〈94・95・96〉	
	小野田豪介（佛教大学大学院生）〈94・95・96・97〉	
	米川仁一（橿原考古学研究所主任研究員）〈94・95・96・97〉	

市川良文（龍谷大学大学院生）〈94・95・96・97〉

小林利晴（国学院大学大学院生）〈95〉

大山幹成（京都大学大学院生）〈95〉

佐藤右文（撮影技師）〈95・開棺調査〉

中島皆夫（長岡京市埋蔵文化財センター調査員）〈95・96〉

杉本和樹（奈良国立文化財研究所撮影技師）〈95・96・97〉

坂本和子（古代オリエント博物館研究員）〈96・新疆文物考古研究所調査〉

田中清美（大阪市文化財協会長原事務所長）〈96〉

吉川和孝（京都造形芸術大学大学院生）〈96〉

吉田恵二（国学院大学教授）〈96・97〉

内田賢二（ジェックテクニカルマネージャー）〈96・97〉

近藤知子（京都市埋蔵文化財研究所研究員）〈96・97〉

加藤里美（国学院大学大学院生）〈96・97〉

古手川博一（国学院大学大学院生）〈96・97〉

稲益晃一（龍谷大学大学院生）〈96・97〉

井上　正（佛教大学教授）〈97・新疆文物考古研究所調査〉

石田志朗（元山口大学教授）〈97〉

栗田一生（国学院大学大学院生）〈97〉

中国側隊長　韓　翔（新疆ウイグル自治区文化庁文物処処長）〈1988・90・93・94〉

岳　峰（新疆ウイグル自治区文物局局長・文化庁庁長助理）〈95・96・97〉

学術隊長　王炳華（新疆文物考古研究所所長）〈91・92・93・94・95・96〉

于志勇（新疆文物考古研究所副所長）〈91・92・93・94・95・96・97〉

隊員　熱傑布・玉素甫（和田地区文物管理所所長）〈88〉

伊弟利斯・阿不都熱蘇勒（新疆文物考古研究所副所長）〈88・90〉

王経奎（新疆ウイグル自治区文化庁外事処副主任）〈88・90・92・93・94・95・96〉

盛春寿（新疆ウイグル自治区文物局副局長）〈88・91・92〉

李　肖（新疆文物考古研究所館員）〈90〉

劉文鎮（新疆文物考古研究所館員）〈90・91〉

阿合買堤・熱西堤（新疆文物考古研究所文保室主任）〈91・92・93・94・95・96・97〉

張鉄男（新疆文物考古研究所館員）〈91・92・93・94・95・96・97〉

沙比提・阿合買提（新疆博物館館長）〈92・93・94・95・96〉

劉玉生（新疆文物考古研究所撮影技師）〈92・94・95・96・97〉

劉宇生（新疆ウイグル自治区外事弁公室副主任）〈93〉

景　愛（国家文物局中国文物研究所研究員）〈93〉

劉樹人（華東師範大学遥感研究所所長）〈93〉

陳　芸（華東師範大学遥感研究所講師）〈93〉

王　博（新疆博物館館員）〈93〉

肖小勇（新疆文物考古研究所館員）〈93〉

伊　力（新疆文物考古研究所測量技師）〈93・95・96・97〉

佟文康（新疆文物考古研究所助理館員）〈93・94〉

李　季（国家文物局文物三処処長）〈94〉

楊　林（国家文物局文物二処副処長）〈94〉

楊逸疇（中国科学院地理研究所研究員）〈94〉

王守春（中国科学院地理研究所研究員）〈94〉

王邦維（北京大学教授）〈94〉

李文瑛（新疆文物考古研究所館員）〈94〉

王宗磊（新疆文物考古研究所助理館員）〈94・95・96・97〉

李　軍（新疆ウイグル自治区文物局外事室室員）〈95〉

任式楠（中国社会科学院考古研究所所長）〈95〉

孟凡人（中国社会科学院考古研究所研究員）〈95〉

斉東方（北京大学助教授）〈95〉

楊　晶（国家文物局中国文物研究所研究員）〈95〉

王　軍（国家文物局文物二処副処長）〈95・開棺調査〉

王亜蓉（中国社会科学院歴史所古代服飾究所室研究員）〈95・開棺調査〉

呂恩国（新疆文物考古研究所研究室主任）〈95・96〉

呉　勇（新疆文物考古研究所研究員）〈95・96・97〉

阮秋栄（新疆文物考古研究所助理館員）〈95・96・97〉

伊斯拉斐尓·玉蘇甫（新疆博物館副館長）〈96〉

邢開鼎（新疆文物考古研究所副研究員）〈96〉

趙　静（新疆文物考古研究所助理館員）〈96〉

張樹春（新疆文物考古研究所工作人員）〈96〉

阿迪力·馬木提（和田地区文物管理所所員）〈96〉

張玉忠（新疆文物考古研究所副所長）〈97〉

羊毅勇（新疆文物考古研究所副研究員）〈97〉

尼加提·肉孜（新疆文物考古研究所助理館員）〈97〉

龔国強（中国社会科学院考古研究所新疆隊隊長）〈97〉

柳洪亮（吐魯番地区文物局局長）〈97〉

Research organization: The research has involved various fields of top-class specialists both in Japanese and Chinese universities as mentioned above. Because of space limitations, name of individuals and their affiliated institutions are abbreviated in terms of English translation.

III 日中共同ニヤ遺跡学術調査　143

干上がったニヤ河ぞいに北上し、ニヤ遺跡を目指す天津テレビ「泊客中国」取材班3台の小型沙漠車
2017年6月天津テレビドローン撮影

沿干涸的尼雅河北上进入尼雅遗址的天津电视台"泊客中国"采访组的3辆小型沙漠车　2017年6月天津电视台无人机航拍
The three small-sized desert vehicles driving north along the dried Niya River heading for the Niya ruins to cover in the Tianjin TV "China Right Here"　The drone filming shots by Tianjin TV in June 2017

点在する遺構に接近する天津テレビ「泊客中国」取材班の小型沙漠車
2017年6月天津テレビドローン撮影

向散落的遗迹靠近的天津电视台"泊客中国"采访组的小型沙漠车　2017年6月天津电视台无人机航拍
The small-sized desert vehicle approaching scattered relics to cover in the Tianjin TV "China Right Here"　The drone filming shots by Tianjin TV in June 2017

世界最大の木造都市遺跡 ニヤ遺跡を世界遺産に

　2006年8月、中国国家文物局と世界遺産センターは、トルファンで「シルクロード」申請予備会議を開催。中国のほかにカザフスタン・キルギス・タジキスタン・ウズベキスタンなども参加し、行動計画を決議し、国をまたぐ共同申請活動が開始された。

　2007年には国家文物局が6省区48ヵ所の申請を決定。新疆ではキジル千仏洞・ニヤ遺跡をはじめとして、楼蘭遺跡・交河故城・高昌故城・アスターナ墓地・スバシ故城・クムトラ千仏洞・シムセム千仏洞・ベゼクリク千仏洞など12遺跡。2012年登録を目指した。

　2011年12月、タジキスタン・ウズベキスタン側の準備遅れで申請延期と分離申請を決定。規模も縮小、天山山脈周辺に絞られ、ニヤ遺跡や楼蘭などは次段階へ繰り越された。

为世界最大的木结构城市遗址尼雅遗址能够登录为世界文化遗产

2006年8月，国家文物局和世界遗产中心在吐鲁番召开"丝绸之路"申请预备会。除中国外，卡萨克斯坦、吉尔吉斯、塔吉克斯坦、乌兹别克斯坦等也参加了会议，决定了执行计划，开始了跨国联合申请行动。

2007年，国家文物局决定申请6个省区的48处遗址，新疆境内以克孜尔千佛洞、尼雅遗址为首，楼兰遗址、交河故城、高昌故城、阿斯塔纳墓地、苏巴什故城、库木吐拉千佛洞、森木塞姆千佛洞、柏孜克里克千佛洞等12处遗址入选。以2012年登录成功为目标。

由于塔吉克斯坦、乌兹别克斯坦方面的准备不足，2011年12月，决定延期并分开申请。同时缩小规模，锁定在天山山脉周边，尼雅遗址和楼兰遗址等顺延至下个阶段。

The Niya ruins: the world largest wooden ruins for the world heritage

In August 2006, the preliminary conference was held for the Silk Road application by SACH Chinese and the World Heritage Centre in Turpan. Besides China, Kazakhstan, Kyrgyzstan, Tadzhikistan, Uzbekistan, and other countries participated in this conference and decided an action plan. The joint application project extending across national boundaries was commenced.

In 2007, SACH Chinese decided to file 48 sites in six provinces. In Xinjiang, 12 sites were included, such as the Loulan ruins, the ancient cities of Jiao River and Gaochang, the Astana tombs, the Subashi Buddhist Temple Ruins, and the Kumutula grottoes, the Shimsem grottoes, the Bëzeklik grottoes, as well as the Kizil grottoes and the Niya ruins. They aimed to have them registered in 2012.

In December 2011, as a delay in preparation was found in Tadzhikistan and Uzbekistan, it was decided to postpone the application and apply separately. The applied area was also scaled down like limiting only to the areas surrounding Tianshan Mountains which resulted in procrastinating the Niya ruins and Loulan, and others in the next phase.

「一帯一路」歴史交流実例 ニヤ遺跡 中国が着々と保護 後世へ 世界遺産に

"一带一路" 交流历史实例　尼雅遗址得到中国政府全力保护　传与后世　争取成为世界遗产

The actual interaction example of "One Belt, One Road" Steady efforts to conserve the Niya ruins being made by China to be handed down to the next generation to ultimately have it registered as the World Cultural Heritage

※ニヤ遺跡と後述するダンダンウイリク遺跡は保護のため一般公開されていませんので、ご注意ください
出于保护目的，尼雅遗址及下面要介绍的丹丹乌里克遗址尚没有对民众开放，敬请注意
Please note that the Dandanoilik ruins mentioned hereafter as well as the Niya ruins are not open to the public for the sake of conservation

天津TV「泊客中国・五星出東方利中国」ドローン映像（Web放映を撮影）
天津电视台"泊客中国 五星出东方利中国"无人机航拍（摄于网络播映）
The image shot by a drone in the Tianjin TV program, China Right Here: Five Stars Appearing in the East Bring Good Fortune to China (Screenshot)

遺跡のほぼ中央に位置する仏塔で、世界平和と文化財保護を念じる筆者
在位于遗址中心的佛塔 笔者祈祷世界和平和保护文化遗产
In front of the pagoda located in the center of the ruins, I pray for world peace and conservation of cultural assets

ニヤ遺跡調査の食事事情

(公財) 京都市埋蔵文化財研究所　**吉崎 伸**

　調査隊の朝はお粥かインスタントラーメンで始まる。お粥の日は当たりだ。ホウロウ引きのお椀にたっぷり注いでもらい、ピータンや塩漬け卵を添えて食べる。とくに湯がいた塩漬け卵はお粥ととても相性が良い。私はこの食材が特に気に入っていた。ところがこれが曲者なのである。食べ過ぎるとやたらのどが渇く。

　昼は携帯食料が支給される。隊のコックが自作した窯で炊いてくれたナン、魚肉ソーセージ、小さなリンゴかナシ、それに500mℓのミネラルウォーター2本、時折支給される甘い八宝粥の缶詰が主なメニューである。中でも私は、八宝粥の缶詰がお気に入りだった。帰国後も中国物産店へ買い出しに行ったほどである。ただ、ナンには難があった。焼いた当日は柔らかくておいしい、ところが2日もたつと乾燥してやたら固くなる。「これで釘が打てますよ」と隊員が冗談交じりに言っていたことを思い出す。水がなければとても食べられた代物ではない。ここで、水を消費すると午後の作業は地獄となる。朝食の塩卵もボディブローのように効いてきて、渇きに苦しむ。「やはり砂漠だ」と思い知らされる。しかし本当の地獄は帰国してからだった。ある日突然腰に激痛が走り、病院に駆け込むことになった。病名は「尿路結石」、水分不足が続いたことが原因とのこと。約2か月間痛みに耐え、3mmほどの石が排泄された時には本当にほっとした。

　夕食はたいてい羊肉料理である。羊肉はまずくはないが、やたらと固い部分がある。これにあたると歯間に筋が詰まって苦労する。こうして羊尽くしの食事が1か月も続くと体臭が変わってくる。帰国してしばらくは家族から、異臭すると疎まれた。食事が終わると、椀にそのあたりの砂をかけて磨き、汚れを落とす。水が貴重な砂漠ならではの食器洗いだ。

　ところで食用の羊は10頭ほど生きたままベースキャンプの横に繋いであった。2～3日おきに1頭ずつ隊のコックによって食肉にされる。選ばれた羊は群れから引き出されるときはひどく抵抗している。しかし、群れから離されてしまうと途端におとなしく引かれていく。「羊のようにおとなしいとはこのことか」と納得。と殺はイスラムの儀式に乗っ取って厳粛に行われ、瞬く間に毛皮がはがされ解体されていく。羊の肉体構造を知り尽くしているものの手際の良さである。

昼の携帯食料を持つ筆者

　夜は焚火を囲んで酒盛りがはじまる。中国隊の隊員はよく飲むので、真剣に付き合っていては体がもたない。適当なところで切り上げて、自室のテントにこもり、日本から持ち込んだ12年物のウイスキーの減り具合を気にしながら、その日の作業の成果をまとめつつ眠りにつく。

　ニヤ遺跡の調査は食料や水の大切さを身をもって知る調査でもあった。

タクラマカン砂漠調査に思う

六甲山麓遺跡調査会代表　浅岡俊夫

　タクラマカン砂漠とは「死の砂漠」の意。史書には「走る獣、飛ぶ鳥無し」とある。事実、砂時計の砂の様な目の細かな砂が一面に広がった砂の海である。砂漠に入るにはよほど周到な準備がなければ死にに行くようなもの。以前、楼蘭遺跡で中国の地理学者が単独行動をして行方不明に。大がかりな捜査にもかかわらず見つからなかったという記事を思い出す。

　1994年、日中共同ニヤ遺跡調査で初めて砂漠に入った。生き物はまったく目にすることは無いものと思っていた。さにあらず、朝、目が覚めると砂上に小さな足跡が目にとまった。何かいる。出迎えてくれたのはトカゲであった。そして蜘蛛も。ニヤ遺跡の仏塔の傍でキャンプ生活が始まるとネズミに雀のような小鳥、カラスまでが。キジらしき鳥を見た時にはびっくりした。ダンダンウイリク遺跡ではトンボがテントの中へ。嗚呼！生き物がいるんだ。生活しているんだ、と感激した。砂漠は生きているんだと思った。

　砂漠は全体が鱗のような波でおおわれている。波の大きさ、深さはまちまちであるが、深さ2ｍほどの波間に入ると、もう隣はおろか周囲が分からない。瞬間、孤独感が漂い、不安が募った。取り残されてはいけないと、必死によじ登って周囲を確認する。何の目印もない。共に行動する仲間が頼りだ。GPSが頼りだ。だが現地のウイグル人は自分の居場所が分かるという。景色が違うという。目的地まで、右へ曲がって、左へ折れて、と腕を右へ左へふって合図し案内してくれた。我々にはまったく分からない、彼の手先だけがたよりだった。もし、こんな彼を大阪に連れて行ったらどうだろうかと、ふと思った。ビルの谷間を躊躇なく歩けるだろうかと。逆にGPSが必要ではなかろうかと。

　砂漠の調査にGPSは欠かせない。遺跡の位置を記入する地図もないから、GPSの数値（緯度・経度・高度）のみがたよりだ。ダンダンウイリクの分布調査（2004～2006）でのことであった。ある遺物散布地のGPS測定の緯度・経度が間違っていたのである。GPSが誤作動したか、あるいは聞き間違えたか、書き間違えたか。砂漠という異常な状況の中ではあり得ない数値に気づかず調査カードに書き込んでいたのだ。もう二度とその場所へはたどり着けないだろう。まもなくして、GPS（緯度・経度・高度表示）付きのカメラが発売された。これが記録保持のために便利なことは言うまでもなく、直ぐに飛びついた。しかしながら残念なことに、いまは緯度・経度・高度を表示するGPS付きカメラは製造されていない。

　砂漠の分布調査ではできるだけ採取遺物を少なくすることが肝心だ。重い荷物を持ち歩かないためにも。必要な遺物は現地で実測した。次、いつ現地に来られるか分からないし、できるだけ多くの資料を図化しておいた方が報告書づくりにも役立つからだ。

1996年日中共同ニヤ遺跡の発掘調査の思い出

帝塚山学院大学非常勤講師　田中清美

1、ニヤ遺跡93A35の調査

　10月10日から30日まで途中で2日、遺跡の見学に出かけた以外は宿営地の近くの93A35（スタインN. V）の発掘調査に従事した。須弥壇の残る小規模な寺院建物（FS）の床面に散らばる阿弥陀如来など仏教壁画の清掃から着手したが、これは流砂との戦いであった。午前中の作業を終えて昼食後に現場に戻って見ると調査着手時の状態まで流砂で覆われており、午前中の作業が徒労に終わったことを知り絶望感が広がった。気を取り直して須弥壇をハイキング用のシートで囲い、流砂の侵入を防ぐ工夫をしてから清掃を続行したことが思い出される。FC Ⅲ・Ⅳ（スタインN. XV）の調査では、スタインによるものであろう鉛筆書きのある木製品と、これが見つかった近くの丸い穴の中からスコップの先、英字の印刷物の断片が出土した。木製品に鉛筆でＮⅤ XⅣと書かれていることを確認した時、先に見つかったスコップなどを含め、これらはスタインが何かの事情で持ち帰れなかったものであろうと思った。当時は浮かばなかったが今ニヤ遺跡で遭遇した砂嵐のことを思うとき、おそらくスタインも砂嵐に巻き込まれ、あわてて現場から立ち去ったのではないかと。

2、ニヤ遺跡と砂嵐

　タクラマカン砂漠の砂嵐は聞きしに勝るもので、調査終盤日の午後の体験は生涯忘れないだろう。砂嵐は砂漠の地平線に濁った雲のような塊が湧き上がったとたん、それを目にしたウイグル人たちがスコップやキャッチメント（鋤簾の一種）を投げ捨て、一目散に宿営地に向かって走り出し、テントの中に逃げ込んだ直後に起こった。彼らが走り去った直後に、強風と不気味な音とともに砂が横殴りに吹き付けてゴーグルを掛け、耳や鼻、口をスカーフで覆っても体中が砂だらけになる感覚に襲われたのである。先に避難した人に遅れをとりながらも必死で宿営地の個人用テントに転がり込み、入口のジッパーを下ろし砂嵐が止むまでしばらく息を潜めていたことを覚えている。ニヤ遺跡での発掘調査は20日間あまりしか出来ないという話を聞いたが、それが砂嵐を避けるためであることを体験したのであった。かつて玄奘三蔵も、タクラマカン砂漠を旅した折に砂嵐に遭い吹き荒ぶ風砂の音が人の泣き声や呼び声のように聞こえたことを書き記している。昼間でも不気味な砂嵐に夜巻き込まれたらと思うと今でも背筋が寒くなる。流砂は嵐の度に生き物のように移動するため、今年見えていた遺跡が翌年には砂丘で隠れ、前に来たときには無かった遺跡が流砂から顔を出すといった具合に、景観が大きく変わることがある。宿営地の周辺を踏査した時、流砂の中に土器片や石器、鉄滓、焼土などが散布している場所を見たおり、ニヤ遺跡には流砂に覆われた精絶国の未知の遺跡が存在することを感じることができ、神秘に満ちたニヤ遺跡の魅力に胸迫る思いであった。

　近年ニヤ遺跡は仏塔およびその周辺の一部の遺跡が整備され、砂漠公路からも現地の見学が可能になったと聞く。今後も流砂に守られてきたニヤ遺跡の調査と保護に伴いオアシス都市国家精絶国が繁栄していた頃の自然環境や文化など学際的な研究が進展することを期待したい。

砂漠の思い出

佛教大学教授　安藤佳香

　仏教美術の現地調査に困難は尽きない。マニュアル通りにはいかないのである。しかしどんな苦労があっても、美術史の研究者にとって実査はかけがえのない研究の礎である。

　ずいぶん長い間、千差万別の現場で、心身を集中させて仏像と対峙し、調査を重ねてきた。ある時期には灼熱のインドで、単独での調査・撮影もずいぶん行った。大概の経験はしたかもしれない、と思っていた。砂漠に行くまでは。

　恩師である井上正先生を介して、ダンダンウイリク遺跡新出壁画群の写真を拝見したのは、2003年の初頭であった。その量にも驚

心を一にしたラクダ　ひときわ大きいがおとなしいラクダであった

いたが、そのなかの息を呑むような仏のまなざしに心を射抜かれた。後に「西域のモナリザ」と愛称されるようになる仏画との出会いであった。この壁画群発見の一行を率いておられたのが小島康誉先生である。居ても立っても居られないほど、気持ちが高まった。何としても実物に会いたい。

　壁画群はラクダの背に乗せられてウルムチの新疆文物考古研究所に運ばれていた。砂漠から運ばれたばかりの壁画は色鮮やかで、保存処理前の崩れ落ちそうな質感のなかで、圧倒的な存在感を放っていた。私はただただ吸い込まれるように見続けた。そして翌2004年10月、日中共同の調査隊の一員に加えていただき、壁画が発見された現地に入る機会を得た。ついにタクラマカン砂漠に足を踏み入れることになったのである。

　砂漠での調査は想像以上に厳しいものであった。最寄りの集落から出発したラクダ隊で二泊三日、ようやく現地に到達する。一日中、ラクダの背に揺られての移動。しばらくすると、痩せたラクダの背骨と自分の尾てい骨がこすれて痛みが出てくる。それを微妙にかわしながら、延々と旅は続く。これは辛い、こんなことならいっそラクダを降りて歩いたほうがましかと思って試したら、あっという間に熱砂が靴の中に入り込み、歩けなくなる。それならと靴を脱いで歩けば、砂の熱さで足の裏が火傷しそうだ。もう、これはラクダに任せるしかないと諦観のなかにその背に身をうずめていると、なんだかラクダと自分の境界がわからなくなる不思議な境地に達していた。

　辛苦を越えて到達したダンダンウイリク遺跡。壁画発見の場所は砂に埋もれて、しかとは確認できなかったが、あの素晴らしい壁画群が眠っていたおおよその場所に身を置けたことは感慨無量であった。それから数日の間、砂漠での遺跡調査を体験した。私が歩くこともままならなかった過酷な生の現場の中で終始先頭にたってテキパキと動かれる小島先生をはじめ、日中の隊員のエネルギッシュな行動力に頭が下がった。この得難い体験は、私と壁画群、ひいてはシルクロードとの距離をぐっと縮めてくれたように思う。その後度々新疆を訪れ、2007年にはキジル石窟での研究の機会をいただくこととなった。

　ダンダンウイリク遺跡調査の後、ニヤ遺跡に移動した。目の前に現れた仏塔は、砂漠に坐す大仏のように私には見えた。

ニヤ遺跡の仏塔が見えてきた

保護が第一

保护第一／Conservation comes first

V
日中共同ダンダンウイリク遺跡学術調査

中日共同丹丹乌里克遗址学术考察

The Japan-China Joint Scholarly
Research of
The Dandanoilik Ruins

V 日中共同ダンダンウイリク遺跡学術調査

（きっかけ）

　きっかけは佛教大学内ニヤ遺跡学術研究機構顧問の安田暎胤薬師寺現長老夫人であり、奈良女子大学博士課程で玄奘三蔵の取経ルートを研究している安田順惠女史の踏査希望であった。筆者は中国側と1988年にニヤ遺跡やダンダンウイリク遺跡などをふくむ西域南道の遺跡群調査の覚書（59頁）を交わし、ニヤ調査で大きな成果を上げていたので、許可は比較的容易であった。

　ダンダンウイリク（丹丹烏里克）遺跡は1896年1月にスウェーデンの地理学者ヘディンが発見。その情報によりスタインが1900年12月に大量の壁画や「桑種西漸伝説」板絵などを発掘した。1905年に米国の地理学者ハンティントンが踏査し、1928年にはドイツのトリンクル隊員でスイスの植物学者ボスハートが踏査した。それ後、所在が定かでなくなったが1996年、石油探査隊に同行した新疆文物考古研究所隊が再発見し遺跡の位置が明確となった。その情報をもとに翌年スイスのバウマーが非正規調査をおこなった。このように世界中の探検家や考古学者の興味をひいてきたが、大沙漠の奥深く位置することと、未開放地域に位置することなどの理由から、本格的調査はおこなわれていなかった。

　遺跡はタクラマカン沙漠南縁・チラ（策勒）の北方約120kmに残る仏教都市である。北緯37度46分・東経81度04分一帯に寺院址・住居址など70ヵ所の遺構が東西約2km・南北約10km（周辺をふくむ）に分布し、8世紀頃に衰退したと推測されている。本遺跡の東方に位置するニヤ遺跡とは約145km隔てている。海抜は1250m前後。名称は「象牙の家」を意味する。唐代には「傑謝」と称された。

　契机是担任佛教大学内尼雅遗址学术研究机构顾问的药师寺副住持（后任管主）安田暎胤的夫人（当时在奈良女子大学就读博士课程）安田顺惠女士，为了研究玄奘三藏的取经之路希望能去实地踏查。我在1988年与中方签署了西域南道（包括尼雅遗址和丹丹乌里克遗址）遗址群考察意向书（59页），加之在尼雅的考察取得了重大成果，因此比较容易地获得了许可。

　丹丹乌里克遗址是1896年1月被瑞典地理学家赫定发现的，斯坦因依据赫定的资料于1900年12月进行了大规模的发掘，收集了大量的壁画及"桑种东传"木板画。1905年美国地理学家亨廷顿进行踏查，1928年德国特林克勒队队员、瑞士植物学家博斯喀进行踏查。之后所在地不明，1996年，随同石油勘探队进入的新疆文物考古所调查队再次发现并确定遗址位置，依据该信息，瑞士的鲍默进行了非正规调查。如上所述，尽管引起了全世界探险家和考古学者的极大兴趣，但是因为地处大漠深处而且尚未开放，始终未能进行正规考察。

　遗址是残留在塔克拉玛干沙漠南缘、策勒以北约120公里的佛教城市。位于北纬37度46分、东经81度04分一带，在东西约2公里，南北约10公里（包括周边地区）的范围内分布着寺院遗址和住宅遗址等70余处遗迹，推测该遗址衰退于公元8世纪左右、与遗址以东的尼雅遗址相距145公里。海拔在1250米左右，遗址名称的含义是"象牙之家"，唐代称其为"杰谢"。

All this idea originated with Ms. Junkei Yasuda who is the wife of the present Patriarch of Yakushiji Temple Eiin Yasuda having assumed the position of the special adviser at the Academic Research Organization for the Niya Ruins, Bukkyo University. She studied the route how Xuanzang Sanzang had obtained Buddhist sutras and wished to trace that exact route. Since I signed the memoranda of agreement (page 59) on the research of ruins in the Western Regions' Southern Route including the ruins in Niya and Dandanoilik with China in 1988 and had achieved the great results, it was easy to get the permission.

　The Dandanoilik ruins was discovered by Swedish explorer and geographer Hedin in January 1896. In December 1900, Stein, having been informed of this discovery, excavated a huge amount of murals and the panel paintings depicting "the legendary princess who had exported silkworms to the Western Regions." In 1905 American geographer Huntington made a survey, and in 1928 a member of the German Trinkler's team Bosshart, a Swiss botanist, explored there, as well. Since then, although it had not been known exactly where it was located, the staff of the Xinjiang Archaeological Institute that accompanied an oil exploration team rediscovered the ruins in 1996, and clarified its location. Based on this information, a Swedish named Baumer made an illegal survey. As seen above, while explorers and archaeologists across the world have shown interests, a full-fledged research was not conducted because of its location lying far deep within the great desert, as well as being an unopened area.

　The ruins had been the Buddhist nation survived in the area lying 120 km to the north of Cele located at the southern edge of the Taklamakan Desert. 70 relics such as the remains of temples and houses were distributed in the area of 2 km east to west and 10 km north to south including the surrounding area about 37 degrees and 46 minutes north latitude and 81 degrees and 4 minutes east longitude. The ruins was estimated to have been discarded around 8th century. The Niya ruins situates about 145 km east of the ruins. It is more or less 1,250 meters above sea level. The ruins' name means an ivory house. It was also referred to as Jiexie in the era of the Tang Dynasty.

ダンダンウイリク遺跡略位置図
丹丹乌里克遗址简略位置图
Brief map of the Dandanoilik ruins

スウェン・ヘディン（1865-1952）とオーレル・スタイン（1862-1943）
（『近代外国探検家新疆考古档案史料』より）
斯文·赫定（1865-1952）、奥莱尔·斯坦因（1862-1943）（摘自《近代外国探险家新疆考古档案史料》）
Sven Hedin (1865-1952), Aurel Stein (1862-1943), *The Archives of Modern, Foreign Explorers in Xinjiang*

2002
第一次調査（予備調査）

　2002年10月25日〜11月9日、新疆文物局と「日中共同ダンダンウイリク遺跡学術調査」（佛教大学内ニヤ遺跡学術研究機構・新疆文物局主催、国家文物局批准）を試行した。日本側は筆者を隊長に安田順惠ら8名、中国側は盛春寿文物局長・張玉忠新疆文物考古研究所副所長を隊長に李軍文物局主任・張鉄男・佟文康・買提・卡斯木ら7名、サポート隊ふくめ計31名であった。隊員一覧は219頁記載。タクラマカン沙漠は日本の約9割に相当する面積。広大な沙漠での調査は困難を極める。今もヘディンやスタイン探検時と殆ど変らない。国道315号線の小都市于田よりケリヤ河沿いに北上、四輪駆動車も悪路に度々スタック。約120kmに約6時間。小集落でラクダに乗り換え。3時間かけてようやく出発。41頭のラクダ隊が水量ゆたかなケリヤ河を渡河するのは壮観だった。

　2002年10月25日至11月9日，与新疆文物局试行"中日共同丹丹乌里克遗址学术调查"（佛教大学内尼雅遗址学术研究机构、新疆文物局主办，国家文物局批准）。以笔者为队长、安田顺惠包括在内有8名日方队员，中方以文物局盛春寿局长、新疆考古文物所张玉忠所长为队长，李军等7名队员，加上后勤队合计31名。队员名单在219页有记载。塔克拉玛干沙漠的面积相当于日本国土面积的百分之九十，在广袤的沙漠内进行考察的难度与赫定和斯坦因时期不相上下，极其艰难。从位于315号国道的小镇于田出发沿克里雅河北上，四轮驱动车也常常抛锚。大约120公里竟然走了6个小时，在一个小村子改乘骆驼时要花费3个小时才能出发。41头骆驼排队渡过水量丰富的克里雅河的景象非常壮观。

From October 25 through November 9, 2002, we, together with the Xinjiang Cultural Assets Bureau, have made a trial exploration of the Japan-China joint scholarly research of the Dandanoilik ruins which was led by the Academic Research Organization for the Niya Ruins, Bukkyo University and the Xinjiang Cultural Assets Bureau and ratified by SACH Chinese. There were 31 members in total, assistants included, consisting of eight Japanese members, including Junkei Yasuda and I as team leaders, and seven Chinese members, including Cultural Assets Bureau Director Sheng Chunshou, Vice-Director of the Xinjiang Archaeological Institute Zhang Yuzhong as team leaders, and Li Jun. The lists of the members are referred to on pages 219. The Taklamakan Desert covers the area about 90% as large as that of Japan. The survey in the vast desert entailed extreme hardships. There was little difference from the time when Hedin and Stein had explored there. We drove northward along the Keriya River from a small city, Yutian, on National Highway 315. Even 4WD vehicles were frequently stuck in the rough dirt road. It took us about six hours to cover around 120 km. We switched our ride to camels at a small village. And it took three hours to prepare for departure. Yet, it was a magnificent view that 41-camel's team was crossing the affluent Keriya River.

Ⅴ　日中共同ダンダンウイリク遺跡学術調査　159

ラクダに揺られて遺跡をめざす2002年隊
乘着骆驼，摇晃着向遗址前进的2002年队
The 2002 team on a swaying camel heading for the ruins

　GPSに入力した新疆文物考古研究所隊測位の遺跡位置を目指していくつもの大砂丘を越えて進んだ。2日目も西へ西へ前進。ラクダの歩行距離は砂丘を迂回するため、直線距離の1.5倍ほどになる。大沙漠の地平線に太陽がおちると急速に寒くなる。限られた日程のため暗くなっても前進。3日目の午後2時すぎにようやく遺跡東端に到達。一同から歓声があがった。到達の喜びとラクダに乗らなくてもよいという安堵感からだ。ラクダ歩行距離で約50km、10月30日、日本人としては初の公式到達。中国隊やラクダ使い、運転手らサポート隊のおかげである。

　以输进GPS的新疆文物考古研究所队测定的遗址位置为目标一路前行，越过了几个大沙丘。第二天继续一路向西，骆驼需要在沙丘间迂回前进，实际行走距离是直线距离的1.5倍。当太阳落入大沙漠的地平线以下时，气温骤然下降，但是由于日程有限，天黑后也要继续前进。第三天下午2点多，我们终于到达了遗址东端。一行人发出欢呼声，欢呼来自到达后的喜悦和不用再骑骆驼的放松感。骆驼的行走距离大约是50公里。10月30日我们成为第一位以官方形式进入遗址的日本人，这都得益于中方队员、驼工、司机等后援队的努力。

　We advanced across a number of mega dunes toward the ruins' location positioned by the Xinjiang Archaeological Institute via GPS. On the second day, too, we headed off for farther westward. As camels always make a point to detour dunes, their walking distance usually increases 1.5 times more than when going straight. It's getting drastically cold when the sun sets into the horizon of the great desert. Notwithstanding, we advanced even after dark due to the limited schedule. On the third day, we finally reached the east edge of the ruins after 2 pm. The whole members cheered because of not only the joy of arrival, but the relief of a no more camel ride. We covered approximately 50 km in terms of a camel distance. On October 30, it was the first officially authorized visit by Japanese. It was all thanks to the Chinese team and assistants like camel masters and 4WD drivers.

2002年隊(部分)／2002年队(部分队员)／The team 2002 (part)

仏寺遺構 悠久の時を経て／佛寺遺址 经过漫长的岁月／Buddhist temple remains: Having survived for a thousand and several hundred years

Ⅴ　日中共同ダンダンウイリク遺跡学術調査　161

法隆寺旧壁画の源流の実物資料ともいえる壁画発見

　目的であった到達が達成できた喜びにひたる間もなく、分かれて初歩的分布調査を開始。前方で叫び声。中方隊員が露出した壁画を発見。風のいたずらか仏様のお顔が地表に。盛局長と張副所長の指揮で保護のために緊急試掘を実施。慎重に砂を取り除くと次々と壁画が。焼損した法隆寺「鉄線描」壁画の源流ともいえる「屈鉄線」壁画であった。千数百年ぶりにお出ましになった御仏を拝しおもわず合掌。日本側は略式法要を行った。各遺構GPS登録、地表散布遺物収集も行った。

　享受了片刻到达目的地的喜悦后，马上投入到分布调查之中。正在观察建筑构造，前方传来了高呼声，中方队员发现了裸露在外的壁画，是风在调皮吗？佛像尊容现于地表之上。在盛局长和张副所长的指挥下，紧急实施保护性试发掘。谨慎地拨开沙子，壁画一点点地显露出来，是可以称之为已烧毁的法隆寺"铁线描"壁画之源的"屈铁盘丝"壁画，面对时隔千百年重露真容的佛祖，不由得合掌祭拜。日方举行了简单的法式。用GPS登记各个遗迹。收集地表散落文物。

With little time to enjoy our arrival at the targeting destination, we started to conduct an introductory distributional research breaking into several groups. I heard a loud glad cry in front. A member of the Chinese team found a mural exposed on the ground surface. Maybe due to fickle gusty wind, the face of the Buddha appeared at the surface of the ground. We proceeded with an immediate trial excavation for conservation under the direction of Bureau Director Sheng Chunshou and Vice-Director Zhang Yuzhong. With careful removal of sand, a mural appeared one after another. They were the murals drawn by "flexed iron-line" from which the fire-damaged mural of Horyuji Temple drawn by Tessenbyo "wire-line", originated. I spontaneously joined my hands in prayer with the pleasure of seeing the divine face of the Buddha that showed up after having been buried for a thousand and several hundred years. We, Japanese, practiced informal Buddhist memorial service. Each relic was registered via GPS and antiquities scattered on the ground were collected, as well.

仏寺遺構　壁画発見直後／佛寺遗址　刚刚发现壁画后／Right after the discovery of the remains of a Buddhist temple and murals

近づくのが張副所長・撮影中が李主任
走过来的是张副所长　正在拍照的是李主任／Vice-Director Zhang approaching, Shot by Chief Li being

発掘現場／发掘现场／The excavation site

Ⅴ　日中共同ダンダンウイリク遺跡学術調査　　163

発掘現場／发掘现场／The excavation site

V 日中共同ダンダンウイリク遺跡学術調査　165

壁画断片とテラコッタ断片
壁画残片和赤陶残片／The fragments of murals and terracotta pots

陽が落ちると急に寒くなる
太阳落山 气温骤降／Getting suddenly cold after sunset

この時は本格発掘の準備をしておらず、張玉忠中方隊長率いる考古研究所隊が急ぎ態勢を整え、翌月再び遺跡へはいり約2週間にわたって発掘。大沙漠奥深くで発掘し、ラクダと車で、大型の壁画を破損させずに約1400km離れたウルムチの研究所まで運ぶことは並大抵ではない。その時にボスハートの残した名刺なども回収された。

因为当时没有作正规发掘的准备，张玉忠副所长带领的考古研究所队紧急调整态势，于下个月再次进入遗址，历时两周开展发掘。大漠深处进行发掘，在保证大型壁画不受损伤的前提下，用骆驼和汽车运回位于1400公里以外的乌鲁木齐的研究所，实属不易。同时收集到了博斯喀遗留的名片等。名片的背面用英语写着"相信能够在我们留下报纸的这里有所发现的可怜的后来人啊，祈祷你们好运。特林克勒、博斯喀 1928.3.25"。

Having failed to fully prepare for excavation at that time, the team members of the Xinjiang Archaeological Institute headed by Leader of the Chinese team Zhang Yuzhong urgently positioned themselves and returned to the remains in the following month to excavate for about two weeks. It was a serious challenge to carry a large mural excavated deep inside the great desert without damage all the way to the Institution in Urumqi about 1,400 km away. In the meantime, the business card and other things left by Bosshart were also collected.

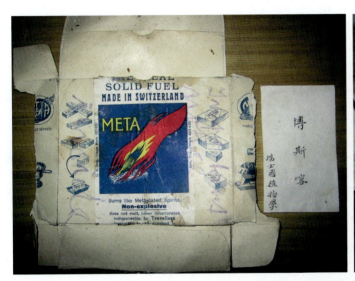 

ボスハートが遺跡に残した固形燃料箱・漢字の名刺・1927.12.9の新聞
博斯喀留在遗址的固体燃料箱、汉字名片、1927年12月9日的报纸
The outer case of solid fuel, the business card in Chinese, and the newspaper dated December 9, 1927 which were left by Bosshart

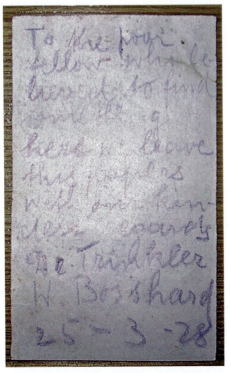

"To the poor fellow who believed to find something here we leave this papers with our kindest regards. E. Trinkler, W. Bosshart. 25-3-28"

名刺の裏には英語で「我々が新聞を残したここで何かを発見できると信じる可哀想な後継者に対して良きことを祈る。トリンクラー、ボスハート、1928.3.25」と記されている。

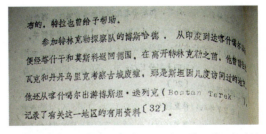

『新疆探察史』に記されたボスハートのダンダンウイリクほか踏査／《新疆探察史》里记载的博斯喀对丹丹乌里克等遗址的踏查／Exploring Dandanoilik and other places recorded by Bosshart in *The Exploration History of Xinjiang*

Ⅴ　日中共同ダンダンウイリク遺跡学術調査　167

CD-1（スタインD15）　東西28.7m・南北15.7mの大型遺構
东西约28.7米、南北约15.7米的大型遗迹
The large-scale remain covering 28.7 m from west to east, 15.7 m from north to south

研究所へ運んだ壁画／运到研究所的壁画／The murals carried to the Institute

テラコッタ断片／赤陶残片
The fragments of terracotta pots

運びこんだ壁画を開封／打开运来的壁画／Opening the carried murals

壁画部分／部分壁画
A part of the mural

壁画発見を報じる朝日新聞／报道发现壁画的朝日新闻／*Asahi Shimbun* reporting the discovery of the murals

2003
壁画保護・研究開始

当初は試行のみの計画であったが、2003年1月、佛教大学内ニヤ遺跡学術機構会議で、壁画は内容（仏・菩薩・供養者・動物などと豊富）・量（約10㎡）・質（高度の洗練された表現力）ともに優れ、「西域仏教はもとよりアジア古代仏教絵画史の研究に欠かせない」との判断から、本調査研究を「日中共同ニヤ遺跡学術調査」の関連事業とすることが承認された。同月、上記方針に対して新疆文物局より同意するとの回答をえた。

4月～5月、井上正・安藤佳香・切畑健・筆者が新疆文物考古研究所で張玉忠・李文瑛らと壁画の予備研究を開始。井上正は「内容は豊富、西域壁画の最高傑作のひとつ、文献にある『用筆緊勁にして屈鉄盤絲の如し』そのものを見ているようだ」と最高水準の評価を与えた。調査後、井上正・安藤佳香らはトルファンの石窟壁画も参観した。この時は中国で「サーズ」が流行中で、関空から北京への乗客は我々4人の日本人と帰国する中国人3人だけだった。北京空港は閑散としていた。

最初只是试行计划，2003年1月，在佛教大学内尼雅遗址学术研究机构的会议上，认为壁画无论从内容（佛、菩萨、供养人、动物等十分丰富）上，还是量（约10平方米）和质（高度提炼的表现力）上都很优秀，"研究西域佛教不必赘言，在研究亚洲古代佛教绘画史方面也不可或缺"，同意将该调查研究作为"中日共同尼雅遗址学术研究"的关联事业。当月，新疆文物局回答同意上述方针。

4月至5月，开始预备研究。井上正高度评价道"内容丰富，堪称西域壁画中最高杰作之一，仿佛看到了文献中描述的'用笔紧劲且如屈铁盘丝'"。调查结束后，井上、安藤佳香等参观了吐鲁番的石窟壁画，那时中国爆发SARS，从关西空港到北京的飞机上只有我们4个日本人和3名回国的中国人。北京机场空空荡荡。

Though it had been planned on a trial basis at first, in January 2003, since the murals were evaluated as extremely distinguished not only in content (abundant Buddhas, Buddhist saints, prayers and animals), but in quantity (such a scale as large as about 10 square meters) and quality (with highly sophisticated, expressive faculties) and determined as the ruins' research was essential for "Studies of the Western Regions' Buddhism, as well as ancient Buddhism painting history of Asia," the project was authorized as a related part of the Japan-China joint scholarly research of the Niya ruins at the conference of the Academic Research Organization for the Niya Ruins, Bukkyo University. In the same month, we received a response of accepting the above-mentioned concept from the Xinjiang Cultural Assets Bureau.

From April through May, we started the preliminary research of the mural at the Xinjiang Archaeological Institute. Tadashi Inoue admired the mural stating, "Its content is rich and it is one of the finest Western Regions' mural masterpieces. Exactly as being said in a literature, I'm just feeling like watching "the brushstrokes are emphatically contrasted, what with some parts being as powerful as an iron wire and other parts being as fine as a thin thread." After researching, Tadashi Inoue and Yoshika Ando visited Turpan to observe the grottoes' murals, too. At that time, the SARS scare was running rampant in China and passengers from Osaka to Beijing were only four Japanese of us and three Chinese going home. Beijing Airport was quiet and empty.

壁画観察／观察壁画／Observing the mural

乗客は7人のみ／只有7名乗客／Seven passengers only
15時の北京空港／15点的北京机场／Beijing Airport at 3 pm

Ⅴ　日中共同ダンダンウイリク遺跡学術調査　171

西域のモナリザ

如来が描かれた壁画を目にした私たちは、その眼差しと微笑みを拝し、思わず「西域のモナリザ」と叫んだ。レオナルド・ダ・ヴィンチのモナリザを彷彿させたからである。

描写如来的壁画映入眼帘，其眼神、其微笑令我们情不自禁地喊道"西域的蒙娜丽莎"，因为她让我们仿佛看到了列奥纳多·迪·达芬奇的蒙娜丽莎。

Taking a look at a part of the mural where Buddha is depicted, we spontaneously exclaimed by seeing its eyes and smile, "The Mona Lisa in the Western Regions." Because it instantly reminded us of the Mona Lisa by Leonardo da Vinci.

筆者2018.03.17 天津美術館講演「古代壁画と現代美術」でルーブル美術館ガラス越しのモナリザと対比したPPT画面より
笔者于2018年3月17日在天津美术馆作"从古代壁画到当代艺术"演讲时PPT上与隔窗拍摄的蒙娜丽莎作品的对比画面
PPT slide of my lecture on The Ancient Mural and the Contemporary Art at Tianjin Arts Museum on March 17 2018, which shows the comparison with a picture of the Mona Lisa taken through glass at Louvre Museum

「用筆緊勁にして屈鉄盤絲の如し」
(張彦遠『歴代名画記』唐晩期)
"用笔紧致如屈铁盘丝"（张彦远《历代名画记》唐晚期）
"The brushstrokes are emphatically contrasted, what with some parts being as powerful as an iron wire and other parts being as fine as a thin thread" (From Record of Famous Painters of All the Dynasties by Zhang Yanyuan in the later Tang Dynasty era)

2003
国家文物局 正式許可

2003年7月、訪日した盛春寿局長一行との打合せをへて9月、保護研究協議書に筆者と艾尔肯・米吉提新疆文物局副局長が調印し、10月には国家文物局より正式許可を取得した。12月には艾尔肯副局長・張玉忠らと打合せ、中国側許可のもと壁画残片を持ち帰り、奈良国立文化財研究所の協力により分析をおこなった。

2003年7月，经过与访日的盛春寿局长一行协商后，9月，与新疆文物局艾尔肯・米吉提副局长在保护研究协议书上签字，10月，取得国家文物局的正式许可。12月，与艾尔肯副局长、张玉忠等协商，在征得中方同意后，带回壁画残片，请奈良国立文化财研究所进行分析。

In July 2003, the party headed by Bureau Director Sheng Chunshou visited Japan to have a meeting. Afterward, Vice-Director of the Xinjiang Cultural Assets Bureau Aierken Mijiti and I singed the memorandum of understanding for conservation and studies in September. I received a formal approval from SACH Chinese in October. I had talks with Vice-Dirctor Aierken Mijiti and Zhang Yuzhong in December to bring home fragments of the mural under the approval of the Chinese side, and analyzed them with the cooperation of Nara National Research Institute for Cultural Properties.

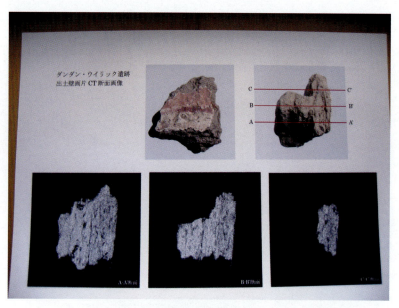

分析結果（部分）

分析结果（部分）／The results of the analyses (part)

協議書

协议书／The memorandum of understanding

調印しパチリ

签字／Taking a picture after the signing

2004

保護研究原案策定

2004年3月、日中双方は井上正・安藤佳香・切畑健・孫躍新・筆者に岡岩太郎・辻本与志一を加え、馬世長・鉄付徳・佟文康らと新疆文物考古研究所で保護研究原案を策定、双方は柔軟な考えと先進技術により保護を行うことで一致し、庫熱西・買合蘇提新疆副主席に報告した。

2004年3月，日中双方在新疆考古研究所商定保护研究方案，双方就运用灵活思维和先进技术进行保护事宜达成一致意见，向新疆库热西·买合苏提副主席汇报。

In March 2004, the Japan-China joint team developed a draft for conservation and studies at the Xinjiang Archaeological Institute. Both sides agreed to preserve the murals in a flexible way of thinking as well as by using sophisticated technology, which was reported to Vice-Governor Kurexi Maihesuti.

喧々諤々打合せ／热烈讨论／Heated discussion

壁画保護研究正式スタートを報じる新疆日報
报道壁画保护研究正式启动的新疆日报
Xinjiang Daily reporting the conservation and the research of the murals having been officially launched

喧々諤々打合せ／热烈讨论／Heated discussion

V 日中共同ダンダンウイリク遺跡学術調査 177

2004
国家文物局専門家委員会　保護原案　承認

2004年5月、艾爾肯・米吉提・張玉忠・鉄付徳・井上正・沢田正昭・辻本与志一・孫躍新・筆者が北京科技大学での国家文物局専門家委員会の王丹華・潘路ら6委員との審議会合に出席し保護原案を説明した。これは国家文物局の規定により計画が適正か科学的かを審査するもので、承認された。

2004年5月，在北京科技大学召开国家文物局专家委员会审议会，向出席会议的王丹华和潘路等6位委员介绍了保护方案，要依据国家文物局的规定审核计划是否妥当、是否科学，喜获批准。

In May 2004, the original plan for conservation was explained to the council consisting of six members of the specialist committee for SACH Chinese, such as Wang Danhua and Pan Lu at University of Science and Technology Beijing. This council reviews whether or not the project meets appropriately and scientifically the requirements imposed by SACH Chinese. And it was so authorized.

2004
第二次調査

2004年10月10日〜27日、第二次調査を敢行した。新たに浅岡俊夫・安藤佳香・孫躍新・鉄付徳らを加え、サポート隊・取材班ふくめて計34名。スタインが貴重遺物を発掘した南部遺構群など26ヵ所の遺構をGPS登録し模式図を作成、本遺跡が西域南道の〝仏教聖地〟と思われる古代仏教都市であることを確認した。地表散布遺物収集。調査とは別に、NHKと中国中央テレビが「新シルクロード」制作のため同行した。ニヤ遺跡も再訪した。

2004年10月10日至27日，实施第二次调查。包括后勤队、采访组在内合计34名成员，对斯坦因发现了重要文物的南部遗迹群等26处遗迹进行GPS登记、制作模式图，确认该遗址是西域南道"佛教圣地"的古代佛教都市，收集地表散落文物。调查同时，NHK和中国中央电视台为制作"新丝绸之路"也随同拍摄。再次访问尼雅遗址。

From October 10 through 27 in 2004, the second research was conducted with 34 members in total, including assistants and reporters. We registered 26 remains via GPS such as series of remains in the southern part where Stein had excavated valuable relics and created those pattern diagrams to verify the said remains as those of the ancient Buddhist city so-called "The Buddhism sacred site." Antiquities scattered on the ground were collected. Besides research, NHK and Central TV accompanied us to prepare The New Silk Road. We also revisited the Niya ruins.

オーバーヒートする車、駱駝に装備を積み込む、西へ西へ、今日はどこで野営
水箱沸腾了的汽车、将装备固定在骆驼身上、一路向西、今天在哪里露营呢
Overheated vehicle, loading equipment on camels, heading west and west down west, and searching for a place to camp

住居址模式図作成
制作住居模式图／Creating the pattern diagram of a residential remain

2004年隊（部分）／2004年队（部分队员）／The team 2004 (part)

2004
保護処理開始

　専門家委員会の保護原案承認をへて材料・薬剤などの準備をおこなった。一部は岡岩太郎・辻本与志一から無償提供を受けた。2004年11月、各種準備ととのい岡岩太郎・辻本与志一・亀井亮子・孫躍新・張玉忠・鉄付徳・佟文康・劉勇・何林・筆者らは双方の技術を活かし壁画保護処置を開始した。また富澤千砂子が模写を行った。岡は「新疆側は充分な技術水準にある。汚れを完全に取り除くことなく、表面の凹凸も残し千数百年前の風格がしのばれるようにしよう」と提案し、張玉忠・鉄付徳も同意した。

　为征得专家委员会对保护方案的认可，我们准备了材料和药剂等。有一部分是由冈岩太郎、辻本与志一无偿提供的。2004年11月，各项准备就绪，发挥双方技术优势，开始对壁画进行保护处理。富泽千砂子进行了临摹。冈提议"新疆方面具备一定的技术水准。不完全去除污垢，而是保留表面凹凸，令千百年前的样子依稀可见"，张玉忠和铁付德对此表示赞同。

　Based on the authorization of the specialist committee, we started to prepare materials and chemicals. Some of them were offered from Iwataro Oka and Yoshikazu Tsujimoto free of charge. In November 2004, having fully prepared every necessary arrangement, we started performing conservation treatment for the murals making use of both sides' techniques. Chisako Tomizawa reproduced them. Iwataro Oka suggested saying, "Xinjiang specialists have techniques at a sufficiently high level. It's better not to completely remove stein. Leave rugged surface, so that we can recall the elegance of over thousand years ago." Zhang Yuzhong and Tie Fude also agreed.

砂などが付着した壁画
附着沙子的壁画
The mural stained with sand and others

Ⅴ　日中共同ダンダンウイリク遺跡学術調査

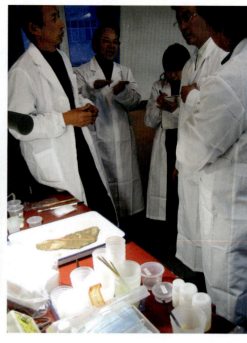

意見を出し合いベターな具体的方法を決定
各自发表意见 决定最佳方案
Better methods being decided through discussion

付着した砂などを取り除く
去除附着的沙子
Removing attached sand and others

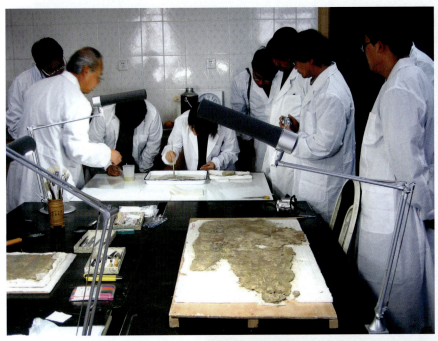

断片で実験し本番
用断片实验后再正式开始
First testing with a fragment, then actual practice

西域のモナリザ模写
临摹西域的蒙娜丽莎
Reproducing "The Mona Lisa in the Western Regions"

V　日中共同ダンダンウイリク遺跡学術調査　181

「用筆緊勁にして屈鉄盤絲の如し」
（張彦遠『歴代名画記』唐晩期）
"用笔紧致如屈铁盘丝"（张彦远《历代名画记》唐晚期）
"The brushstrokes are emphatically contrasted, what with some parts being as powerful as an iron wire and other parts being as fine as a thin thread" (From Record of Famous Painters of All the Dynasties by Zhang Yanyuan in the later Tang Dynasty era)

修復前の壁画／修复前的壁画／The mural before restoration

修復後の壁画、全ての壁画保護に約2年を要した／修復后的壁画　要修复所有壁画大约需要2年
The mural after restoration　Taking about two years to conserve all the murals

Ⅴ　日中共同ダンダンウイリク遺跡学術調査　185

2005
保護・研究継続

　2005年1月、井上正・安藤佳香・筆者が新疆文物考古研究所で張玉忠・佟文康らと保護処置の進展確認と研究をおこなった。安藤佳香は「新出壁画に見られる法隆寺金堂旧壁画の源流を思わせる鉄線描には、ホータンの王族に出自をもつ名画家尉遅乙僧の画風をしのばせるものがある。精彩に富む瞳の動きは、拝者の眼と心に深く訴えかけてくる。世界的名画の出現であるといっても過言ではない」とコメントした。筆者は盛春寿局長と小河墓地発掘現場を慰問した。

日中で研究
中日共同研究／Japan-China collaborative research

　2005年1月，在新疆文物考古研究所确认保护处理进度并进行研究。安藤佳香说"从壁画使用法隆寺金堂原有壁画之源头的铁线描上，能看出和田王族出身的著名画家尉迟乙僧的画风，惟妙惟肖的眼神仿佛向观者的眼睛和内心倾情诉说着。说她是世界名画的出现也不为过"。笔者与盛春寿局长一起去小河墓地发掘现场慰问。

　In January 2005, both parties confirmed development of conserving treatments and also conducted studies at the Xinjiang Archaeological Institute. Yoshika Ando made the following comment. "Wire-line drawing seen in the newly discovered mural which makes me feel the origin of the old wall painting of the Horyuji Temple's Golden Pavilion. It reminds me of the style of Yu-chi Yi-seng, the distinguished painter with the royal roots of Hotan. The movement of vividly shining eyes appeals deeply into the eyes and heart of worshippers. It is not too much to say that this is the emergence of the world-class masterpiece." Then Bureau Director Sheng and I visited members of the excavation team on Xiaohe ruins for encouragement.

2005
NHK「新シルクロード展」に出陳

　2005年1月〜12月、NHK「新シルクロード」が放送され、本調査隊検出壁画や前年調査が紹介された。4月〜12月、115頁に記述のように「新シルクロード展」が江戸東京博物館・兵庫県立美術館・岡山デジタルミュージアムで開催され、本隊検出「西域のモナリザ」など多数が出陳され話題となった。筆者らは数ヵ所で調査紹介講演、安藤佳香は4月と8月に上記会場で研究をおこなった。

　2005年1月至12月，NHK播出"新丝绸之路"，介绍了本调查队出土的壁画和前一年度的调查情况。4月至12月，如115页所示，"新丝绸之路展"在江户东京博物馆、兵库县立美术馆、冈山数码博物馆展出，本调查队出土的"西域的蒙娜丽莎"等多件文物出展，引起轰动。笔者在多地介绍调查、发表演讲，安藤佳香也于4月和8月在以上会场进行研究。

　From January through December in 2005, The New Silk Road was televised by NHK to introduce the murals excavated by this research and the research made in the previous year.

　From April through December, as mentioned in the page 115, The New Silk Road Exhibition was held at the Edo-Tokyo Museum, the Hyogo Prefectural Museum of Art, and the Okayama Digital Museum where "The Mona Lisa in the Western Regions" and others

張副所長／张副所长／Vice-Director Zhang

NHK放映画面と講演会冊子／NHK播放画面及演讲会册子
The screen covered by NHK and the lecture brochure

detected by the team were displayed. It gathered a lot of attention. We delivered a lecture to introduce the research at several venues. Yoshika Ando conducted research at the above-mentioned venues in April and August.

江戸東京博物館展示会場
江户东京博物馆展览会场／The exhibiting venue of the Edo-Tokyo Museum

2005
国際シンポジウム開催

　2005年8月、日中双方は佛教大学四条センターで「日中共同ダンダンウイリク遺跡学術調査国際シンポジウム」を開催し、福原隆善佛教大学長・中井真孝同教授・杉本憲司同教授・安藤佳香・浅岡俊夫・岡岩太郎・孫躍新・呂家伝新疆文化庁書記・李軍・張玉忠・鉄付徳・栄新江北京大学教授・筆者らが挨拶や発表をおこない、約200人が参加した。同センターと大学宗教文化ミュージアムで写真展も開催した。同写真展はNHK神戸放送局・岡山市デジタルミュージアムへ巡回した。

　2005年8月，日中双方在佛教大学四条中心召开"中日共同丹丹乌里克遗址学术调查国际研讨会"，约200人参加。同时在该中心和大学宗教文化博物馆举办图片展。该图片展还在NHK神户放送局、冈山数码博物馆巡回展出。

In August 2005, the international symposium on Japan-China Joint Scholarly Research Project of the Dandanoilik Ruins was convened at the Shijo Center of Bukkyo University with about 200 participants. The photo exhibition was also held at the Bukkyo University Museum of Religious Culture as well as at this Shijo Center. This exhibition also traveled the NHK Kobe broadcasting station and the Digital Museum of Okayama city.

日程と会場／日程和会场／Schedule and venue

2005
第三次調査

　2005年9月、筆者は調査協議書（05・06年分）を張玉忠と調印した。10月7日～11月1日、新たに乾哲也・奥山大石・村上智美・劉国瑞・阿里甫江・尼牙孜・呂宗宜・李東を加え、サポート隊ふくめ計24名で調査をおこなった。南北約12km・東西約5kmの範囲を調査、新たに円形遺構など約60ヵ所を登録。測量技師の参加をえて、7487ポイントを測量し地形図を作成するなど大きな成果をあげた。筆者らは疲労度を確かめるため遺跡から車乗換地点まで徒歩で帰った。調査終了後にダマゴゥ仏寺の塑像・壁画を参観した。資金提供から10年かかったホータン博物館の開館式に出席し、新疆側と共に出田和久奈良女子大学教授・安田順惠らを小河墓地へ案内した。12月、安藤佳香・筆者が新疆文物考古研究所で壁画研究を行った。

　2005年9月，笔者与张玉忠签署调查协议书（05・06年），10月7日至11月1日，包括后勤队在内的24名队员在南北约12公里、东西约5公里的范围内实施调查，登记了圆形遗迹等60多处新遗迹，测量技师参与调查，测量了7487个点并制作地形图，取得巨大成果。笔者等为确认疲劳程度，从遗址徒步到换车地。调查结束后参观了达玛沟佛寺的佛像和壁画。提供资金的十年以后出席了和田博物馆的开馆仪式，与新疆方面一起带领奈良女子大学出田和久教授参观了小河墓地。12月，在新疆文物考古所进行壁画研究。

In September 2005, Zhang Yuzhong and I signed the memorandum of understanding for the research in 2005 and 2006. From October 7 through November 1, we conducted the research with 24 members, including attendants, covering the area roughly 12 km from north to south and 5 km from east to west. While we additionally registered about 60 sites such as a circular remain, thanks to the participation of a survey engineer we made a survey on 7,487 points to create topographic charts. These were great achievements. We returned on foot from the ruins to the spot to ride a vehicle to check out our level of tiredness. After completing research, we observed statues and murals at Damagou Temple and attended the opening ceremony of the Hotan Museum which took 10 years to complete since I initially had funded for it. Then, I guided Professor of Nara Women's University Kazuhisa Ideta through the Xiaohe ruins with the Xinjiang team. In December, we conducted research of the mural at the Xinjiang Archaeological Institute.

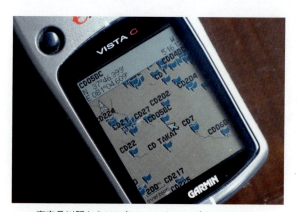

東京品川駅から2005年ベースキャンプまでは5161km
从东京品川站到2005年大本营的距离是5161公里
5161kms from Shinagawa Station in Tokyo to the base camp in 2005

協議書
協議书／The memorandum of understanding

"沙漠の舟"ラクダに助けられて遺跡を目指す
在"沙漠之舟"骆驼的帮助下向遗址前进
Heading for the ruins with the help of so called "desert boat," a camel

測量／测量／Surveying

夕食後も遺物実測など／晚饭后实测文物／Measuring actual dimensions of antiquities even after supper

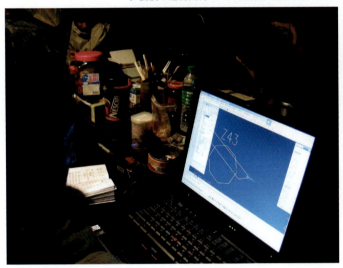

友好 共同 安全 高質 節約

ダンダンウイリク遺跡と関係深いダマゴゥ仏寺
与丹丹乌里克关系密切的达玛沟佛寺
Damagou Temple being closely related with the Dandanoilik ruins

2005年隊（部分）／2005年队（部分队员）／The team 2005 (part)

V　日中共同ダンダンウイリク遺跡学術調査　189

CD-30 謎の円形遺構

　2005・06年に調査した円形遺構は謎に満ちている。幅11m前後の粘土床がほぼ正円形に取り巻き、内径約80m外形約100m。城壁の東側には長さ15m、幅10mほどの張り出しがあり、その上面の粘土床は赤く焼けており、枘穴のある20cm角の柱が散乱している。スタインも「古代の円形城壁遺構」と記している。ニヤ遺跡の南方城址（96頁）・北方遺跡（95頁）と合わせて解明が待たれる。

　2005・06年调查过的圆形遗迹充满谜团。在宽约11米的粘土床上几乎围成一个正圆形，内径约80米，外径约100米。城墙东侧有长约15米，宽约10米的突出部分，上面的粘土床烧成红色，带榫眼的20CM角柱散落一地。斯坦因也记载了"古代圆形城墙遗迹"。与尼雅遗址的南方城墙遗址（96页）及北方遗址（95页）一样，有待明确。

　The circular remain researched in 2005 and 2006 is filled with mysteries. A clay-floor surrounds it almost in a complete circle with width of more or less 11 meters. The inside diameter is about 80 m and the outside is about 100 m. There is a jetty in the eastern side with a length of 15 m and width of 10 m, and the surface of a clay-floor was burned in red. Pillars 20 cm square with mortises were scattered around. Stein also noted this as ancient circular castle-wall remains. Along with the southern castle remains (p.96) and northern relics (p.95), unraveling the mysteries is much-expected.

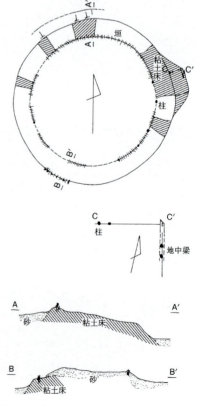

図25　CD-30略測図（全体平面図は略測1/200
　　　A-A'、B-B'、C-C'は略測1/40）

190

Ⅴ　日中共同ダンダンウイリク遺跡学術調査　　191

2006
壁画保護完了審査合格

　2006年6月、本調査隊の成果もあり、国家文物局により本遺跡は「全国重点文物保護単位」に昇格した。7月、全壁画保護処置が完了し、潘路・馬家郁による国家文物局専門家委員保護完了審査会が新疆文物考古研究所で開催され、盛春寿局長・鉄付徳・張玉忠・岡岩太郎・沢田正昭・筆者が出席し、保護処置は承認された。付帯意見として壁画周囲の色調統一が示され、承認報告書は国家文物局へ提出された。

　2006年6月，本考察队取得了成果，国家文物局将该遗址升级定为"全国重点文物保护单位"，7月所有壁画保护处理完成，在新疆文物考古研究所召开由潘路、马家郁主审的国家文物局专家委员保护完成审查会，保护处理得到肯定，提出附带参考意见：一致壁画周围的色调，向国家文物局提交了认可报告书。

　In June 2006, partly because of the achievements made by our team, the Dandanoilik ruins was promoted to the Chinese Cultural Assets of Important Protection by SACH Chinese. In July, since the conserving treatments of the entire mural were completed, the committee members of SACH Chinese, or Pan Lu and Ma Jiayu, to examine completion of protection gathered at the Xinjiang Archaeological Institute and the said treatments were endorsed. As a supplementary opinion, it was recommended that color of unity should be made on the frame of the mural. Thus, the report of the approval was submitted to SACH Chinese.

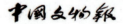

保護完了を報じる中国文物報／报道了保护完成消息的中国文物报／*Chinese Cultural Resources News* reporting the completion of conserving work

2006
第四次調査

　2006年10月9日〜11月8日、新たに竹下繭子・阮秋栄・韓善鋒が加わり、サポート隊ふくめ計19名で調査を実施。沙漠車とラクダを併用した。スタイン報告書記載の「ラワク」と「D17」の探査を試みたが発見できなかった。遺跡北方ふくめて遺構・遺物散布地など約20ヵ所を新たに登録。これまでの実績が認められ国家文物局の発掘許可（2006年161号）を

えて、複数の遺構を発掘した。寺院址も状況確認をおこない内容豊富な壁画を撮影し、保護のため埋め戻した。これらの結果、西域における〝仏教聖地〟としての本遺跡の全容を把握し、現地調査を終了した。

2006年10月9日至11月8日，包括后勤队合计19人实施调查。沙漠车和骆驼并用。尝试探查了斯坦因报告书中记载的"热瓦克"和"D17"，但是没有发现。登记了包括遗址北方在内遗迹、文物散落地在内的20多处新遗迹。之前的调查业绩得到认可，取得了国家文物局的发掘许可（2006年161号），发掘几处遗迹。寺院遗址状况也得以确认，拍摄了内容丰富的壁画，出于保护目的，将遗址回填。基于上述调查成果，基本掌握了该遗址作为"佛教圣地"的全貌，实地调查结束。

From October 9 through November 8, 2006, the research was conducted with 19 members in total, including assistants. Both a desert vehicle and camels were used. We failed to find the Rawak stupa and D17, which are described in the Stein's report. Yet, we newly registered about 20 sites, such as remains and sites with antiquities scattered in pieces on the ground including the northern part. Under the official authorization of SACH Chinese (the 161st issue, 2006) which had shown their recognition of our outstanding performance ever, we excavated several remains. We also confirmed the conditions of the temple remain, shot murals with abundant content, and buried them back for conservation. All of these investigations have added up to the conclusion that the whole picture of the ruins was assumed to verify as "the Buddhist sacred site" in the Western Regions. Thus, we have completed the research on site.

2006年隊（部分）／2006年队（部分队员）／The team 2006 (part)

炎天下の発掘は重労働／烈日炎炎下的发掘是重体力劳动／Excavation under the blazing sun was tough work

CD-1（上）・CD-17（スタインD14?・下）発掘後／CD-1（上）、CD-17（下）发掘后／CD-1 (above) and CD-17 (below) after excavation

CD-10（スタインD2）試掘し撮影し、埋め戻した寺院遺構／対 CD-10（寺院址）试行发掘，拍照之后回填了
Temple remain buried back after excavating to shoot CD-10

CD-10 試掘状況

保護のため発掘は最小限に留めた　試掘し撮影、埋め戻した寺院遺構　盗掘痕が痛々しい
为保护将发掘控制在最小限度　试发掘、摄影，回填后的寺院遗址　盗掘痕迹触目惊心
Excavation was minimized for conservation A temple remain being excavated on a trial basis, shot, and buried back Acutely painful to see the remain left after having been stolen

Ｖ　日中共同ダンダンウイリク遺跡学術調査　　197

皆で発掘／合力发掘／Excavating all together
筆者はどこにいるでしょう／猜猜笔者在哪里／Where would you find me?

2007
壁画研究・遺物実測

　2007年3月、安藤佳香・筆者は新疆文物考古研究所で盛春寿局長・于志勇・張玉忠らとニヤ報告書第三巻やダンダンウイリク報告書の打合せを行い、大量の修復後壁画を研究した。ダマゴゥ仏寺壁画も調査するとともに、ラワック遺跡を参観した。同月、浅岡俊夫らが考古研究所で、ダンダンウイリク遺跡出土遺物約100点を実測した。

　2007年3月，在新疆文物考古研究所商议尼雅报告书第三卷及丹丹乌里克报告书，研究了大量修复后的壁画。在调查达玛沟佛寺壁画的同时，参观了热瓦克遗址。同月，在考古研究所，实际测量了大约100件丹丹乌里克遗址的出土文物。

　In March 2007, we discussed the third volume of the Niya ruins report and the Dandanoilik ruins report at the Xinjiang Archaeological Institute and studied the post-treatment restoration murals. We conducted research on the mural in Damagou Temple and also visited the Rawaq ruins. In the same month, we measured the actual dimensions of about 100 antiquities unearthed in the Dandanoilik ruins at the Archaeological Institute.

考古研究所で壁画研究
在考古所进行壁画研究
The research of the murals at the Archaeological Institute

ダマゴゥ仏寺壁画
达玛沟佛寺壁画／The murals at Damagou Temple

2007
国際シンポジウム開催

　2007年11月、前述のように「日中共同シルクロード学術研究国際シンポジウム」を佛教大学四条センターで開催し、福原隆善学長・杉本憲司・八木透・安藤佳香・浅岡俊夫・片山章雄東海大学教授・艾尓肯・米吉提副局長・張玉忠・于志勇・栄新江北京大学教授・巫新華中国社会科学院考古研究所新疆隊長・孫躍新・筆者らがニヤ調査をふくめて挨拶や発表を行った。

　2007年11月，如上所述，在佛教大学四条中心召开"中日共同丝绸之路学术研究国际研讨会"，与会者的致辞和论文内容包括尼雅调查。

　In November 2007, as referred to above, The international symposium on the Japan-China collaborative scholarly research in the Silk Road was held at the Shijo Center of Bukkyo University. The addresses and presentations were delivered, on the Niya research included.

発表要旨／发表要旨／The summary of the presentations

2007
報告書出版

　2007年9月、ダマゴゥ仏寺博物館開館式に参加した。11月、調査研究保護の成果を浅岡俊夫・安藤佳香・岡岩太郎・沢田正昭・孫躍新・周培彦・盛春寿・張玉忠・栄新江・呂宗宜・劉国瑞・古麗比亜・阿里甫江・尼牙孜・屈涛・阮秋栄・巫新華ら諸氏の尽力をえて『日中／中日共同ダンダンウイリク遺跡調査学術報告書』（日本語版）としてまとめ文部科学省オープン・リサーチ・センター整備事業（平成15～19年度）関連刊行物として出版した。

　2007年9月，参加达玛沟佛寺博物馆开馆仪式。11月，在大家的努力下，将调查研究保护成果汇编成《日中/中日共同丹丹乌里克遗址调查学术报告书》（日文版），作为文部科学省公开调查中心整备事业关联刊物出版。

　In September 2007, I attended the opening ceremony of the Damagou Temple's Museum. In November, the achievements of research, studies and conservation were compiled to be published with the title of The Report of the Japan-China Joint Scholarly Research of the Dandanoilik Ruins (Japanese version) as a related publication of the development project of the MEXT's Open Research Center thanks to the supports of various people.

V　日中共同ダンダンウイリク遺跡学術調査　201

ニヤ調査ふくめて大沙漠での調査・発掘・保護・研究、そして報告書・シンポジウム……
並大抵ではない。諸氏ご尽力の一端を理解たまわれば幸いである。
包括尼雅考察在内，在大漠深处调查、发掘、保护、研究，以及报告书、研讨会……．非比寻常。如能理解各位所付努力，甚感欣慰。
It was far from easy to conduct research, excavation, conservation, and studies in the great desert, and then carry out reports, symposium, and so forth, not to mention the case of the Niya research. I would be very much obliged, should you understand even a bit of exertions made by various people.

日中／中日共同
丹丹烏里克遺跡学術調査報告書

2007
日中共同ダンダンウイリク遺跡学術調査隊
中日共同丹丹烏里克遺址学术考察队

Dx.18916『大暦十五年（780）傑謝鎮牒為徴牛皮二張事』

文書の前端下部2行を欠損、紙の継ぎ目後に于闐文4行を書き、上下を欠損するが、裏面に11行の于闐文を書く。図版は『俄藏敦煌文獻』第17冊、281頁を参照。

1　靴鞍牛皮二張
2　牒得舉稱："奉處分□
3　因恐賊默來侵抄，辰宿至要鼓擎相應〔者〕，□
4　自各牒所由處。"牒舉者，准狀各牒，火急限〔當
5　日内送納，遲料附者，故縣。
6　　　　　　大暦十五年四月一日、判官果毅□□進□
7　　　　　　知鎮官大將軍張順。

D.V.6（S.5864）『大暦十六年（781）二月六城傑謝百姓思略牒』

文書の下部が少々破損する。沙知、呉芳思編纂『斯坦因第三次中亞考古所獲漢文文獻（非佛經部分）』②，313頁。

1　阿磨支師子下胡書典高施掠　胡書典□
2　牒：思略去年五月内，與上件二人贓，准作錢六□□
3　思略放了，經今十個月，丁不得，贓不還。伏望
4　乞追徴處分，謹牒。
5　　　　　　大暦十六年二月　日六城傑謝百姓思□

Dx.18926+SI P 93.22+Dx.18928『大暦十六年（781）傑謝合川百姓勃門羅濟賣野駝契』

当文書は二枚に切断されており、直接接合できる。上部はやや破損するが、下部は完全に破損する。文書は二国語で書かれる。本文は于闐語と漢文で間隔を置いて書かれる。第8行の"錢主"以下は于闐語で漢文の上方の空白に書かれる。図版は『俄藏敦煌文獻』第17冊、287ページ、288ページの上部参照。熊本裕氏（Hiroshi Kumamoto）"Sino-Hvatanica Petersburgensia (Part I)", *Manuscripta Orientalia*, 7.1, 2001, pp.3-9には二国語の文書に対する考釈がある。またSI P 93.22の残片（Saka Documents, VII, pl. 67e）をDx.18926とDx.18928の間の上部につなげ合わせている。この点はMargarita I. Vorob'eva-Desjatovskajaが原文による確認を取っている。本文そのまま引用する。

1　　　　　　野駝壹頭父拾歲
2　大暦十六年六月廿一日，傑謝合川百姓勃〔門羅濟〕
3　等，為徒次負税錢，遂將前件駝賣□
4　作駝〔價錢〕壹拾陸阡文。其錢及駝〔當日〕
5　〔交〕相分付了，後有識認，一仰〔賣主知當，〕
6　不関買人之事。官有政法，〔人從私契，〕
7　兩共平章，畫指為記。

— 29 —

D.I遺構について記述した中で、千仏壁画の他、案内人のトゥルディが以前ここで発掘した彫像も含めて、多くの石膏の仏像を発見したことを特筆している。スタインは時々、持って帰れないものをある遺構の中に置いて次回まで保存するようにしていた。とすればあるいは、バウマーが発見したこれらの石膏像は、スタインが故意に残した物かもしれない。バウマーの発見は学術面において重要な意義を持ち、その3人組の仏像の図版は2004年に英国図書館で行なわれたシルクロード展示会の図録『シルクロード　貿易、戦争と信仰』に収録されたため、学者達はそれらの画像をめぐって文章を書き議論し始めた。しかし、我々は、このような勝手に発掘することは違法な行為であり、シルクロードに位置する重要な埋蔵文化財の保護の面からも深刻な問題をもたらした事を指摘しなければならない。

2002年10月、新疆文物局と新疆文物考古研究所、日本佛教大学ニヤ遺跡学術研究機構の共同調査隊は、ダンダンウイリクに入り、ある仏寺の壁画が風で地面に露出しているのを発見した。同年11月、新疆文物考古研究所はその壁画の緊急発掘を行い、仏寺の壁の下部に残っていた千仏像、雑神像、鉢を手に持った一列の騎馬像の壁画などを剥がし取り、ダンダンウイリク遺跡の新資料を採取した。ところが興味深いことに、この寺院のある壁の下からドイツ語の新聞などが出てきた。新聞のほかに*Neue Zürcher Zeitung*（『新チューリッヒ民報』、図13）と*Schweizer Illustrierte Zeitung*（『スイス画報』、図14）もあり、また固体燃料の紙箱が挟まれており、箱の中には1928年にダンダンウイリクへ入ったことを示したボスハート（W. Bosshart）の名刺（図15）が一枚入っていた。紙箱の一面には「Please see inside」（中を見てください）と書かれており、もう一面には「Important matters inside」（中に重要なものが入っている）と書かれていた。名刺には、中央に漢語で「博斯略」と書かれているが、それは当時のボスハートが使った漢語の名前であり、左下に「スイス国植物学」と書き、自分の国籍と身分を表

図13　トリンクラー探険隊が残した『新チューリッヒ民報』

図14　トリンクラー探険隊が残した『スイス画報』

図15　トリンクラー探険隊の紙箱とその中の名刺

図16　トリンクラーが撮った仏寺の壁画写真

— 51 —

Dx.18916『大暦十五年（780）傑謝鎮隊為徴牛皮二張事』
文書の前端下部2行を欠損、紙の継ぎ目後に于闐文4行を書き、上下を欠損するが、裏面に11行の于闐文を書く。図版は『俄藏敦煌文献』第17冊、281頁を参照。
1　鞡鞁牛皮二張□
2　牒得舉稱："奉處分□
3　因恐賊獸来侵抄，辰宿至要薮聲相應〔者〕，□
4　自各牒所由處。"牒舉者，准狀各牒，火急限〔當〕
5　日内送納，運糧附者，故牒。
6　　　　　　大暦十五年四月一日，判官果毅□進□
7　　　　　　　知鎮官大將軍張順。

D.V.6（S.5864）『大暦十六年（781）二月六城傑謝百姓思略牒』
文書の下部が少々破損する。沙知、呉芳思編集『斯坦因第三次中亞考古所獲漢文文献（非經部分）』②、313頁。
　　　阿磨支師子下胡書典高施㨾　胡書典
1　牒：思略去年五月內，與上件二人驢，准作錢六□
2　思略放丁，經今十個月，丁不得，驢不還。伏望□
3　乞追徹處分，謹牒。
4　　　　　大暦十六年二月　日六城傑謝百姓思□□

Dx.18926+SI P 93.22+Dx.18928『大暦十六年（781）傑謝合川百姓勒門羅濟賣野駞契』
当文書は二枚に切断されており、直接接合できる。上部はやや破損するが、下部は完全に破損する。文書は二国語で書かれる。本文は于闐文と漢文で間隔を置いて書かれる。第8行の"錢主"以下は于闐語で漢文の上方の空白に書かれる。図版は『俄藏敦煌文献』第17冊、287ページ、288ページの上参照。熊本裕氏（Hiroshi Kumamoto）"Sino-Hvatanica Petersburgensia (Part I)", Manuscripta Orientalia, 7.1, 2001, pp. 3-9 には二国語の文書に対する考釈がある。またSI P 93.22の残片（Saka Documents, VII, pl. 67e）をDx.18926とDx.18928の間の上部につなげ合わせている。この点はMargarita I. Vorob'eva-Desjatovskajaが原文による確認を取っている。本文そのまま引用する。
1　野駞壹頭父拾歳
2　大暦十六年六月廿一日，傑謝合川百姓勒〔門羅濟〕
3　等，為役次負稅錢，遂將前件駞賣□
4　作駞〔價錢〕壹拾陸阡文。其錢及駞〔當日〕
5　〔交〕相付了，後有識認，一仰〔賣主知當，〕
6　不關買人之事。官有政法，〔人從私契，〕
7　兩共平章，畫指為記。

表1　ダンダンウイリク遺跡分布調定成果表①
（北緯：N、東経：E）

番号	遺構番号	位　置	高度(GL)	遺　体	備　考
1	CD-1	N37°46.565' E81°04.747'	1251	建物跡	胴石出土
2	CD-2	N37°46.636' E81°04.586'	1251	果園樹跡群	胴石出土
3	CD-3a	N37°46.510' E81°04.386'	1251	建物跡	壁画塑影設眉頭柱　騎仏 スタインD18
4	CD-3b	N37°46.394' E81°04.363'	1250	以上跡	スタインD8?
5	CD-3c	N37°46.93' E81°04.370'	1251	建物跡	農業門具
6	CD-3d	N37°46.497' E81°04.361'	1249	以上跡	2棟の建物 スタインD8?
7	CD-3e	N37°46.672' E81°04.365'	1248	建物跡	
8	CD-4	N37°46.972' E81°04.377'	1257	以上跡	壁画・塑仏　2002発掘調査 スタインD1
9	CD-5	N37°46.651' E81°04.542'	1254	建物跡	窯
10	CD-6	N37°46.643' E81°04.554'	1251	建物跡	旅者の墓
11	CD-7	N37°46.282' E81°04.751'	1253	建物跡	古くに壁面の剝 スタインD7「護国寺」史料
12	CD-8	N37°46.271' E81°04.75.1'	1255	以上跡	スタインD6
13	CD-9	N37°46.672' E81°04.965'	1249	円台地?	
14	CD-10	N37°46.156' E81°04.168'	1245	以上跡	回字形建物 スタインD2
15	CD-11	N37°46.157' E81°04.185'	1249	以上跡	2棟の建物 スタイン「貝に開けた建物」
16	CD-12	N37°46.161' E81°04.182'	1248	以上跡	2棟の建物 スタインD3
17	CD-13	N37°46.166' E81°04.191'	1249	建物跡?	高い柱1本
18	CD-14	N37°46.180' E81°04.195'	1249	建物跡	スタインD11
19	CD-15	N37°46.171' E81°04.195'	1254	以上跡	スタインD10
20	CD-16	N37°45.642' E81°04.491'	1254	建物跡	
21	CD-17	N37°46.692' E81°04.991'	1252	建物跡	青銅製　塑仏 スタインD14?
22	CD-18	N37°46.161' E81°04.924'	1249	建物跡	木製鍵 スタインD14?
23	CD-19	N37°46.703' E81°04.865'	1250	建物跡	絵細陶器 スタインD14
24	CD-20	N37°46.699' E81°04.867'	1252	寺院跡	塑仏 スタインD14
25	CD-21	N37°46.453' E81°04.350'	1249	泉湧跡	木製鍵
26	CD-22	N37°46.331' E81°04.314'	1254	寺院跡	壁面建築材
27	CD-23	N37°46.720' E81°03.710'	1255	建物跡	2棟の建物　木製鍵　陶製紡輪車

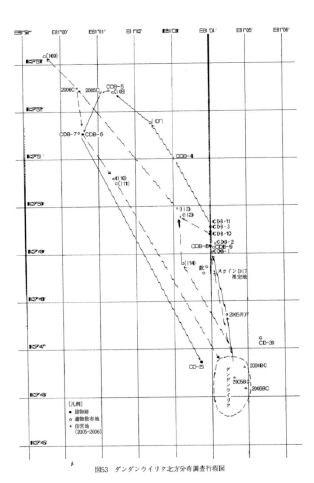

図53　ダンダンウイリク北方分布調査行者図

表3　ダンダンウイリク遺跡出土銭貨一覧表

番号	出土地点	種　類	初鋳年	大きさ（縦×横×厚さ）mm	備　考
1	CD-1北側	無文銭		19.55×21.20×1.95	半損
2	CD-1北側	無文銭		14.05×8.10×1.15	剪輪銭　半損
3	CD-1北側	無文銭		16.35×16.20×1.00	剪輪銭　半損
4	CD-7	開元通宝	621年	24.80×24.75×1.90	
5	CD-7	開元通宝	621年	25.50×25.75×2.05	背上月
6	CD-7	開元通宝	621年	26.45×27.00×1.95	
7	CD-5	開元通宝	621年	25.50×25.40×2.40	
8	CD-26	無文銭		23.90×23.60×1.20	
9	CD-241	不明		23.65×23.50×1.20	
10	CD-243	乾元重宝	758年	21.30×21.70×1.40	表裏の内郭にズレ
11	CD-226	無文銭		21.40×21.05×1.15	
12	CD-218	無文銭		20.10×20.40×1.10	剪輪銭
13	CD-218	無文銭		16.95×18.25×1.15	剪輪銭
14	CD-218	無文銭		17.10×14.90×1.20	六角加工　剪輪銭
15	CD-218	無文銭		17.95×17.00×1.30	13に付着　剪輪銭
16	CD-218	無文銭		16.85×17.45×1.40	12に付着　剪輪銭
17	CDB-2	無文銭		9.60×9.50×1.50	
18	CDB-2	無文銭		14.15×14.30×1.25	剪輪銭
19	CDB-3	無文銭		18.15×17.45×1.00	剪輪銭
20	CDB-4	無文銭		12.50×12.30×1.60	
21	CDB-7	無文銭		21.45×21.70×1.25	採取後に破損

2006年に採取）と2004年に採取した2枚の18枚がある。そのうち銘文のあるのは7枚である。内訳は開元通宝（初鋳621年）が5枚、乾元重宝（初鋳758年）が2枚である。その中には、2004年にCD-1東側で採取した開元通宝とCD-2で採取した乾元重宝の2枚が含まれる。開元通宝のうち、CD-7で採取した5の背面の上部には月印（上月）が鋳出されている。10の乾元重宝は、表裏の内郭がずれており、鋳型のずれが看取される。無紋銭の中にはかなりの剪輪銭が含まれ、14のように六角形に剪輪されたものもある。その多くは剪輪五銖銭だろうと思われるが、断定できない。図版24。

英博物館の木板画には馬の頭に太陽と月を戴いているのに対しCD-4：02の4頭目にはないことである。なお、大英博物館の木板画では馬の尾を束ねているがCD-4：02中の1頭目も同じように束ねている。このような細部の問題点は、供養者の種族などを研究するうえで役立つと思われる。しかし、ボロをめがけて急降下して来る黒鳥が何を意味するのかは明らかでない。

3．CD-4：04壁画にある地神の形象

地神（地天）の形象は于闐地区の仏寺遺跡の壁画に多く見られる。1982年、フガイウライク（布盖鳥士来克）仏寺遺跡で、仏足の間に座って合掌礼拝している女性の壁画が見つかった。この女性の頭部からは光波らしき波線が発せられている（図4）。これはまさしく堅牢地神である。『金光明経・堅牢地神品』には、堅牢はかつて大願成就したことがあり、よって『金光明経』を説法する人があれば、彼女は大地から現れて、法座の下に、その人を護持する、と説かれている。

CD-4：04壁画の中では、仏足の下で地神と見られる濃い髪と髭を生やした像が仏足を持ち上げている。それは明らかに男性であって、経典に説かれていることと符合していない。しかし、それも地神と見てよいだろう。また、この地神は折返し襟の服を左前に着て、腰に帯を締め、まったく現地人と同じ装束で世俗化している。これは、おそらく現地の信仰の中で仏教芸術を理解するために形象を変化させたものであろう。

クチャ（庫車）県キジルガハ（克孜・尕哈）14窟の右側通路の内壁に堅牢地神が描かれている。それは女性像で、亀兹に礼拝する王族の供養者を持ち上げている（図5）。

その他、敦煌莫高窟にも五代時代の第98窟の右側門壁に于闐国王李聖天の供養像があり、その像の下に、雲気とともに地下から湧き出した女性の地神が李聖天の両足を持ち上げている（図6）。

以上の資料を検証することにより、于闐や亀兹、敦煌地区における地神の形象の発展過程を知る手がかりが得

図3 ダンダンウイリク遺跡出土の木版画
（スタイン発掘・大英博物館蔵）

図4 ホータン・フガイウライク仏寺遺跡出土の地神壁画

図5 キジルガハ第14窟右通道内側の地神壁画

図6 敦煌莫高窟98窟（五代）の于闐王李聖天供養像を支える地神

図13 CD-1F2発掘平面・立面図

（3）CD-17建物遺構の発掘調査

CD-17（図14、図版55～58）は、ダンダンウイリク遺跡の北方地区の北部に位置する。地理座標は北緯37°46.692′、東経81°04.934′、海抜は1252mである。

この建物遺構は、地表観察から東西に並ぶ3部屋で構成されていることが読み取れるように。自然および人為的な破壊により砂の堆積が浅く、少し発掘すると、地山と地中梁が現れてきた。壁の残高は0～0.5m（南壁が少し高い）である。建物の規模は、東西の長さ13.7m、南北の幅5.6m、面積77㎡である。部屋の番号は東から西へ付け、東の部屋がF1、真ん中の部屋がF2、西の部屋がF3となる。F2とF3の間は幅約1.1mの廊下で隔てられている。

F1は、平面が南北の長方形を呈し、長さ5.6m、幅4.6mの規模をもつ。床面は堅く固められているが、表面に厚さ約10cmの家畜の糞が堆積している。北壁には略長方形の長さ1.0m、幅0.9mの竈を設えた跡がある。入口は家屋の北東角にあり、西向きに開く。その幅は0.9mである。

図10 壁画表面の整理作業

作業に必要な材料や道具は、全てラクダに乗せ、何日もかかって運ばねばならず、その調査は慎重の上にも慎重に計画せねばならなかった。発掘によって出土する壁画の数量や大きさなどがはっきりしない上、調査中に遭遇する予見できない状況に対応するためにも、準備する材料や機材を多めに調達するなど、その準備におわれた。壁画の剥ぎ取りは2002年11月に行なったが、その時は昼間が暑く、夜になると大変冷え込んだ。現場へ持って来た水や化学試薬は、夜に凍結してしまい、その状態が翌日の午前まで続き、毎日、仕事のできる時間帯が制限された。また、よく風が吹いたため、壁画の表うちや補強に大変困難が強いられた。風砂が強いときには、壁画の剥ぎ取りの作業をやむなく中止せざるを得なかった。壁画を持ち帰り用に包装するための挟み板も、現場で臨時に作らねばならなかった。このように、砂漠の過酷な環境の中での壁画の剥がし取り作業は、非常に難しく、高度な技術が求められた。壁画表面の汚れの洗浄など、現場でできない技術的作業は、実験室に持ち帰ってから行なわねばならなかった。

(a) 現場での壁画表面に対する整理　発掘調査の手順に従い、まず現場を撮影し、図面に記録するなど順次、仏寺遺跡に対し調査が進められていく。調査された作業現場で、露出した壁画の表面を逐一清掃する。清掃には軟毛ブラシを使い、露出した壁画の表面に沿って、同じ方向で、ゆっくりと壁画の表面に付着している砂やホコリを掃う。この作業に際して、砂やホコリと壁画表面の顔料層との摩擦を避けるために、まず小さな区域から始めて、次第に拡大していった（図10）。時間や現場の条件に制限があり、壁画表面に付着している強固な汚れなどは、現場での洗浄を諦め、実験室に戻ってから入念に洗浄することにした。

(b) 模写　壁画は、出土した状況を即座に写真撮影で壁画表面の当初の状態を記録し、さらにトレーシングペーパーでもって壁画表面の図像を模写した。入念に模写することが大事であるが、できるだけ従来の図案を忠実に写すことに気を取られ、模写の動作や模写用の材料によって壁画表面に危害を加えないように気を配った（図11・12）。

図11 壁画の模写作業

図12 壁画の模写図

（4）中国との技術協力進展に向けて

中国への個人旅行が自由になった1980年代初頭から、私は度々当地を訪れている。表具技術の源流である中国で、北京や上海の装潢技術者と修理材料や技術について議論したいという希望や、西安の壁画を是非見たいという興味から、私の中国通いが始まった。保存科学の専門家とともに様々な現場を訪れるうちに、私たちの装潢技術による修理経験から、材料や技術についての情報を提供できる部分があるのではないかと考えられた。その後、1990年代から現在に至るまで、西安や新疆ウイグル自治区、内モンゴルなどにおいて、墳墓壁画等の修理に技術協力を続けていく中で意見交換や技術交流が進展した。このような流れを受けて、2004年、ダンダンウイリク遺跡壁画の保存作業にあたって、現地で共同作業を行う機会を得た。現地滞在中、同時に、絵画技法の究明や記録作製を兼ねて、富沢千砂子氏による壁画片の模写も行われた。

ダンダンウイリクの壁画修理を行う新疆文物考古研究所では、既にフランスの技術が導入され、ヨーロッパ式の壁画修理技術のノウハウを習得している。前述したように、日本において大谷探検隊により将来された西域壁画を修理する際にも、欧米の技術を取り入れ日本の技術を融合させる形で修理技術が確立された。その成果は、法界寺阿弥陀堂修理においてひとつの形をなし、現在の日本における壁画修理のひとつの完成形となった。2004年の日中間における技術協力では、お互いに持っている技術の交換をしながら、その中で特に日本の技術が導入できる点について話し合った。

2004年11月初旬に日本側から技術者が派遣され、数個の断片にて表打ち及び裏面処理の一部を行い、日本で行った壁画処置の事例を紹介した。作業工程は次の通りである。まず、作業対象となる壁画片の観察、撮影を行った後、壁画片の埃を払った。そして、表打ちを行うために表面に樹脂を塗布し、一日おいて1層目の表打ちを行った。1層目の表打ちが完全に乾いたことを確認して2層目の表打ちを行い、それも完全に乾いたことを確認してから壁画を裏返した。壁体は既に薄くされていたため、ここから裏面処理に入った。まず、裏面に貼り付けるカーボン繊維のシートを作成する。次に、壁画裏面の強化とカーボン繊維による裏打ちものための下地という2つの意味から、樹脂（PB72：20％）を塗布する。アセトンと樹脂（PB72：5％）を使いカーボン繊維を貼り付け、その上からさらに固定するために樹脂（PB72：10％）を塗布する。この状態で半日ほど置いたあと、壁画を表に返し、水を用いて表打ちを除去する（図17）。

このような具体的な作業紹介、協議を経た結果、中国や欧米では行われていない、布苔による表打ち及び高分子以外のものによる表面の強化が導入されれば、よりよい結果が得られるのではないかという点で合意され、実際の作業工程の一部に日本の技術が導入された。

図17 工程写真　表打ち除去の様子

郭線はいわゆる鉄線描と呼ばれるもので、「この地域特有の肥痩のない均一な線」とされる。

さて、この地域の画家としてつとに著名なのがホータン（于闐国）の王族にその出自が求められる尉遅乙僧である。張彦遠『歴代名画記』では唐朝の三大画家の一人として、呉道玄、閻立本と並び称され、七世紀後半から八世紀初頭にかけて、長安・洛陽で多くの寺院壁画を制作したことが記されている。乙僧には兄の甲僧がおり、その兄も画才があって西域の母国に在住していたという。父の尉遅跋質那もまた隋代に活躍した画家であった。その作風について、父跋質那は「瀧落にして気概あり」、乙僧の方は「用筆緊勁にして鉄を屈し絲を盤まらせるが如し」と張彦遠は評している。ここにいう「屈鉄盤絲」が乙僧の描線についての評言であることは疑いない。

この「屈鉄」という語を語源として日本ではじまったと思われるのが「鉄線描」という用語である。わが国ではこの語は主に法隆寺旧金堂壁画の描線を語る際に用いられてきたが、奈良・平安時代の仏画にも数多い実例がある。そして旧金堂壁画の鉄線描の源流は、その陰影法とともに西域にあるとし、さらに西域系の尉遅乙僧の流れに属するものであるとしたのは滝精一（1873〜1945）であった。

滝氏は法隆寺旧金堂壁画の描線を「細くして肥痩なく、如何にも強く弾力性のものを屈曲したるの感ありて、即ち謂う所の屈鉄盤絲に外ならず」として両者を結びつけたのである。しかしながら、評語としては残っているが、これまではそれに合致する作例が伴っていなかったのである。

そして遂にこの「屈鉄盤絲」を彷彿とさせる描線がダンダンウイリクの新出壁画に見い出されたことは刮目に値する。新出壁画のうち、もっとも卓越した力量を示す②如来図に描かれた大型の如来立像（図3・4）である。肉身の輪郭線は伸びやかにして柔らかい筆使いを示し、単純に肥痩のない緊張感のある線という枠を超えたものであることはすでに述べた。肩に力の入らない、自信に満ちた熟練した線がそこにはみられる。それに対して④如来像及び諸神図の如来坐像の肉身の輪郭線は、やや神経質な細線である。肥痩の度合いは少なく、やや硬質で文字通りの鉄線描に近い。また①如来図の肉身輪郭線では、一段と太輪の、息を詰めて引いたような鉄線描が示される（図1・2）。このようにひとまずは同じ鉄線描という描法分類に括られるとはいえ、個々の描線の特質はけっして一様ではない。とりわけ傑出した②如来立像では、情感を湛えた鉄線描という実に高い境地を成していること、そして清新な初発性を感じさせることなどに再度注意を払っておきたい。

これと同じような様相が法隆寺旧金堂壁画にも認められる。旧金堂壁画の十二面のうち、六号壁がもっとも優れた作風を示していることは衆目の一致するところである。仏・菩薩の輪郭線には、まったく肥痩がないとはいえず、むしろ多少の肥痩が線に生命感を与えている（図52）。伸びやかな手指の線には立体感が宿り（図53）、新出壁画②如来立像のそれと通じ合うところが感じられる（図54）。一方、一号壁では描線はより細くなり、肥痩の度合いも増し、線にこもる弾力性も感じとれる（図55）。また二号壁のさらに細くなった描線には六号壁ではみられなかった繊細な情感が宿っている。従来「鉄線描」として括られてきた法隆寺旧金堂壁画

— 258 —

表1　日本古代顔料一覧

種類	九州装飾古墳	高松塚古墳壁画	法隆寺金堂壁画	上淀廃寺出土被災壁画片
赤	不純なベンガラ（酸化鉄を含む赤色の土など）	ベンガラ（Fe₂O₃）・朱（HgS）	ベンガラ・朱・鉛丹（Pb₃O₄）	ベンガラ・朱・鉛丹
黄	黄色粘土	黄土（含水酸化鉄を主成分とした黄土）	黄土・密陀僧（PbO）	黄土・密陀僧（鉛丹が被熱生成の可能性もある）
緑	緑色岩石粉末（海緑石・セラドナイトなどの粘土鉱物を含む緑色泥岩等）	緑青（CuCO₃・Cu(OH)₂）	緑青	緑青
青	—	群青（2CuCO₃・Cu(OH)₂）	群青	群青
白	白色粘土	不明　漆喰壁の表面から鉛白（2PbCO₃・Pb(OH)₂）を検出しているが、壁画の顔料としては未確認	白土	白土
黒	炭素（煤）黒色鉱物（鉄・マンガンなど）	墨	墨	墨
紫	—	—	混合物（赤色と紺青色系顔料の混色か）	—

肩にかけた袋にはベンガラ（酸化鉄を主成分にした赤土）が使用されている。肌色（肉色）には朱と白色顔料を混合して用いていると推定している。白色顔料に関しては、鉛白（塩基性炭酸塩、2PbCO₃・Pb(OH)₂）・白土などの存在を確認しているものの、壁画に使用された成分は今後の分析結果を待つしかない。男子像の首にかける袋は黄色を呈しており、これらは黄土（主な化学成分は含水酸化鉄が主成分）を使用している。緑色や青色には、緑青（塩基性炭酸銅、CuCO₃・Cu(OH)₂）、群青（2CuCO₃・Cu(OH)₂）を使用しており、最もよく知られる岩絵具である。また、輪郭線や衣文様、男子像の上衣などには黒色の墨が使われている。

寺院壁画としては法隆寺金堂壁画や上淀廃寺出土の壁画片などがあげられる。これらの壁画顔料の同定に関しては、試料を採取して分析したものもあるが、なかには古代顔料の分析経験の豊富な化学者たちによる肉眼的な鑑定による報告もある。およそ7系統の色材が存在し、11種類以上の顔料が使われていることがわかっている（参考文献3）。日本における古代の顔料を概観すると、およそ7系統の色で、11種類の顔料の存在を推定することができる（表1参照）。

法隆寺金堂壁画では、昭和の大修理が開始された昭和9年頃から金堂の解体修理にともなう事前の準備が進められた。1930年代の調査報告書によると、第6号壁について調査を行い、8種類の顔料の確認をしている。紅・赤色の朱、橙赤・緒・茶色としての酸化鉄、黄色の黄土、緑の緑青、黒色の松煙墨（炭素）、紫色については朱と紺青色の何かを混合したものと推定している。白色の胡粉もしくは白土、赤色の鉛丹（四三酸化鉛、Pb₃O₄、一酸化鉛PbOを400〜500℃で長時間熱してつくる）、黄色の密陀僧（一酸化鉛、PbO黄色または赤黄色の粉末）、そして青色の群青である。

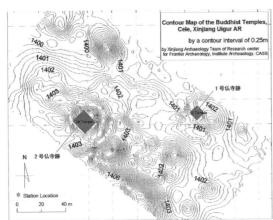

図1　タマゴゥ・トブルクトン仏寺遺跡の遺構配置と微地形

図2　タマゴゥ・トブルクトン1号仏寺遺構の全景写真

the research of history of ancient Asian Buddhist paintings. It was thus determined that Japanese and Chinese researchers would work together on the study and protection of the murals, and a dedicated joint project was launched in 2003. After 4 years in 2006, the protective restoration of the murals was completed using state-of-the-art technology developed by China, Japan and other countries. In 2005 when the restoration work was still underway, a TV program jointly created by China Central TV and NHK (Japan Broadcasting Corporation) called "New Silk Road" presented part of the restored murals. Among the murals shown in the program, the figure of *tathagata*, which has been called the "Mona Lisa of the Western Regions", received a great response. It was exhibited in the "New Silk Road Exhibition" hosted by NHK and made a strong impression on the Japanese public.

The discovery and excavation of these murals also gave rise to renewed recognition of the significance of the Dandan Oilik Site, prompting the need to study their size and extent, and the state of preservation of the remnants and a distributional survey was planned. As a result, the distributional survey of the site was carried out for 3 years between 2004 and 2006 by a Japanese-Chinese joint Dandan Oilik expedition team, wherein the scattering locations of remnants and important artifacts were registered using GPS data and measured with Total Station surveying instruments. In the final year of the project in 2006, part of the remnants was excavated and surveyed.

The current report summarizes the 2002 urgent excavation survey, distributional survey, excavation of part of the remnants, and the findings of the protection and study of the murals.

Chapter 1 looks at the location of the remains and the history of their survey and research.

Chapter 2 describes the results of the distributional survey and measurements using the Total Station surveying instruments. The distributional survey showed that the remains stretched for 3 km in every direction, and 70 sites were registered, including the remnant of a circular castle wall, 45 buildings, a rough-woven fence, 2 hearths/cooking stoves, 11 kilns and 10 orchard remains. Fifteen of the 45 building remnants were Buddhist temple related facilities. The team also tried to locate the remains of a pagoda which Stein had claimed to have found in a location about 12 km north to the Dandan Oilik, which was not successful but led to the registration of 11 sites including some buildings and kiln remnants and scattered artifacts. A distribution map, survey map and measured drawings of the collected artifacts are presented as the findings of the distributional survey.

Chapter 3 describes the urgent excavation survey of the remains of the CD-4 Buddhist Temple, as well as the survey results of the CD-3a, CD-1 and CD-17 sites excavated in

2009
北京大学と「漢唐西域考古：ニヤ・ダンダンウイリク」 国際シンポジウム開催

2009年11月、118頁に記述のように日中双方は北京大学・中国社会科学院とシンポジウムを北京大学考古文博学院で開催した。右頁はダンダンウイリクに焦点をあてシンポジウムを報じる新疆日報。

2009年11月，如118页所述，中日双方与北京大学、中国社会科学院共同在北京大学考古文博学院召开研讨会。右页是报道了将焦点放在丹丹乌里克的此次研讨会的新疆日报。

In November 2009, as stated on page 118, the Japan-China joint team held the symposium at School of Archaeology and Museology of Peking University together with Peking University and the Chinese Academy of Social Sciences. The right-hand page shows Xinjiang Daily reporting the symposium focused on Dandanoilik.

2009
報告書（中国語版）出版

2009年11月、張玉忠中方隊長の尽力で『丹丹烏里克遺址－中日共同考察研究報告』が出版された。本書は2007年に刊行した日本語版の中国語版であるが、一部に欠落と追加があった。

2009年11月，在中方队长张玉忠的努力下，《丹丹乌里克—中日共同考察研究报告》出版。该书是2007年所出日文报告书的中文版，但是在内容上有部分删除和添加。

In November 2009, The report on the China-Japan joint studies and research on the Dandanoilik ruins was published thanks to the enormous efforts by Chinese Team Leader Zhang Yuzhong. Although this is the Chinese version of the same book in Japanese published in 2007, there were missing parts and some additions.

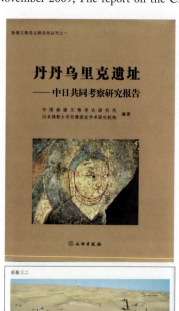

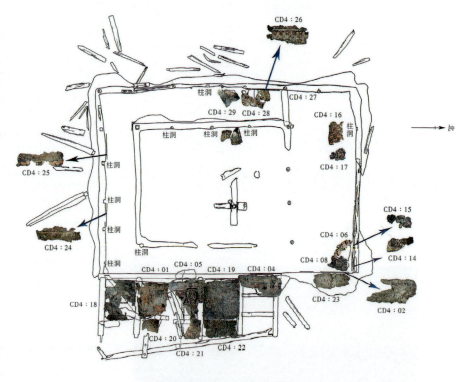

発掘遺構CD-4と壁画検出位置
发掘遗迹CD-4和壁画出现地
The excavated relic CD-4 and the detected position of the mural

丹丹乌里克故事——
历史尘埃中的繁华佐证

2010
張春賢書記へ報告

2010年8月、新疆トップの張春賢中国共産党新疆委員会書記と会見した。張書記より「4月末就任以来、新疆党委員会で外国人と会見するのは初めて、それほど評価している、今後も協力する、提案があれば遠慮なく」との発言に応じて、「文化財保護は経済活動にも結びつくので更に強化を」とお願いし、ニヤ・ダンダンウイリク調査の両報告書を提出した。

2010年8月，与新疆最高领导、中国共产党新疆委员会张春贤书记会晤。张书记说"自4月底就任以来，您是我在新疆党委会见的首位外国人，可见评价之高。今后将继续支持，如果什么建议，请不要客气"，对此我恳请道"保护文化遗产也关系到经济活动，要进一步加强"，提交了尼雅、丹丹乌里克两遗址的调查报告书。

In August 2010, I had talks with Secretary of the Xinjiang Committee of the CCP Zhang Chunxian, or the Head of Xinjiang. He told me, "I have appreciated you so highly enough to meet you as the first foreigner at the Xinjiang Committee since I assumed this position at the end of April. As I will support you from now on, too, please don't hesitate to tell me whatever proposals you might have." So, I suggested, "Would you please further promote cultural conservation because it will lead to an increase in economic activities?" Then I presented him with the research reports of both Niya and Dandanoilik.

2012
ウルムチでのシンポジウムで発表

2012年10月、121頁記述のようにウルムチで開催された国際シンポジウムで日中双方が本調査についても発表した。

2012年10月，如121页所述，在乌鲁木齐召开的国际研讨会上，中日双方就本考察也发表了论文。

In October 2012, as referred to on page 121, both the Japanese and the Chinese members made their presentations in the international symposium held in Urumqi.

2013
佛教大学でシンポジウム・写真展開催

2013年3月、キジル千仏洞保護協力・ニヤ調査もふくんだ『新疆での世界的文化遺産保護研究事業と国際協力の意義』出版。11月には122頁記述のように日中双方は国際シンポジウムで本調査についても発表した。

2013年3月，包括克孜尔千佛洞保护协力、尼雅考察内容在内的《新疆世界性文化遗产保护研究事业与国际合作的意义》一书出版。11月，如122页所述，中日双方在国际研讨会上就本考察发言。

In March 2013, I released a book titled The Projects to Preserve and Research World-class Cultural Heritages in Xinjiang and the Significance of International Cooperation, which includes Kizil, Niya, and Dandanoilik. In November, the Japanese and the Chinese members made their presentations on this research at the international symposium as mentioned on page 122.

シンポジウム会場／研讨会会场／The symposium venue

歓迎会（部分）
欢迎会（部分）／Welcome party (part)

2017
NHK「シルクロード・壁画の道をゆく」放映

2017年10月、52頁記述のように放送された本番組でダンダンウイリク壁画と法隆寺金堂壁画との関連が詳しく紹介された。

　2017年10月，52頁提到的节目中，对丹丹乌里克壁画与法隆寺金堂壁画的关联性作了详尽的介绍。

　In October 2017, as referred to on page 52, the relations between the mural at Dandanoilik and that of the Golden Pavilion at Horyuji Temple were described in detail in this program.

屈鉄線と鉄線描、NHK画面より
屈铁线与铁线描，摄于NHK画面
Flexed iron-line and iron-line: sources; NHK's screen

2018
天津テレビ「西域蒙娜麗莎」放映

　2018年1月、天津テレビ「泊客中国」が筆者特集3番組を放映。「西域蒙娜麗莎」で西域のモナリザと法隆寺壁画との関連も取り上げられた。

　2018年1月，天津电视台"泊客中国"播放了笔者的三集专题节目，"西域蒙娜丽莎"中也涉及了西域蒙娜丽莎与法隆寺壁画的关联。

　In January 2018, Tianjin TV covering China Right Here featured me in its three programs where they took a look at the relations between the Mona Lisa in the Western Regions and the mural of Horyuji Temple in its program of "The Mona Lisa in the Western Regions."

画法が一致、歴史資料が交流を物語っていると（Web放映を撮影）
画法一致、历史史料在诉说着交流（摄于网络播映）
Brushwork is precisely the same. Historical materials have proven existence of interaction. (Screenshot)

保護打合せ　　　　　　　　　　壁画　　　　　　　　　　模写
商议保护／Discussion on conservation　　壁画／The mural　　临摹／Reproduction

人々のたくましい生活を物語る出土品
出土文物反映出人们的顽强生活
The unearthed articles telling people's energetic lives

V 日中共同ダンダンウイリク遺跡学術調査 211

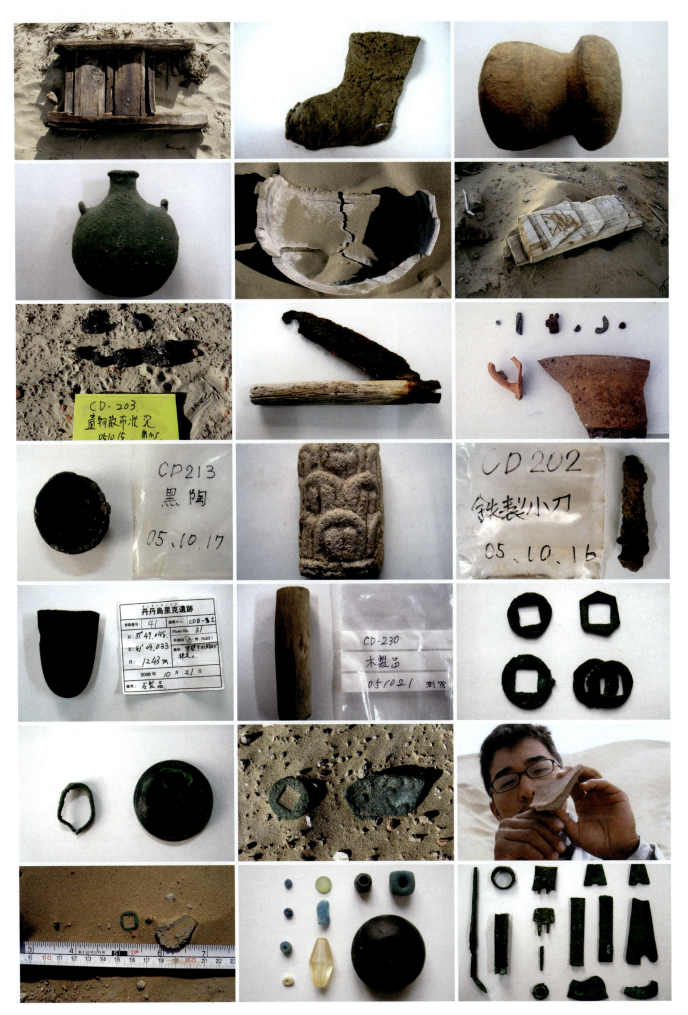

V 日中共同ダンダンウイリク遺跡学術調査

皆で世界的文化遺産保護研究するゾ〜

冬は零下40度、春は砂嵐、夏は40度超。調査に適した10月〜11月も一日の温度差は40度。共同調査成功乾杯！ 計画・交渉・調印・許可・組織・調整・分布調査・測量・発掘・保護・研究・報告書・シンポジウム・資金……乾杯！

冬季零下40度、春季黄沙漫天、夏季高温40度。适合调查的10月至11月间的昼夜温差也要40度。为共同考察的成功干杯！为计划、交涉、签字、许可、组织、调查、分布调查、测量、发掘、保护、研究、报告书、研讨会、资金……干杯！

Temperature plunges to 40 degrees below zero in winter, sand storm blows in spring, and temperature goes up to over 40 degrees in summer. While research was conducted during the period of a stable weather condition such as October through November, a temperature difference between night and day is 40 degrees.

Cheers for the success of the collaborative research! Planning, negotiation, signings, authorization, organizations, arrangement, distribution researches, survey, excavations, research, reports, symposium, funds, and a lot more; Cheers for everything!

Ⅴ　日中共同ダンダンウイリク遺跡学術調査　215

前方の大砂丘の更に向こうの遺跡での調査を終えて帰路につく2005年隊　ラクダ隊をひきつれて徒歩で帰った際に撮影
对越过前面大沙丘还需前行才能到达的遗址进行调查后，踏上了归途的2005年队　率骆驼队徒步返回的时所摄
The 2005 team, on their way back after finishing research at remains lying far away from the great dune seen forward
Being shot on our way back on foot leading the camel team

成果概要

　研究領域が多岐にわたることもあり、後述のように多くの機関の研究者が参加した。専門分野は文化財管理・国際協力・考古学・建築学・仏教美術史・文化財保護・模写・測量などである。これら多くの方々の努力により、次のような成果をあげることができた。

- 寺院・住居・円形城壁・炉・窯・果樹園など70ヵ所の遺構と遺物散布地約30ヵ所を確認し、GPSなどで経緯度を登録し、遺跡分布図を作成した。
- 光波測量により、各遺構・周辺地形図を作成した。
- 大量の国宝級壁画を発見し保護のために緊急発掘した。
- それらの壁画の保護と研究を行った。
- 銅貨など多くの遺物を収集し研究を開始した。
- 国家文物局の許可をえて、数遺構を発掘し貴重な知見をえた。
- 数ヵ所の寺院址を試掘し状況確認をおこない内容豊富な壁画を撮影し、保護のため埋め戻した。
- これらの結果、西域における"仏教聖地"としての全容を明らかにした。

成果概要

　因为涉及多个研究领域，如后所述，众多机构的研究者都有参与。专业领域有文化遗产管理、国际合作、考古学、建筑学、佛教美术史、文化遗产保护、临摹、测量等，在这些众多人士的努力下，取得了如下成果。

- 发现寺院、住居、圆形城墙、炉、窑、果树园等70处遗迹和30处文物散落地，用GPS记录经纬度制作遗迹分布图。
- 通过光波测量，制作各个遗迹、周边地形图。
- 发现大量国宝级壁画，紧急进行保护性发掘。
- 对上述壁画进行保护和研究。
- 收集了许多铜币等文物并开始研究。
- 获国家文物局许可，发掘多处遗构，获得宝贵新知。
- 对几处寺院遗址进行试发掘，确认状况，拍摄内容丰富的壁画后将遗址回填。
- 基于上述成果，弄清了西域"佛教圣地"的全貌。

Summary of achievements:

Since the scope of studies extends over a wide range of fields, a number of researchers from various organizations participated in this project as being referred to below. Specialized fields include the management of cultural assets, international cooperation, archaeology, architectonics, the history of Buddhist art, conservation of cultural assets, reproduction, and survey. People in these fields had made tireless efforts, which has resulted in the following achievements:

- Confirming about 70 relics, such as temples, dwelling sites, circular castle walls, fireplaces, kilns, and orchards, and about 30 sites with dispersed remains followed by registering their latitude-longitude locations via GPS to create the distributional diagram of the relics.
- Creation of the surrounding topological chart of each remain via light wave survey.
- Discovering a large quantity of national-treasure class murals and urgently excavating them for conservation.
- Conserving and studying those murals.
- Collecting many remains such as coppers to initiate research.
- Under the authorization of SACH Chinese, excavating several remains to gain valuable insights.
- Making a trial excavation on several temples' remains to confirm their conditions and shoot the murals with abundant content all of which were buried back for conservation.
- As a result, we have pieced together the full details of "the Buddhist sacred site" in the Western Region.

（調査組織）

　日中共同ダンダンウイリク遺跡学術調査隊の組織は下記の通りである。現地調査参加年度は〈 〉に記入した。役職は当時のものを使用した。（参加年度順）

　中日共同丹丹烏里克遺址学術調査队的组织形式如下所示。参加实地调查的年度计入〈　〉中，职位是出版报告书时所任的职务（以参加年度为顺）

　Described below is the organization chart of the Japan-China joint

scholarly research team of the Dandanoilik ruins. The participated year is noted in parentheses. The official positions are at the time of participation. (In order of the year participated)

日本側隊長　小島康誉（佛教大学内ニヤ遺跡学術研究機構代表）〈2002・04・05・06〉
　　副隊長　浅岡俊夫（六甲山麓遺跡調査会代表）〈04・05・06〉
　　　隊員　安田順惠・岸田善三郎・岸田晃子・清田怜子・中造和夫・高田和行・高田洋子（第一次予備調査隊）〈02〉
　　　　　　安藤佳香（佛教大学教授）〈04〉
　　　　　　近藤　謙（佛教大学アジア宗教文化情報研究所学芸員）〈04〉
　　　　　　孫　躍新（佛教大学内ニヤ遺跡学術研究機構研究員）〈04・05・06〉
　　　　　　村上智見（奈良大学大学院生）〈05〉
　　　　　　乾　哲也（奈良大学大学院生）〈05・06〉
　　　　　　奥山大石（奈良大学大学院生）〈05・06〉
　　　　　　竹下繭子（奈良大学大学院生）〈06〉
中国側隊長　盛春寿（新疆ウイグル自治区文物局長）〈2002〉
　　　　　　張玉忠（新疆文物考古研究所副所長）〈02・04・05・06〉
　　　隊員　張鉄男（新疆文物考古研究所館員）〈02〉
　　　　　　托呼提・吐拉洪（新疆文物考古研究所館員）〈02〉
　　　　　　李　軍（新疆ウイグル自治区文物局主任）〈02・04〉
　　　　　　佟文康（新疆文物考古研究所館員）〈02・04・05・06〉
　　　　　　買提・卡斯木（和田文物局館員）〈02・04・06〉
　　　　　　鉄付徳（中国国家博物館文物科技保護研究中心教授）〈04〉
　　　　　　劉国瑞（新疆文物考古研究所館員）〈05〉
　　　　　　李東（中国石油東方公司測量技師）〈05〉
　　　　　　阿里甫江・尼牙孜（新疆文物考古研究所館員）〈05・06〉
　　　　　　呂宗宜（中国石油東方公司測量技師）〈05・06〉
　　　　　　阮秋栄（新疆文物考古研究所館員）〈06〉
　　　　　　韓善鋒（中国石油東方公司測量技師）〈06〉

保護・研究・模写メンバー（現地調査以外）

日本側：井上正（飯田市美術博物館長）　沢田正昭（国士館大学教授）　切畑健（大手前大学教授）　岡岩太郎（岡墨光堂社長）　辻本与志一（アート・プリザヴェーション・サービス代表）　亀井亮子（岡墨光堂社員）　富澤千砂子（六法美術社長）

中国側：馬世長（北京大学教授）　劉勇・何林（亀茲石窟研究所員）

Research organization: The research has involved various fields of top-class specialists both in Japanese and Chinese universities as mentioned above. Because of space limitations, name of individuals and their affiliated institutions are abbreviated in terms of English translation.

寒い　暑い　疲れる　美味しい！　ゴミ拾い

VI

関連活動

相关活动

Related Projects

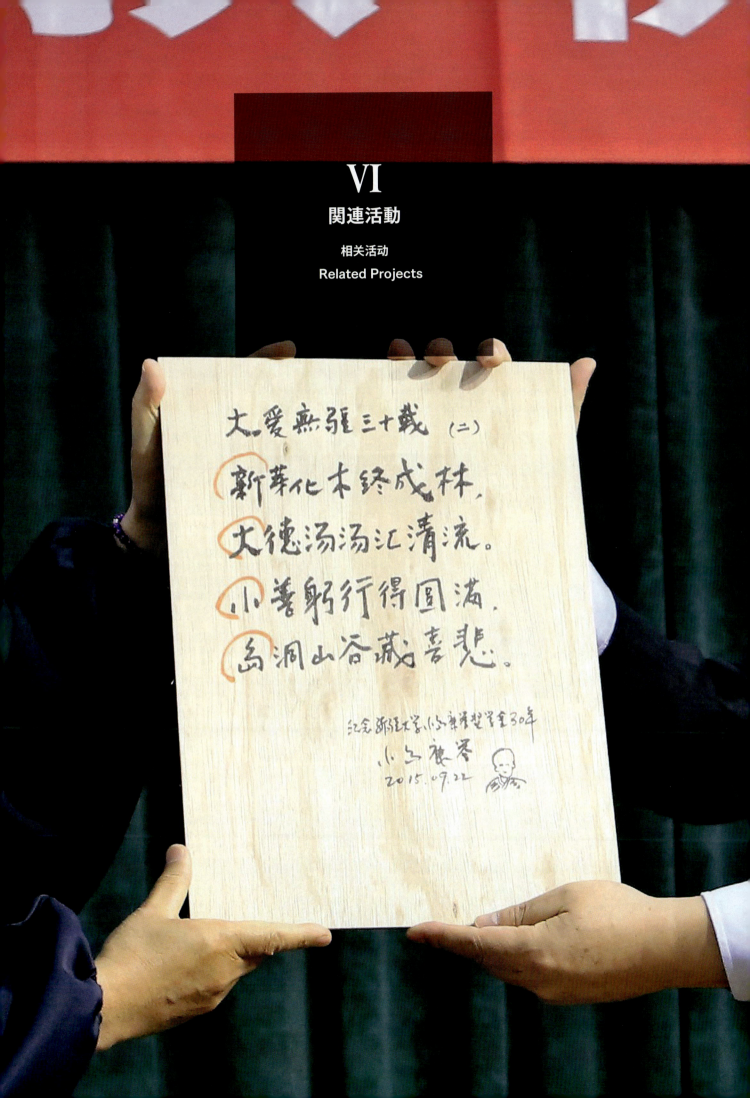

Ⅵ 関連活動

1982
各種寄付開始

　1982年より民生向上のため各種寄付を行っている。ウルムチ仏教寺院建設・改水項目・ホータン＆ミンフゥン＆チラ博物館建設・政府機関FAX機器・新疆文物考古研究所エレベーター・ウルムチ＆ホータン福祉施設各種物品・新疆図書館図書購入・新疆日報撮影機材＆パソコン設備・カパクアスカン村各種物品・大学研究項目・農業用井戸掘削・街路灯設置・小学校＆幼稚園修理など多岐にわたっている。四川地震義捐金などは友人らと提供した。

　1982年开始，为提高民生，进行了各种捐款。乌鲁木齐佛教寺院建设、改水项目、和田・民丰・策勒博物馆建设、传真设备、新疆文物考古研究所电梯、福利机构的各种物品、图书馆购入图书、新疆日报摄影器材和电脑设备、卡巴克阿斯坎村的各种物品、农业用井的挖掘、设置路灯、小学校及幼儿园的修缮等，涉及各个方面。还与友人一起为四川地震灾区捐款。

　I have made various contributions for the sake of enhancement of people's livelihood since 1982: construction of the Urumqi temple, agriculture water improvement projects, construction of museums in Hotan, Minfeng, and Chira, fax machines, the elevator for the Xinjiang Archaeological Institute, various supplies for welfare facilities, purchase of books for libraries, filming equipment and computer devices for Xinjiang Daily, various goods for Kapakeasican village, research projects of universities, water well drillings for agricultural use, placement of street lamps, repairing elementary schools and kindergartens. Along with friends of mine, I made the relief donation for the Sichuan earthquake.

雪克来提·扎克尔会见小岛康誉
发挥顾问优势
关注新疆发展

新疆日报 2015.4.8

本报乌鲁木齐4月7日讯 记者李行报道：4月7日，自治区党委副书记、自治区主席雪克来提·扎克尔会见了自治区人民政府文化顾问、日本友人小岛康誉。

小岛康誉先生自1982年至今，先后访问中国新疆140多次，主要致力于保护研究世界性文化遗产、培养人才、促进中日两国人民的理解和友好工作，与新疆各界有100多个合作项目。

雪克来提·扎克尔对小岛康誉的到来表示欢迎，对小岛康誉先生多年来对新疆文化和教育事业所作的贡献表示感谢。他说，小岛康誉先生是中日友好使者、新疆人民的老朋友，多年来一直关心新疆的教育、文化事业，为新疆的文物保护、教育、扶贫等各项事业倾注了大量心血，在增进日本各界群众对新疆多民族文化的了解方面做了许多有益的工作。国家提出"一带一路"战略构想，新疆要建丝绸之路经济带核心区，希望小岛先生充分发挥自治区政府文化顾问的优势，为加强中国新疆与周边国家文化交流，往来多提意见建议。今年是自治区成立60周年，欢迎小岛康誉先生在大庆期间回新疆多走走、多看看，更多关注新疆的发展建设。

小岛康誉表示，多年来见证了新疆的发展，作为一名多年关注新疆发展的外国人，想在自治区60周年大庆时出一点绵薄之力。他表示，在新疆大学设立的小岛康誉奖学金今年已到30年期限，他希望再延长5年时间，提高奖学金额度，并想制作一个宣传新疆的纪录片，同时对新疆贫困地区、文化遗址等项目提供援助资金，为自治区60周年大庆献礼。

小岛康誉为我区图书馆捐款

本报乌鲁木齐7月15日讯 记者一鸣报道：昨天晚上，日本友人、自治区人民政府顾问小岛康誉把10万元人民币捐赠给自治区图书馆。

多年来，小岛康誉情系新疆，多次为新疆的文化、考古、文物事业捐赠，并设立"小岛康誉文化奖"，用以奖励文化界有突出贡献的人士，受到自治区党委和人民政府的好评。

新疆日报 2000年7月17日

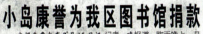

ありがとう一日100回運動
大きな愛に境界はない
Random Acts of Kindness

1986
新疆大学奨学金設立

　1986年から人材育成を目的に小島奨学金を提供している。中国重点大学のひとつである新疆大学で最も早い奨学金、計4600名余に贈呈した。当初は生活費半年以上に相当した金額に意味があったが奨学金制度が増えた現在はその名誉が重視されている。授与式には新疆政府副主席・新疆大学書記・学長・新疆政府幹部らが出席し、学生にとって栄えの日であり、学長の「小島精神に学ぼう」挨拶に毎年拍手が鳴りやまず、授与式後にサインに殺到するほど。現時点での契約は2020年までである。

　1986年开始，以培养人才为目的，开设小岛奖学金。这是中国重点大学之一的新疆大学最早开设的奖学金，已经合计向4600多学生发放了奖学金。初期的金额相当于学生们半年的生活费，意义重大，在奖学金项目日益增多的现在，更被看重的是它的荣誉性。新疆政府副主席、新疆大学书记和校长、新疆政府干部等出席授予仪式，是学生们倍感光荣的日子，校长"学习小岛精神！"的致辞每年都令掌声不断，仪式结束后，学生们蜂拥而至要求签名。目前的协议截止到2020年。

I have granted Kojima scholarships for nurturing human resources since 1986. 4,600 students have received the scholarships in sum total at Xinjiang University, one of the major universities in China. This scholarship was the first of this kind in Xinjiang and had value equivalent to half-year cost of living at the time. Nowadays, however, as many scholarships are available, this scholarship symbolizes the well-deserved honor. For example, Vice-Governor of Xinjiang, the Secretary and the President of Xinjiang University, and the senior staff members of the Xinjiang Region have attended the award ceremony. This ceremony has been taken as a very treasured occasion for awarded students. Whenever the president addresses, "Let's learn the Kojima spirit," sustained applause followed and I am overwhelmed by floods of students asking for my autograph after the ceremony. The agreement term is valid until 2020 as of today.

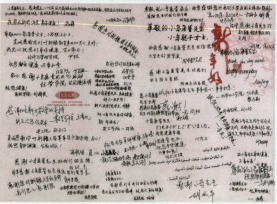

1988
各種代表団派遣開始

　1988年から新疆を理解いただくために各種代表団派遣を行っている。海部俊樹元首相・佐藤観樹元自治大臣・日中友好協会・自治体国際化協会・各種メディア・参観団など多方面にわたる。「一帯一路」の先駆けであるウルムチ対外交易会では展示ブースも設置いただいた。人民劇場で日本側の中国琵琶・日本舞踊・三味線・民謡・ピアノなどと新疆交響楽団・歌舞団との日中音楽会も開催した。一部は企業・団体との共同である。

　1988年开始，为增加大家对新疆的了解，组织派遣了各类代表团。海部俊树前首相、佐藤观树原自治大臣、日中友好协会、自治体国际化协会、各类媒体、参观团等，涉及各个方面，还在堪称"一带一路"先驱的乌鲁木齐贸易洽谈会设立展台。在人民剧场举办中日音乐会。有一部分是与企业和团体合办的。

　In order to enhance understanding of Xinjiang, I have dispatched a number of delegates in a whole variety of fields since 1988, such as former Prime Minister Toshiki Kaifu, former Minister of Home Affairs Kanju Sato, Japan-China Friendship Association, the Council of Local Authorities for International Relations, the various media, and sightseeing parties. The display booth was kindly set at the Urumqi Foreign Trade Fair which had spearheaded the policy of "One Belt, One Road." The Japan-China joint concert was hosted at the People's Hall, as well. Some of them were collaborations with other companies or groups.

新疆日報 2000年7月23日

本报乌鲁木齐7月22日讯 记者张玲报道：今天晚上，乌鲁木齐人民剧场座无虚席，自治区党委副书记克尤木·巴吾东、自治区副主席买买提明·扎克尔和近千名观众一同出席了日本名古屋访华艺术团与新疆歌舞团联合举办的2000乌鲁木齐之夏中日文化交流晚会。

以日本友人、新疆维吾尔自治区人民政府文化顾问小岛康誉先生为顾问、以日本著名舞蹈家竹内善菊为团长的日本访华艺术团的艺术家们演出了具有浓郁日本民族风情和古朴典雅的歌舞音乐节目，博得了观众们的阵阵掌声。

新疆歌舞团的艺术家们也在今天的晚会上表演了精彩歌舞音乐节目。

日本名古屋访华艺术团来疆访问演出
克尤木·巴吾东观看演出

1989
各種講演・写真展・出版開始

　1989年より相互理解促進のために文化財保護研究活動や日本・新疆の紹介を日中両国で行っている。講演は浄土宗・臨済宗・佛教大学・京都大学・奈良女子大学・中央大学・早稲田大学・愛知大学・名古屋外国語大学・NHK「新シルクロード展」会場・東京中国文化センター・広島県立美術館・新疆政府・新疆文物局・新疆博物館・新疆大学・新疆師範大学・北京大学・清華大学・中国伝媒大学・天津科技大学・同済大学・天津美術大学・天津大学・大連大学・中国歴史博物館・天津美術館・大英図書館などにおいてである。写真展は佛教大学・栄地下街・北京図書館・清華大学で行った。出版は『シルクロードの点と線』・『鉄木尓・達瓦買提詩集』（日本語版）・『王恩茂日記』（日本語版）など多数。なお喜多郎公演とフランク・ステラ作品北京展は実現しなかった。

　1989年开始，为增进相互理解，在中日两国分别开展文化遗产保护研究活动、互相介绍日本和新疆。在净土宗、佛教大学、NHK"新丝绸之路展"会场、东京中国文化中心、新疆政府、新疆文物局、新疆博物馆、新疆大学、新疆师范大学、北京大学、清华大学、中国传媒大学、天津大学、大连大学、中国历史博物馆、天津美术馆、大英图书馆等地举办演讲。在佛教大学、荣地下商业街、北京图书馆、清华大学等地举办摄影图片展。出版《丝绸之路的点与线》、《铁木尓・达瓦买提诗集》（日文版）、《王恩茂日记》（日文版）等多本书籍。

For the purpose of promoting mutual understanding, I have been engaged in activities since 1989, such as conservation and research of cultural assets, and introduction of Japan, Xinjiang and vise versa, both in Japan and China. The introductory lectures were held at Jodo Buddhist Sect, Bukkyo University, the venues of The New Silk Road Exhibition hosted by NHK, China Cultural Center in Tokyo, the Xinjiang Government, The Xinjiang Cultural Assets Bureau, the Xinjiang Museum, Xinjiang University, Xinjiang Normal University, Peking University, Tsinghua University, Communication University of China, Tianjin University, Dalian University, the National Museum of China, Tianjin Arts Museum, the British Library, and other places. The photo exhibitions were held at Bukkyo University, Sakae Underground Shopping Center, the National Library of China, and Tsinghua University. Publications include Points and Lines on the Silk Road, The Poetry Anthology of Tiemuer Dawamaiti (Japanese version), The Diary of Wang Enmao (Japanese version), and a lot more.

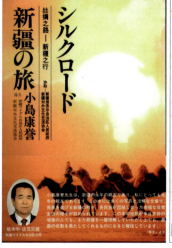

VI 関連活動

1990

各種仲介開始

1990年から経済・教育・メディアなど多方面からの依頼に応じて仲介を行っている。外国との交渉は煩雑であり、仲介者がいれば比較的スムースである。伊藤忠商事と新疆政府、野村證券と新疆政府、奈良女子大学と新疆大学、芝浦工業大学と新疆工学院、守口東高校とウルムチ第一高校、NHK・東海テレビ・テレビ東京と新疆政府・新疆文物局、NHKと新疆文物局……各種契約など多数である。違法調査で拘束された邦人教授らのお詫びの仲介も日中双方から要請をうけ行った。このような各種仲介でも国際運賃はじめ諸費用も自己負担し、謝礼なども一切辞退した。ビジネスでなくボランティアだから。

1990年开始，应经济、教育、媒体等多方面要求进行斡旋。与外国的交涉很繁琐，如果有斡旋者居中，会相对顺畅些。促成了伊藤忠商事与新疆政府、野村证券与新疆政府、奈良女子大学与新疆大学、芝浦工业大学与新疆工学院、守口东高中与乌鲁木齐第一高中、NHK・东海电视台・东京电视台与新疆政府・新疆文物局、NHK与新疆文物局签约等，数目众多。还斡旋促成了因违法勘察而被捕的日本人教授去道歉。上述各种斡旋、居间工作时的国际交通等各种费用都是笔者自己支付，也不要任何酬谢，因为这不是商业行为，是志愿活动。

I have served as an intermediary in response to requests from various fields, such as economics, education, and the media, since 1990. Negotiations with other countries are somehow complicated one way or another but would go smooth given an intermediary available. I have played an intermediary role between Itochu Corporation and the Xinjiang Government, Nomura Securities and the Xinjiang Government, Nara Women's University and Xinjiang University, Shibaura Institute of Technology and Xinjiang Technology Academy, Moriguchi-higashi High School and Urumqi First Junior and Senior High School, TV corporations like NHK, Tokai, or Tokyo and the Xinjiang Government, or the Xinjiang Cultural Assets Bureau, and a whole variety of contracts. I served as an intermediary of an apology for Japanese professors having been arrested for illegal research. Even for this kind of intermediary work, I paid out of my own pocket, such as airfares and various expenses, and declined to receive any honorarium. It was because of a volunteer work, unlikely a business work.

中澤忠義伊藤忠商事副社長一行活動を連日報じる新疆日報
连日报道伊藤忠商事副社长中泽忠义一行活动的新疆日报
Left-hand page: *Xinjiang Daily* reporting the activities of the party headed
by Vice-President of Itochu Corporation Tadayoshi Nakazawa on consecutive days

我区再次查处日本公民非法测绘案

本报乌鲁木齐4月27日讯 记者兴科、通讯员张麒、艾山江·艾尼瓦尔、实习生张倩报道：4月24日，自治区测绘局对日本国公民相马秀广等四人在艾比湖区域实施的一次性测绘的非法行为，依法作出责令停止其违法测绘活动、给予罚款、没收测绘工具和测绘成果的行政处罚。

这是继2006年4月10日，自治区测绘局查处日本株式会社国土情报研究所人员在和田非法测绘案之后，又一起查处外国人来华非法测绘案件。

经查，2007年3月5日，日本国公民相马秀广、村田泰辅、远藤邦彦、洼田顺平四人受日本国综合地球环境研究所委托，携带两部手持GPS接收机和地形图，在中国科学院新疆生态与地理研究所研究员穆某某的带领下，驱车进入艾比湖区域。在进行生态环境演变考察活动中，擅自实施了一次性测绘活动，违反了《中华人民共和国测绘法》《外国的组织或者个人来华测绘管理暂行办法》的有关规定。

得知此事后，自治区人民政府文化顾问、中日友好人士小岛康誉先生责成并带领日本国综合地球环境学研究所佐藤洋一郎从日本国专程到新疆。佐藤洋一郎对其下属来疆实施非法测绘的行为，进行了反省和道歉，并递交了道歉信。

自治区测绘局局长李全战说，四名日本国公民的违法测绘活动，是对中国法律法规的严重不尊重。这种行为不利于中日科研合作。希望日方今后不再发生类似事件。

李全战还向日方赠送了《中华人民共和国测绘法》《外国的组织或者个人来华测绘管理暂行办法》等法律法规；并对小岛康誉先生的关注和积极协调表示感谢。

新疆日报 2007年4月28日

無許可調査とお詫びの筆者仲介を報じる新疆日報
报道了违法勘察及笔者促成道歉的新疆日报
Xinjiang Daily reporting unauthorized research and me serving as an intermediary for an apology

本件は読売・京都新聞も日本側教授の実名入りで報道した
读卖新闻和京都新闻也公开教授实名报道了该事件
This case also reported by *Yomiuri* and *Kyoto Shimbun* with Japanese professors' real names

1993
各種代表団招聘開始

　1993年から新疆政府主席代表団やウルムチ市書記・市長代表団・新疆文化庁書記代表団・文物局長代表団・新疆大学代表団・企業家代表団・教師代表団・生徒代表団など各方面の代表団多数を招聘し、大きな効果をあげている。なにかと理解されていない日本を知ってもらうには「百聞は一見にしかず」である。一部は関係団体と共同での招聘。

　1993年开始，邀请新疆政府主席代表团和乌鲁木齐市书记・市长代表团、新疆文化厅书记代表团、新疆文物局长代表团、新疆大学代表团、企业家代表团、教师代表团、学生代表团等各个方面代表团访日，取得了重大成果。要想让大家了解尚不熟悉的日本，就是"百闻不如一见"。有一部分是与相关团体共同邀请的。

　Since 1993 I have invited many delegates such as those headed by the Chairman of Xinjiang and the Secretary, the mayor of Urmqi, the Secretary of the Cultural Agency, the Director of the Cultural Assets Bureau, and of those who belonged to Xinjiang University, a corporation, education, a student union, and so on. And I have found it very effective and relevant to have people understand Japan, "Seeing is Believing" as they say. Some of these invitations were made jointly with other institutions.

VI 関連活動 233

1998
希望小学校建設開始

　1998年より教育環境改善のため新疆政府外事弁公室・新疆青少年発展基金会と僻地に日中友好希望小学校5校舎を建設した。多民族地区であるので、漢・ウイグル・モンゴル族など民族バランスも考慮している。一部は上岡長作・喜多野高行・遠藤さち子・涂善祥・安田暎胤氏らの拠出もえた。

　1998年开始，为了改善教育环境，与新疆政府外事办公室、新疆青少年发展基金会一起在偏远地区建设了5所希望小学。因为是多民族地区，需要平衡汉、维吾尔、蒙古族等民族关系。一部分来自他人捐助。

　For improvement of educational environments, I have funded for the construction of five Japan-China Friendship Hope Elementary Schools in the backcountry with the supports of the Foreign Affairs Office of the Xinjiang Government and the Xinjiang Youth Development Foundation since 1998. We have always kept it in mind to take the balance of various races, such as Han, Uyghur, and Mongol, due to its characteristics as a pluralistic region. Some parts of the funds were contributed by some friends of mine.

VI 関連活動

1999

新疆文化文物優秀賞設立

　1999年、新疆政府外事弁公室・新疆文化庁・新疆文物局と「小島新疆文化文物優秀賞」を設立した。文化遺産の調査・保護・研究・継承を実践するのは、最終的には人であり、その育成こそ重要と開始した。張玉忠の示唆をえた。本年までに373人・組織を表彰し、鼓舞している。授与式は新疆政府副主席・文化庁書記・庁長・文物局長・政府幹部などが出席し盛大に開かれ、文化文物管理や研究者ばかりでなく歌舞継承者やニヤ遺跡保護管理人といった第一線の人たちの大きな励みになっている。現時点の契約は2020年までである。これ以外に中国文物保護基金会に1993年から5年間毎年研究者2名の日本の専門機関での研修制度を設けた。

　1999年，与新疆政府外事办公室、新疆文化厅、新疆文物局共同设立"小岛新疆文化文物优秀奖"，要实践文化遗产的调查、保护、研究、传承，最需要的是人才，终极需要就是人才。经张玉忠提示，开始了这个项目。截止今年，共表彰和鼓励了373个个人和团体。新疆政府副主席、文化厅书记和厅长、文物局长、政府干部出席颁奖仪式，十分隆重。不仅是文物管理和研究者，对歌舞传承人、尼雅遗址保护管理员等活跃在第一线的工作人员都是极大的鼓励。目前协议签至2020年。除此之外，还于1993年在中国文物保护基金会设立了为期5年、每年派2名人员赴日本专业机构研修的制度。

　In 1999, the Foreign Affairs Office of the Xinjiang Government, the Xinjiang Cultural Agency, the Xinjiang Cultural Assets Bureau, and I founded the Kojima awards for outstanding performances for Xinjiang cultures and relics. Human resources are the ultimate source to perform investigations, conservation, research, and inheritance of cultural heritages. In considering the significance of nurturing those performance capabilities, this project was launched with the suggestion of Zhang Yuzhong. A total sum of 373 awards, including people and organizations, were presented thus far, which has inspired increased motivation in them. The ceremony of awards presentation has been taken place magnificently every year with attendance of Vice-Governor of the Xinjiang Region, Secretary of the Cultural Agency, Director-General of the Xinjiang Cultural Agency, Bureau Director of the Xinjiang Cultural Assets Bureau, and senior staff members of the Xinjiang Region. These rewards have been received by people active in the front lines, such as not only administrators and researchers of cultural assets but successors to traditional songs and dances and even a security guard for the Niya ruins. These awards have served as powerful encouragement for them. The term of this agreement is valid until 2020. Apart from this, I established a specialist development program within the Chinese Cultural Relics Protection Foundation which has annually given two researchers an opportunity to study at the Japanese institutions for five years from 1993.

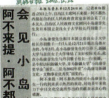

1999
シルクロード児童育英金開始

　1999年よりウルムチ市政府と貧困児童に育英金を提供している。急成長してはいるが貧困地区では学用品を買えない家庭もまだあり、学習条件改善のためであり、累計約1600人に達している。あわせて学校へ温水器・寄宿舎布団・学用品なども寄贈している。一時期は友人からも寄付をえた。

　1999年开始，与乌鲁木齐市政府共同向贫困儿童提供育英金。尽管经济急速发展，但是偏远地区一些家庭还是买不起学习用品，该资金用于他们改善学习环境，累计有约1600人受捐。同时还向学校赠送热水器、宿舍用棉被和学习用品等。有一段时期，还获得了友人们的捐助。

　I have provided poor children with scholarships in concert with the Urumqi City Government since 1999. Despite rapid economic growth, there still are many households that can't afford to buy school supplies in poor areas, which should enhance learning environments. Recipients have come to about 1,600 pupils. Along with this initiative, I have donated water heaters, beds for the use of a dormitory, and school supplies for schools. Some parts of the funds were contributed by my friends.

大愛無疆

ありがとう一日100回運動
大きな愛に境界はない
Random Acts of Kindness

烏魯木斉晩報　2000年7月16日

小岛康誉昨到永丰乡为贫困儿童发放奖学金

本报讯（记者刘金栋）昨天上午，乌鲁木齐县永丰乡中学的学生像过节一样汇集在学校操场，日本友人小岛康誉第二次向该乡贫困儿童发放了2万元奖学金。副市长隋吉平参加发放仪式。

小岛康誉先生是自治区人民政府文化顾问，我市荣誉市民。他多次访问过新疆，为自治区文化、经济、教育事业做过突出贡献。去年7月小岛先生自愿与我市外办签订协议，设立"丝路贫困儿童奖学金"，每年为我市100名贫困儿童每人提供200元奖学金。发放仪式上，小岛康誉还向永丰乡中学赠送了价值5000元人民币的学习用品。

2000
中国歴史文化遺産保護網開設

2000年、鄔時夏・張書権・楊金栄・孫躍新・周培彦らの尽力をえて「中国歴史文化遺産保護網」www.wenbao.netを開設した。鉄木尔・達瓦買提全人代副委員長の列席をえて人民大会堂で起動式を行った。当時はネット開設には困難が伴った。経済急発展の一方で、破壊もすすんでいる。文化遺産保護意識を啓蒙するための公益性ネットであり、高い評価をえている。設立資金は筆者が負担したが、現在は孫躍新・周培彦夫妻が拠出している。一部に友人の寄付も含んでいる。筆者は国際協力を「一帯一路実践談」と題し発信中。

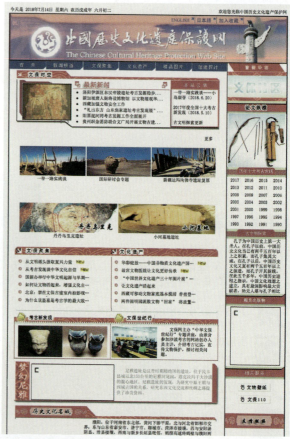

2000年，经过努力，创建了"中国历史文化遗产保护网"（www.wenbao.net），全国人大副主席铁木尔·达瓦买提出席了在人民大会堂举行的启动仪式。当时创办网站要伴随许多困难。经济迅速发展的同时，破坏也在加剧。这个旨在启发文化遗产保护意识的公益性网站获得高度评价。创办资金是由笔者提供的，现在则依靠孙跃新·周培彦夫妇出资。部分资金来自友人资助。笔者在网站以"一带一路实践谈"为题持续发文，宣传国际合作。

I launched www.wenbao.net to preserve Chinese historical, cultural heritages in 2000. The operation ceremony was taken place with attendance of Vice-Chairman of the NPC Tiemuer Dawamaiti at Beijing's Great Hall of the People. At that time, to establish a network site entailed lots of hard work. While being in the midst of rapid economic progress, environmental destruction has been deteriorating. The network site is for the public to raise conservation awareness of cultural assets which has been highly valued. I owed the launching fund but the operation cost has been offered by Mr. Sun Yuexin and Ms. Zhou Peiyan along with our friends' contributions. I am myself releasing messages for international cooperation as titled One Belt, One Road in Action.

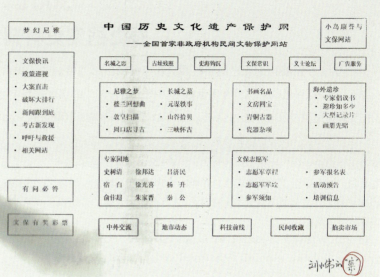

2017年十大考古发现
（按年代早晚排序）

2018年4月10日，为期两天的2017年度全国十大考古新发现终评会在北京结束，入围终评的26个项目进行了演示汇报，评委会经过评议和投票，选出2017年度全国十大考古新发现。4月10日下午，中国文物报社和中国考古学会联合召开新闻发布会，公布了2017年度全国十大考古新发现。

1、新疆吉木乃通天洞遗址

发掘单位：新疆维吾尔自治区文物考古研究所 北京大学考古文博学院
项目负责人：于建军

简介：

作为新疆境内发现的第一个旧石器时代洞穴遗址，通天洞遗址完整保存着从旧石器时代到3500年前古人类生活、居住的遗存，不但是旧石器考古的重要收获，也是新疆北部史前考古文化序列构建的重大突破。阿尔泰山与塔尔巴哈台山之间相对平坦的山谷从旧石器时代开始，一直就是重要的文化传播与交流通道，这种特点在青铜时代、早期铁器时代的遗存中也有所表现，为阿勒泰地区史前考古打上了一以贯之的底色，对于研究中国乃至东亚地区旧石器时代文化的丰富性、多样性，与欧亚大陆西部远古文化的相关性等，以及探讨尼安德特人、丹尼索瓦人群的迁徙扩散，具有重要的学术意义。

2001
歷史檔案史料刊行開始

2001年より新疆档案館と同館収蔵史料を共同出版している。史料を研究者に提供することが目的である。これまでに出版したのは『近代外国探検家新疆考古档案史料』・『中瑞西北科学考察档案史料』・『スタイン第四次新疆探検档案史料』・『清代新疆建置档案史料』である。一部はほかの档案館収蔵史料を含んでいる。

2001年开始，与新疆档案馆共同出版该馆档案史料，目的是向研究人员提供史料。迄今为止出版了《近代外国探险家新疆考古档案史料》、《中瑞西北科学考察档案史料》、《斯坦因第四次新疆探险档案史料》、《清代新疆建置档案史料》。部分书中还收录了其他档案馆收藏的史料。

In order to provide researchers with historical records, I have jointly published historical materials to be stored in the Xinjiang Archives Center of since 2001. They include: The Archives of Modern, Foreign Explorers in Xinjiang; The Archives of Chinese-Swedish Scientific Studies on Northwest China; The Archives of the Stein's Fourth Expedition to Xinjiang; and The Archives of Xinjiang Province in the Qing Dynasty. For your information, some of them are from other archives centers.

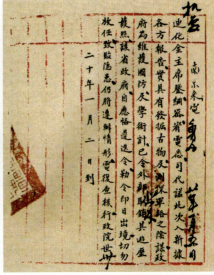
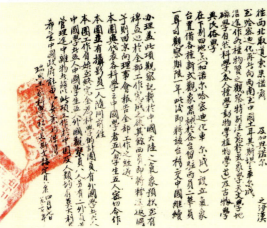
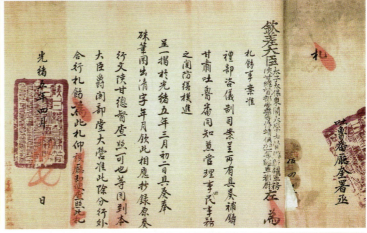

新疆日报 2010.11.30 【文史书架】

边疆史研究的重要资料

《清代新疆建置档案史料》出版发行

□ 杨新才

由自治区档案馆、日本佛教大学尼雅遗址学术研究机构共同合作出版的《清代新疆建置档案史料》于日前面世。

这是一部以反映清代新疆特别是新疆建省以来有关军政机构设置、官员职掌、施政纲略为主要内容的史料集，所选史料均出自自治区档案馆馆藏资料。

相对于历史上各个朝代而言，清朝是在历代中央政府对新疆实行管理基础上对新疆管理体制实行重大变革并最后集大成的朝代，其中又以光绪十年（1884年）新疆建省为界，分为前后两个时期。前期，清朝政府在新疆实行的是军府制。乾隆二十七年（1762年）十月，清廷正式在新疆设立总统伊犁等处将军（简称伊犁将军），作为清政府在新疆的最高军事、行政长官，代表中央政府总揽全疆各项军政事务。后期，新疆建省，这是中央政府治理新疆的重大变革。建省后，地方行政交由各道、府、州、县办理，伊犁将军虽得到保留，但权力大大缩小。同时废除伯克制度，减轻税赋和商业税，实行更为优惠的移民实边政策，采取各项政策恢复农业、发展副业生产、兴办文教等，而这都是这一变革所带来的重大变化。这一变革，对于维护祖国统一、开发西北边疆、增加各民族间的交流，曾起到了巨大的作用。

该档案史料较明晰地勾勒出了这一时期的发展脉络，在为史学研究者提供可靠的第一手资料的同时，也为今天新疆的经济建设和社会各项事业的发展提供了借鉴与参考。

这次编辑出版《清代新疆建置档案史料》是日本佛教大学尼雅遗址学术研究机构与自治区档案馆的第四次合作。自治区人民政府文化顾问小岛康誉先生作为尼雅遗址学术研究机构的代表，奔波在新疆与日本间，为中日文化交流不懈努力，在他的牵线下，尼雅遗址学术研究机构与自治区档案馆合作，之前已编辑出版了《近代外国探险家新疆考古档案史料》《中瑞西北科学考察档案史料》和《斯坦因第四次新疆探险档案史料》，在国内外受到广泛关注。

小岛康誉：一个感动全新疆的日本人

筆者の新疆活動を報じる
中国文物報／中国文物报
报道了笔者在新疆的活动
Chinese Cultural Resources News covering my activities in Xinjiang

VII

国際協力の意義

国际合作意义
The Significance of
International Cooperation

Ⅶ 国際協力の意義

世界には約200の国家があり、約3300の民族がいる。それぞれの歴史・宗教・体制・文化・言語などは異なる。国益は異なり主張はぶつかり合う。戦争・紛争・テロ・差別……が世界で頻発している。相互理解はたいへん困難であり、だからこそ相互理解の努力が必要である。相互理解を促進し平和を守る一環として国際協力の重要性がある。国家のみならず企業や個人レベルでも必要な「共生」・「共育」・「循環型」活動である。

21世紀は国際協力の世紀ともいえる。文明が急速に発展し、各国の相互依存が日に日に濃密になった結果である。いまや世界76億人は運命共同体となった。国際協力は20世紀中葉から言われ始めた。筆者も1982年初めて新疆を訪れたころは、国際協力といった概念は乏しかったが、各種貢献を続けるうちに徐々に公共外交といった考えが形成されてきた。

日本人が内向きになりつつある。激動つづく世界、国論さだまらぬ日本。国家の存続と繁栄によって支えられている国民の生活向上のためにも外向きになり、世界で活躍する人がさらに増えることを望むひとりである。本稿で事実を坦々と長々と記録してきたのは、国際協力実践に少しでも参考になればと願うからでもある。日本では貢献をかくすことが「美徳」とされる風潮があるが、世界はそうではない。日本国・日本人が世界各国で実践しつづけている国際貢献は世界の人々にどれだけ知られているであろうか。いや日本人でさえ殆ど知らない。国も団体も個人も、もっと堂々と発信してこそ、世界から信頼をえることが出来るといえよう。

我が国は国際協力面でも先進的地位を占めている。税金からの政府開発援助（ODA）といった資金面ばかりでなく、国際協力機構（JICA）や国際協力銀行・青年海外協力隊・シニア海外ボランティアなど組織や制度も整っている。また多くのNGOや企業・個人が活動されていることは嬉しいかぎりだ。

国家や外交官だけでなく、政治家や公務員はもとより観光客・ビジネスパースン・研究者・留学生・一般市民などすべての人が公共外交の一翼を担っていることを意識し自覚ある言動が必要とされるのが21世紀であろう。

新疆師範大学で日本語を教育する岡本和恵海外青年協力隊員（左端）
在新疆师范大学教日语的海外青年协力队员冈本和恵（左端）
Japan Overseas Cooperation Volunteers' member Kazue Okamoto (far left) teaching Japanese at Xinjiang Normal University

全世界约有约200个国家、约3300个民族，各自的历史、宗教、体制、文化、语言都不尽相同。国家利益不同，主张也会发先生冲突，世界上，战争、纠纷、恐袭、歧视……等频发。相互理解十分困难，所以才需要为加深相互理解而努力，作为促进理解、保护和平的一环，国际合作意义重大。不仅是国家，企业和个人也需要"共生"、"共育"、"循环型"活动。

21世纪也可以说是国际合作的世纪。文明急速发展，各国间相互依存是关系日益加深的结果。目前世界上的76亿人是命运共同体。20世纪中叶就开始说国际合作。1982年初次访问新疆时，笔者的国际合作概念也很淡薄，是在持续推进各种贡献中逐步形成了公共外交的构想。

日本人逐渐趋于内向，动荡不安的世界、争论不休的日本。国家的存续和繁荣直接关系国民生活，为了提高国民生活水准，真心希望出现更多勇于向外，在世界舞台活跃的人。之所以在本稿中长篇大论地陈述事实，就是希望能对国际合作的实践活动提供一些参考。在日本，对所贡献秘而不宣是一种"美德"，但国际习惯并非如此。日本国及日本人在世界各国推进的国际贡献有多少为世界人民所知呢？没有！连日本人自己都不知道。国家、团体、个人都应该勇敢地发声，才能够取得国际信赖吧。

国在国际合作方面处于领先地位，不仅有源于税款的政府开发援助资金，国际协力机构、国际协力银行、青年海外协力队、老年海外志愿者等组织和制度也很完善。还活跃着许多NGO、企业和个人，令人欣喜。

我国家和外交官、政治家和公务员自不必说，即使是游客、商务人员、学者、留学生、一般市民，都应该意识到自己也是公共外交一分子，自觉注意言行，这也是21世纪所需要的。

There are about 200 nations across the world and around 3,300 races. Each of their history, system, institution, culture, language, etc. differs from each other. So as their national interest does, people crash claiming conflicting ideas. We have frequently seen war, confliction, terrorism, prejudice, and others all over the world. Mutual understanding is almost next to impossible to achieve. That's the very reason why effort is all the more needed to achieve mutual understanding. International cooperation plays significant part to nurture a spirit of mutual understanding to secure peace. Coexistence, shared education, and recycling-oriented activities are crucial issues to be dealt with on the level of businesses and individuals as well as nations,.

The 21st century is, in other words, the century of international cooperation. This underlies the fact that civilization has drastically developed and mutual dependency among nations has increasingly deepened. People as many as 7.6 billion have come to share a common destiny in the world today. International cooperation was beginning to emerge around the middle of the 20th century. When I first visited Xinjiang in 1982, I myself had a low level of awareness regarding international cooperation. In making the said various contributions, the thought of public diplomacy has gradually been formed.

Many Japanese have now become rather introverted because of its unstable national consensus in the ever-changing world. I am one of those who wish that Japanese should get extroverted and work actively in the world to improve their own people's livelihood, which I believe is essential for the existence and the prosperity of Japan itself. The reason why I have long referred to the facts as they are in this thesis is to hope to give references in any way possible to people practicing international cooperation. We Japanese tend to think it a virtue to hide our contributions. It is not so in the world. I am wondering to what extent valuable contributions Japan and Japanese people have made internationally have been informed to the people of the world. Even Japanese have scarcely been communicated. I'm a firm believer in winning the world confidence if Japan, its groups, and its individuals should disseminate their contributions without hesitation.

We hold an advanced position in the field of international cooperation. Besides Official Development Assistance financed by tax revenue, we have established organizations and frameworks, such as the Japanese International Cooperation Agency, the Japan Bank for International Cooperation, Japan Overseas Cooperation Youth Volunteers, and Japan Overseas Cooperation Senior Volunteers. I'm very pleased to see a variety of NGOs, businesses, and individuals being actively committed to their own missions.

I would say that the 21st century needs those who are well aware of sharing a burden for practicing public diplomacy regardless of whether they are sightseers, business people, researchers, international students, or general public, to say nothing of government workers or diplomats.

国際協力実践10ヵ条

筆者は研究者でなく、いわば国際協力手弁当長期実践家である。本書もその立場から活動を紹介してきた。心がけてきた国際協力実践10ヵ条を紹介したい。

国际合作实践10条
My 10 Articles for International Cooperation in Action

笔者并非学者，应该说是自带盒饭国际合作长期实践家。本书也是基于该立场，介绍了活动内容。下面介绍一直铭记心头的国际合作实践10条准则。

Unlikely being a researcher myself, I am a lifelong volunteer for international cooperation. Based on this standpoint, I have described about what I have done thus far. I would like to show you my 10 articles for international cooperation in action that I always keep in mind.

① 使命感をもつ

あまりにも当然のことであるが、何のために国際協力するのかを明確に自覚する必要があろう。あらゆる分野で異なる外国での国際活動では大小様々な衝突がある。そのような際に双方が立ち戻る原点が使命感である。基本理念の明確化である。意義・目的・目標を明確にすべきである。当然ながら双方に同様の意識が必要である。

筆者らは、キジル千仏洞修復保存では「人類共通の文化遺産を後世へ」を、ニヤ・ダンダンウイリク両遺跡調査では「友好・共同・安全・高質・節約」の五大精神を、関連活動では「大きな愛に境界はない」を掲げ活動してきた。

調査五大精神を解説してみる。友好と共同は説明を要しない。沙漠活動は危険がともなう、死に至った例も記録されている。日中隊もルート開発不能による緊急露営、砂嵐に遭遇、ラクダからの落下による脳震盪や骨折、病人発生、車両火災といった突発事故を度々経験している。普段は各自の判断で行動していても緊急時はリーダーの指揮に従う命令系統の一本化が安全確保の要点である。世界的文化遺

ダンダンウイリク壁画保護打合せ成功、乾杯！
丹丹乌里克壁画保护协商成功，干杯！
After a successful meeting to conserve the Dandanoilik murals, Cheers!

産に相応しい高水準の保護研究が必要であり、日中双方の各分野の第一線専門家を組織した。筆者自身が研究者でなく調査保護研究事業の推進者であるので、この点には特に心がけた。感謝しきれない。費用的にも環境的にも節約を心がけた。ただし意思疎通のための潤滑油的部分は削らなかった。大小様々な衝突があった。その度ごとに日中双方は基本理念にもどり解決してきた。

日中両国間の各種会議などでは「戦略的互恵関係」・「WIN-WINの関係」と発言されている。また「日中友好」が叫ばれている。この言葉が頻繁に登場するのはそれが形骸化しているからでもある。264～265頁報道のように「日中友好」を基礎として、第二段階「日中相互理解」、第三段階「日中共同」へ進化すべきと言い続けている。

① 拥有使命感

这是无需赘言的，必须要自我明确为什么要国际合作。在各个领域存在差异的外国推进国际活动会产生各种大大小小的冲突。那时候双方需要回到的原点就是使命感。是基本理念的明确。意义、目的、目标也必须要明确。当然等双方必要具备同样的意识。

笔者等在协力修复克孜尔千佛洞时秉承"将人类共同的文化遗产传与后世"精神；在考察尼雅和丹丹乌里克遗址时秉承"友好、共同、安全、高质、节约"五大精神；推进相关活动时则秉承"大爱无疆"精神。

说明一下调查五大精神，友好和共同无需说明。沙漠活动伴随危险，致死先例也有发生。中日调查队也曾遭遇许多的突发状况：无法拓路而紧急宿营、遭遇沙尘暴、从骆驼上摔下来导致脑震荡和骨折、队员生病、车辆着火等。平时可以自行判断采取行动，但是在紧急时刻，听从领导指挥、实现命令系统的一体化才是保证安全的关键。必须要进行与世界性文化遗产相匹配的高水准保护研究，因此组织了中日双方各个领域的一流专家参加。因为笔者本人不是学者，只是调查保护研究事业的推动者，所以在这方面格外注意，也感恩不尽。无论是费用方面还是环境方面，都不忘节约，但是始终没有削减促进沟通的润滑剂部分。有过大大小小的各种冲突，每次日中双方都是回到基本理念且圆满解决了。

日中两国间的各种会议上"战略互惠关系""双赢关系"的发言不断，高呼"日中/中日友好"。这些言论之所以频繁出现也是因为它们已经形骸化了。如264-265页所示，我一直强调"日中/中日友好"是基础，第二阶段是"日中/中日相互理解"，第三阶段要上升到"日中/中日共同"。

① Keeping a sense of mission

This may sound too obvious, but we may have to be conscious of for what we must implement international cooperation. We have seen a whole variety of large and small conflictions when it comes to performing international activities in any fields. When facing that kind of situation, you have to get back to where you started. That is a sense of mission. What I mean is the clarification of basic philosophy. You should clarify cause, purpose, and goal explicitly. This goes without saying that both sides need to have the same awareness.

We have performed our mission under the theme of "Let's hand down the common cultural heritage of mankind to future generations" at the time of restoration and conservation of the Kizil grottoes while in the case of the research of ruins both in Niya and Dandanoilik, we have maintained the five great principles, or "Friendship, Collaboration, Safety, High Quality, and Frugality." We have worked under the banner of "No Boundaries for Love of Humanity."

Let me elaborate on the five great principles. Friendship and collaboration need no explanation. Activities in the desert entail risks to such a degree as having been recorded deadly. The Japan and China joint team also was often involved in sudden accidents like an emergency camping due to failure to develop a new route, encountering sandstorm, brain contusion, and broken bone caused by falling from a camel, getting sick, and vehicle fire. While it is routinely allowed to act on your own judgment, it is the key point to maintain a unified chain of command to follow a leader's directive to secure safety in an emergency. As it was required to conduct conservation and research on a level high enough to deserve a world-class cultural heritage, I have organized a team consisting of leading professionals both from Japan and China. Not being a professional, myself, but as the promoter of a project for investigations, conservation, and research, I have had my heart set on this point. I cannot thank them enough. I have been mindful of frugality costwise and environment-wise, except for the cost to reduce friction for better interpersonal communication. While we have experienced a whole variety of collisions, large or small, both the Japanese and the Chinese teams have returned to those fundamental principles to solve each issue, accordingly.

At the various conferences between Japan and China, we have more often than not heard "strategic and mutually beneficial relationships" and "win-win relationships," and they have always called for "Japan-China Friendship." Frequent emergence of this word means it has lost substance. As referred to on pages 264-265 of the report, we must enter the second phase based on Japan-China Friendship, which I think you could call Japan-China Mutual Understanding, and then both nations should work together to advance to the third phase, Japan-China Collaboration. I would reiterate this evolution time and again.

② 国益意識をもつ

外国との協力事業が国際協力である。それぞれの国家にはそれぞれの立場があり、それぞれの国益がある。双方が主張を展開、国益を重視するのは当然のことであるが、それは対立の原因にもなりうる。双方が国益を忘れてはならない。筆者は日本を代表して国際協力をしているわけでも、官僚でもなく一市民であるが、我が国の国益を忘れたことはない。中

国人から「中国が好きな日本人は多いが、中国一辺倒の日本人は妙だと思う。貴方は親中派だが意見をハッキリ言うので長く付き合っている」と言われたこともある。

36年にわたる国際協力が対日理解を僅かでも促進したとすれば、それが最大の国益への寄与であろう。中国各地いや世界各地で貢献をつづけている方々も多い。真の外交官といえよう。

② 有国家利益意识

与外国的合作事业是国际合作，各国有各国的立场，也有各自的利益。双方提出各自主张、重视国家利益是理所应当的，但是往往这一点会成为对立的原因。双方都不能忘记本国利益。笔者并不是代表日本在进行国际合作，也不是官员，只是普通市民，但是从未忘记过本国利益。曾经有中国人对我说"喜欢中国的日本人很多，但是对中国一边倒的日本人是奇怪的。您虽然是亲中派，但是发表意见又很直率，所以能够长期交往"。

长达36年的国际合作如果能增进对日理解，哪怕只是一点点，也是为最重要的国家利益作出的贡献吧。在中国各地和世界各地不断贡献的人还有许多，他们可以说是真正的外交官。

② Being Conscious of national interest

Joint undertakings with other countries are international cooperation. Each country has its own standpoint and national interest. It is a matter of course that both of each country express their view and value their national interest, yet it can be a cause for confrontation. Both sides should never forget national interest. Although I am not involved in international cooperation as a representative of Japan or a bureaucrat, I have never forgotten national interest as an ordinary citizen. I was once told, "There are many Japanese who like China, but I think the Japanese who are only on the side of China seem odd. I know you are friendly to China, but you clearly express your own view. That's why I have been getting along with you for a long time."

If my international contribution over 36 years may have somewhat developed an understanding of Japan, it would be my greatest dedication to national interest. There are a number of people who have continuously contributed to China, not to mention other parts of the world. They should be a true diplomat.

③ 握手する

国際協力の基本は相手国の主権・法規・文化の相互尊重である。活動にあたっては反対意見があっても、まずは握手して聞くように心がけた。握手とは相手を尊重することである。我が国での礼に相当するといえよう。握手にも温度差がある。熱烈な握手から早く帰れ、までを体験している。

握手するとは「笑う」とも表現できる。微笑んで近づき「お元気ですか」、「お忙しいでしょう」、「今日も話し合いましょう」などと語りかけながら握手してきた。苦虫をかみ殺したよう顔での握手では「握手」とはいえない。まるで「お前なんかには会いたくないが仕方なく会ってやる」といった握手では協力関係は築けない。そんな態度の相手に対しては力強く握り返し、当方の熱意を伝えるように心がけた。

③ 握手

国际合作的基础是与对象国主权、法规、文化的相互尊重。笔者一直告诫自己：活动时即使有反对意见，也要先握手倾听。握手是尊重对方，在我国属于礼节。握手也是有温差的。从热烈欢迎到企盼离开，都有所体验。

握手也是"微笑"的同义词。微笑着走近，一边问着"身体好吗？""忙不忙啊？""今天也好好聊聊"，一边伸手相握。面带咬死虫子的表情的握手不能称之为"握手"。握手时的感觉就像"根本不想见你，可是又没办法"，这样的握手是建立不起合作关系的。对于这样的握手，笔者告诫自己要用力回应以传达自己的诚意。

③ Offering Handshake

International cooperation is basically to show the other end respect in terms of sovereignty, statute, and culture. Even though someone opposes to what I am planning to do, I first try to shake his hand and listen to that opposition. Handshake signifies respect to others. Bowing in Japan can be corresponding to that. There are a firm handshake and a weak one. I have been through enthusiastic handshake down to "Go home."

Handshake can connote smile, as well. I have approached anyone with smile, saying "How are you?" "Are you busy?" or "Let's enjoy talks." Handshake with a sour face is far from handshake per se. You will never be able to develop cooperative relationships by a handshake as if to say "I could not help meeting you, though I hate to see you." To that kind of person, I have made a point to squeeze his hand back to try to convey our enthusiasm.

④ 主張する

外交とは「協調しながら主張する」ことである。先方の主張を聞いたのちに、主張すべきは大いに主張するが、相手の感情の機微をとらえることが重要であろう。相手の発言をメモし、趣旨を分析し同意できる事項から回答し、同意できない事項は婉曲的であっても明確にその旨を伝え、対案を主張した。

日本側が数名いる場合は、諸氏にそれぞれの考えを述べて頂いた。同意をえるには納得してもらうことが必要である。

VII 国際協力の意義　249

力ずくで押さえ込んだのでは長続きしない。例えば、協力するのだから、資金提供するのだからといった態度では一時的な関係しかできない。

　主張は事実に即して行った。事実を捻じ曲げての発言で主張を通すことは出来てもいつかは剝げ落ちる。重要事項は議事録を作成しサインを得た。準重要事項はメモを渡すなり、帰国後にFAXを送信し記録として残した。活動終了後には概要をまとめた。よって活動記録は膨大である。

　共産党が強い力を持つ中国では、指導者の支持と指示が重要である。本書では殆ど記載しなかったが、新疆党書記・政府主席・副主席とはあわせて100回ほど会見した。会見では先方発言に続いて、当方が会見への感謝・活動報告・計画を発言。事前にイメージトレーニングを行い、メモは一切見ない。聞くことはほぼ分かるので通訳なし、話すときは正確を期すために通訳を通した。指導者には筆者のこれまでの活動からほぼ100％支持発言で応じて頂ける。会見には各組織幹部が同席するので指導者の支持発言効果は大きい。TV各局や新聞各紙でも報道され、指導者の支持が一般の人たちにも広く認識される。おのずと活動しやすくなる。

新疆トップの張春賢書記との会見を報じる新疆日報／新疆日报报道新疆最高领导人张春贤书记接见我
Xinjiang Daily covering the meeting with Secretary Zhang Chunxian, the head of Xinjiang

④ 主张

　所谓外交是"边协调边主张"。在听取对方的主张后，需要主张的要大胆主张，同时又要捕捉对方情感的细微之处，这一点非常重要。记录对方发言，分析主旨，从可以接受的事项开始回答，对于不能同意的事项要既委婉又明确地告知对方并提出对应方案。

　在日方有数人参加时，笔者会请各位陈述自己的想法。要征得同意就需要对方理解。单靠强压是不能持久的。例如：总是以我在帮助你、是我在提供的资金这种态度的话，只能建立短时关系。

　主张也要基于事实。靠歪曲事实的发言通过自己的主张，即使达到目的，有一天也会暴露出来。重要的事情要都写了备忘录并签字。准重要事项也会递上笔记、回国后再通过发传真留下记录。活动结束后写出总结概要。因此，活动记录的数量十分庞大。

　在共产党具有绝对实力的中国，领导人的支持和指示非常重要。本书虽然基本没有记录，我与新疆的党组书记、政府主席和副主席的会面次数多大100次以上。会见时，对方先发言，笔者再依次表示感谢接见、汇报活动、说明计划。笔者会事前练习好，现场不看稿子。因为基本可以听懂，所以不用翻译，只在发言时借助翻译，以保证精确。基于笔者以往的活动，领导人们都以"100％支持"来回应我。会见时会有各组织的干部们在座，因此领导人表示支持的发言，会产生明显的效果。各个电视台和新闻报纸也会报道，领导人的支持态度也会被一般人所广泛了解，自然就便于活动了。

④ Speaking up

Diplomacy is to advocate while collaborating. After listening to the other party's assertion, it is crucial to read the subtleties of their emotion while claiming what's necessary without hesitation. I have put forth a counter proposal after taking a note of counterpart's talks to analyze them and then clearly conveyed why I could not consent somewhat in a euphemistic manner.

When we have several Japanese attendees, each person is urged to deliver their remarks. It is necessary to have them convinced in order to get their consent. Things will not last long if you should force them to consent, saying that we offer assistance or fund, for example, which will end up with a temporary relationship.

I have made my assertion in line with the facts. Misrepresenting them might make it possible to keep your opinion straight, but it will soon wither away. We have prepared the minutes to have them signed when it comes to important issues. As for less important issues, we have handed over a memorandum or sent a fax to record it after returning to Japan. After completion of each project, we have summarized it, which means that activity log is enormous.

As the Communist Party has a strong power in China, the support and directives of leaders are vital. Though I have not touched on much in this paper, I have met the CCP Secretary of Xinjiang, the Governor and the Vice-Governor of Xinjiang about 100 times in total. At the meeting, following their remarks, I expressed my appreciation for the meeting, reported activities, and informed of a coming project. I prepare for a meeting with imagery rehearsal and I talk without using any note. Since I almost understand what they say in Chinese, I do not need an interpreter. When I speak, I communicate through an interpreter to secure accuracy. Recognizing what I had ever done,

the leaders have kindly given me their full support which plays a crucial role because the senior staff at each division has shared a table at the meeting. Each TV station and newspaper, as well, have taken these meetings to report, so that people at large recognize the leaders' support for me. All of that would add up to helping implement my activities.

⑤ 理解する

外国との交渉では当然その立場は異なる。双方が理解しあうことは難しい。理解しようと努力することが重要である。中国ではホテルや大型商店などには保安検査装置が設置されている。係員は「警察POLICE」と表示された防弾チョッキを着用しているが、その人たちは「警官」ではない。このように理解しがたいことはそのまま「理解」するようにしている。

理解するための重要手段が「同働・同食・同眠」であろうか。炎天下の大沙漠で、筆者は彼らと一緒に発掘。誰よりも早く起床し火をおこし、コックが朝食の準備にかかれるようにした。街では同じ部屋で沙漠では同じテントで寝た。会食は経費もかかるしある意味では疲れる活動であるが、積極的に機会を持った。

同働・同食時には笑いを提供した。なにかとプレッシャーの多い中、硬い話は喜ばれない。土産にも気を配った。相手が喜び安くて軽いものを選んだ。例えば、新疆政府主催の筆者訪問30周年記念活動時の感謝宴では「大愛無疆」とサインした北斎の「赤富士」扇子150本。そして日本側諸氏による「大漁節」踊り。新疆大学主催の奨学金30周年記念活動時は自作漢詩。佛教大学宗教文化ミュージアムで開催したシンポジウムの感謝宴ワインは「NIYA」、日中共同隊がニャ遺跡で「五星出東方利中国」を発掘しニャが有名となり、ワインの名前にまでなったものである。

⑤ 理解

在与外国交涉时，立场不同是正常的，双方相互理解很困难。重要的是努力去理解。中国酒店和大型商业设施的安检设备完善，检查人员穿着有"警察POLICE"字样的防弹坎肩，但他们并不是"警察"。对于这样难以理解的事情，我也原样接受并"理解"。

理解的重要手段就是"同勤、同食、同眠"吧。炎炎烈日下的大沙漠中，笔者和大家一起发掘作业。第一个起床生火，方便厨师准备早饭。城镇同屋、沙漠同帐篷睡觉。尽管聚餐既要花钱又要劳神，但我还是积极地创造机会聚餐。

在同勤和同食的时候讲一些笑话，工作压力很大，沉重的话题不受欢迎。在特产方面也很用心，选择对方喜欢，但是又不贵不重的东西。例如：在答谢新疆政府为我举办来疆30周年活动的宴会上，笔者选择了150把有"大爱无疆"签名北斋的"红富士"扇子。同时，日方人员献上"大渔节"舞蹈。在新疆大学主办的奖学金30周年纪念活动时，笔者献上自创汉诗。在佛教大学佛教博物馆召开研讨会的答谢宴上选择"尼雅"干红，中日联合考察队在尼雅遗址发现了"五星出东方利中国"，尼雅由此扬名，甚至成为了葡萄酒的品牌名。

⑤ Mutual Understanding

Negotiations with foreign countries should involve conflicting standpoints. Whereas it is hard to win mutual understanding, an effort to win understanding counts for a lot. They install security inspection devices at hotels and major shopping malls in China. Although those working there wear a bullet-proof jacket indicated as "Police," they are not actual police. I make it a point to try to

understand this kind of incomprehensible thing as it is.

The significant means for understanding might be working, eating, and sleeping together. Under the blazing sun, I excavated with them. I tried to get up earlier than anyone else to fire, so that a cook could start preparing for breakfast much easier. I have always stayed with them in the same class of room in a town, and the same kind of tent out in the desert. Though having dinner together costs a lot and is a tiresome activity in a sense, I have tried to generate this opportunity.

I have provided smile at the time of working and eating together. Serious talks are not welcome in a place under a lot of pressure. I have paid meticulous care to a present, whereby selecting an inexpensive, easy-to-carry one which pleases people. For example, 150 Japanese folding fans with image of Hokusai's Red Fuji and my handwriting "No Boundaries for Love of Humanity" and Japanese participants' dancing with a folk song of Great Catch of Fish at the thank-you party during the activities of the 30th anniversary of my visit sponsored by the Xinjiang Government, my own Chinese poetry at the time of the 30th anniversary of my scholarship awards sponsored by Xinjiang University, "NIYA" wine at the thank-you party of the symposium held in the Bukkyo University Museum of Religious Culture, because Niya became famous as the Japan-China team had excavated the silk brocade "Five stars appearing in the east bring good fortune to China" in the Niya ruins. Ultimately, it has become a wine's brand name.

⑥ 計画する

PLAN・DO・CHECKは基本中の基本。長期・中期・短期計画を作成し臨んだ。とは言っても突然変更時には「柔らかい頭で」で応じた。すべての活動で契約を交わした。合意を明確にするとともに後日の対立にそなえるためでもある。

研究者やメディアなどが許可も得ず、調査研究や撮影している例を度々見聞きする。あるいは楼蘭やニヤ・ダンダンウイリクなどへ無許可侵入する研究者や観光客もいる。

230頁に記した違法測量で拘束された国立大学・国立研究所の教授らは「相手側中国人が許可を取っていると思っていた」との釈明が報道されている。しかし結果的に当人のみならず所属機関そして日本の評判を落とすことになる。また研究成果や撮影資料を持ち出すだけの一方的行為では、20世紀初頭の文化財持ち出しと大差ない。

国際活動では契約を交わし、先方機関の許可を取得し、その確認が必須条件である。相手方研究者が許可証を取得したならば確認しコピーを保存すべきである。日中双方はそれぞれの主権・法規・文化を相互尊重した。前述のように全ての段階で文書による正式許可を取得し覚書や協議書を交わし実施してきた。中でも「中華人民共和国考古渉外工作管理弁法」は度々熟読し遵守した。調印の写真も極力残した。国家文物局の発掘許可書を取得したのは外国人では稀といわれている。

⑥ 计划

计划・实施・确认（PLAN・DO・CHECK）是基本中基本。作出长期、中期、短期计划临战。但是在遇到突发情况时，需要用"柔性思维"来应对。所有活动都签约，这既是为明确双方意图也是为应对日后可能产生的分歧。

学者和媒体等不经允许，擅自进行调查研究和拍照的事情屡见不鲜，还有的学者和游客未经许可闯入楼兰、尼雅、丹丹乌里克遗址等。

关于230页上介绍的因非法测量被拘捕的国立大学、国立研究所的教授们，有报道说他们为自己辩解"我以为合作方的中国人已经取得了许可"。结果是不仅他们本人、包括他们的所在单位、甚至日本国都声誉下滑。另外。带走研究成果和影像资料的单方行为与20世纪初期的文物攫取并无大异。

国际活动中，签署协议、取得对方机构的认可，这是必备条件。如果对方学者取得了许可证，一定要确认并保留复印件。中日双方要互相尊重对方的主权、法规和文化。如上所述，笔者在各个阶段都取得了文件形式的正式许可，签署意向书或协议书后再实施。其中，笔者熟读"中华人民共和国考古渉外工作管理办法"并严格遵守执行。签字时的照片都尽量保留。取得国家文物局发掘许可书的外国人实属罕见。

⑥ Planning

I would say that plan-do-check-action is a basic common principle. I have always prepared plans in short, medium, and long terms when initiating a project. Actually, however, I have flexibly handled things in time of sudden change. I have concluded a contract for any project I have dealt with in order to clarify the agreements and address a conflict in the future.

I've seen and heard lots about the cases where scholars and the media conducted investigations, research, and shooting without authorization. Or I was told that researchers and visitors had intruded in the area of Loulan, Niya, and Dandanoilik without approval.

As I referred to this on page 230, those professors at national universities or national institutions tried to allege, saying that they thought that their Chinese counterpart had acquired the authorization. Eventually, however, those people, their related institutions, and ultimately Japan were discredited. Unilateral action to bring out research achievements and photographed materials does not differ too much from that of having exported cultural assets at the beginning of the 20th century.

In the international activities, it is a prerequisite condition to sign a contract to gain permission and verify that permission. If your counterpart says that they have acquired permission, you have to photocopy it to preserve. Both the Japanese team and the Chinese team would mutually pay due respect to the other party's sovereignty, regulations, and culture. As mentioned earlier, we have received a written official authorization in each and every phase to implement our activities through a memorandum of agreement or a memorandum of understanding. Among other things, I have frequently read and thoroughly observed "The guidelines for management of archaeological negotiation activities of the people's republic of China." I have saved the photos at the signing of a contract as much as possible. I hear that it is quite a rare thing for a foreigner to acquire the excavating permission from SACH Chinese.

⑦ 組織する

ニヤ遺跡・ダンダンウイリク遺跡の大規模調査、同壁画保護、その重要性にふさわしい高レベルの研究者・撮影技師・測量技師・保護技術者・模写専門家を前述したように組織した。諸氏とも超多忙にも関わらず遠く離れた新疆での長期間活動に参加いただいた。さらには大部の報告書作成に膨大な時間を費やしていただいた。各位のご尽力に心からの感謝を改めて表したい。組織したと記したがスムーズに出来たわけではない。調査分野が多領域にわたるため一大学だけでは対応できず、140～142・219頁記載のように多くの大学など研究機関の方々にお願いした。諸氏とも各研究機関の所属、そ

の許可が必要である。所属が異なる故の各種調整も並大抵ではない。

　組織作りに欠かせないのが資金調達である。大規模活動は大金を必要とする。例えば約60人が街から遠く離れた沙漠奥深くへ入り3週間にわたって調査。日本隊約20人の国内交通費・国際航空運賃にはじまり中国隊を含めての新疆内航空運賃・運転手こみ沙漠車レンタル料・ラクダ隊レンタル料・食糧代（運び込む水は約6トン）・調査器材費・諸手当……さらには遺跡保護協力費・報告書数巻刊行・国際シンポジウム度々開催・文物展開催……それらの打合せが電話一本で出来るわけでなく、度々の訪問も必要である。そして複数の人材育成事業・多数の相互理解促進事業と多額にのぼる。ありがたいことに一部は文科省助成や佛教大学補助・畏友数人からの寄付もいただいたが、殆どは筆者負担。給与の大半や配当金・退職金をつぎ込んだが、賄いきれず銀行から借入れるなどした。後半からは株式などを売却してやりくりしている。

　個人での国際協力が普及しない最大の要因はこの資金手当てであろう。筆者も困り果て賞金目当てにいくつかの文化財保護や国際協力の賞に応募したが、選出されなかった。有力推薦者があればと言われた。既得権社会の「仕組み」であろうが残念なことである。

　公開も資金調達とともに欠かせない組織作りの一部である。その成果は極力早く広く公開する必要がある。報告書・シンポジウム・写真集・文物展・プレスリリースなどさまざまな手法が考えられる。インターネット時代となりウエブ発信も重要である。従来、ウエブは印刷物より軽視される傾向にあったが瞬時化と国際化に対応できる利点から逆転しつつあり、筆者も関係者の協力をえて「国献男子ほんわか日記」や「一帯一路実践談」（中国語）を発信している。英語でも発信したいと考えている。

⑦ **组织**

　前面笔者已经提到过，为进行尼雅遗址、丹丹乌里克遗址的大规模考察和壁画保护，组织了与其重要性相匹配的高水准的学者、摄影技师、测量技师、保护技术人员、临摹专家参加。各位在百忙中，专程远道来到新疆长时间参加活动，而且，为编辑大块头的报告书花费了很多时间。再次向各位的尽心尽力表示衷心感谢。说是组织，也并不是顺利达成的。调查领域众多，一所大学难以应对，如，140～142・219所记，请多所大学等研究机构参与。各位分属不同的研究机构，分别需要获得许可，所属机构不同，各种协调也不是一般的难。

　创立组织不可或缺的是筹备资金，大规模的活动就需要大量的资金。例如：60人要远离城镇、深入大漠深处，长达3周开展调查。首先是日本队约20人的国内交通和国际机票，再加上包括中国

1996年度ニヤ機構決算
1996年尼雅机构结算
FY 1996 Niya Organization financial settlement

活動のすべての段階は公開されなければならない。中でも

ニヤ調査プレスリリース
尼雅考察的媒体发表
Niya research press release

队在内的新疆境内机票、带司机沙漠车的租赁费、骆驼租借费、食物（要带6吨水）、调查器材费、各种津贴…、还有遗址保护协力费、出版数卷报告书、多次举办国际研讨会、召开文物展……，关于这些事情的协商，不是打个电话就能解决的，必须要多次到访。还有多个人才培养事业、众多促进相互理解的项目，数额巨大。笔者负担了大部分费用，还幸运地得到了文科省助成金、佛教大学辅助金

VII　国際協力の意義　253

以及数位友人的捐款，笔者投入了大部分工资以及股权分配和退休金，因为还是不够，找银行借款解决。到了后期，靠变卖公司股票支撑。

　　个人国际合作难以普及的最大原因就是资金问题吧。笔者也因为难以维继，申请了多个有奖金的文物保护或国际合作的奖项，全部落选。被告知"有实力人物的推荐的话…"，这也是既有权社会的"体制"吧，令人遗憾。

　　公开也与筹集资金一样是创建组织不可缺少的一部分。必须要对活动的各个阶段加以公示，其中，必须要将成果尽早地广泛公开。有报告书、研讨会、图片展、文物展、媒体宣传等各种方法。

　　互联网时代，网路发声也很重要。以往，网络不如印刷品受重视，但是由于它能对应瞬间化和国际化，正在出现逆转，笔者也在相关人员的协助下，正在连载"国献男子暖心日记"和"一带一路实践谈"（中文版），笔者还考虑用英文发声。

⑦ Organizing

As referred to above, I have organized the right specialists, such as researchers, photographic engineers, survey engineers, conservation engineers, and reproduction mavens whose technical level is high enough for the importance to conduct such a large scale research of the Niya ruins and the Dandanoilik ruins and preservation of the murals in those ruins. Despite the context that every one of them was extremely busy, they kindly participated in this project in Xinjiang far away from home. On top of that, they have spent tremendous amounts of time to prepare a large volume of reports. Here again, I would like to express my hearty appreciation for their great efforts. Whereas I mentioned here that I have organized, it has not gone off smoothly. As researching areas extended over many fields that we could not handle them with only one university and we asked people at a number of universities and research institutions to participate as mentioned on pages 140–142 and 219. They belonged to each one of the research institutions, which means they had to gain the permission from their institutions. The fact that they were a member of various institutions demands a huge amount of energy for arrangement.

Capital procurement is indispensable for organizing any sort of project. A large-scale research demands a lot of money. For example, given that about 60 people research at a site deep inside a desert far away from a town for three weeks, it will require the following expenditures: domestic and overseas transportation costs of about 20 Japanese, flight costs within the Xinjiang Region, Chinese members included, rental fee for desert vehicles with drivers, rental fee for camels with camel masters, the costs of meals including six-ton water to be carried, the costs of researching devices and various allowances, as well as financial assistance to conserve ruins, the publication costs of several volumes of reports, the expenditures to hold several international symposium and cultural assets' exhibitions. All of which cannot be managed with just one phone call, so frequent visits become necessary. Apart from these expenditures, multiple HR projects and many campaigns to promote mutual understanding amount to the huge costs. Fortunately, a part of the costs is subsidized by the Education Ministry and Bukkyo University, and my respectful friends' contributions. Yet, almost all of the expenditures owe to me. I have devoted most of my salary, dividends, and retirement pay. As I could not cover them all, I borrowed from a bank. In the latter half of these undertakings, I have tried to juggle them by selling my share of stock.

This capital procurement might be the biggest factor why international cooperation on an individual basis cannot become widely prevalent. I have once desperately applied for the awards of cultural assets' preservation and international cooperation for the sake of award money, but in vain. I was told that you should have got someone very important to recommend you. It might come from the society based on vested interests, I am very sorry about this.

Along with capital procurement, disclosure is a critical factor in creating an organization. Every single phase of project should be disclosed in public. Among anything, achievements should be released as soon as possible. You can point out a broad range of ways, such as a report, symposium, a photo collection, a cultural assets' exhibition, and a press release. In the age of the Internet, a website release is also quite significant. There has been a tendency to see the website less important than printed matters, but the position has gradually developed the other way around due to its advantage in addressing instantaneously and globally. With the assistance of those concerned, I have been publishing my articles online: The Mellow Diary of an International Dedicator and One Belt, One Road in Action (Chinese). I am planning to disseminate messages in English, as well.

⑧ 我慢する

外国は異国である。立場が異なるのは当然のこと。一例をあげよう。先に紹介した文化・文化財分野の人材を育成する一環としての「小島新疆文化文物優秀賞」は2013年が契約期限であった。その前年に延長を提案した。その後に尖閣諸島が国有化され、日中関係はいっきに冷え込んだ。中国100以上の都市で激しい反日デモが繰り広げられた。筆者が展開している協力事業にも各種影響が出た。本賞延長も同意はえられず、やむなく第15回で終了した。事態が好転すればまた復活の機会も来るだろうと我慢した。2016年に新疆側から延長提案があり、筆者はもとより異存なく同意、9月訪問した際、延長・増額協議書に調印した。

国際協力は外国が主舞台であるからには、先方の意向を重視する必要がある。日本流だけでは進まない。今日にも回答があってしかるべき事柄も数日あるいは数週間を要する。我慢に我慢を重ねたうえで催促するようにした。

我慢は沙漠での大規模調査での必須能力でもある。無人地帯であり、食糧や調査機材などを沙漠車やラクダで運び込まねばならない。天候上調査時期が限られ、10～11月の一ヵ月ほどしか適しておらず、長年を必要とした。生活面でいえば、214頁記載のように厳しい条件であり、強い使命感・強靭な精神力・体力と協調力がないと耐えられない。

⑧ 忍耐

外国即异国，立场自然有所不同。例如：前面介绍过的，为培养文化、文物领域的人才而设立的"小岛新疆文化文物优秀奖"的期限本来是到2013年，到期前一年，笔者提议延长。随后出现钓鱼岛国有化事件，中日关系陷入低潮。中国有100多个城市发生激烈的反日游行。笔者开展的合作事业也受到了各种影响。该奖项的延长未获得同意，15期后只好终止了。笔者相信事态好转后会有机会重新开始的，就耐心等待。2016年新疆方面提出了延长方案，笔者欣然同意，9月访问新疆时，签署了延长、增额协议书。

国际合作的主场是在外国，因此需要重视对方的意向。完全按照日本方式是行不通的。需要当天回复并实施的事项有事也需要几天甚至几周的时间。在忍耐又忍耐下不断催促。

忍耐也是在沙漠实施大规模调查的必备能力。地处无人地带，粮食及调查机器械都必须用沙漠车和骆驼运进去。调查时间受气候条件限制，每年只能在10月至11月的1个月内展开，所以需要持续多年。生活方面也如214页所写的一样，十分艰苦，如果没有强烈的使命感、顽强的意志力、体力和协调力是无法忍受的。

⑧ Being patient

Overseas nations are all alien. Naturally, their standpoints are different from each other. Let me show you one instance, the expiring year of the Kojima awards for outstanding performances among Xinjiang cultures and relics which have been initiated with the theme of nurturing HR in the field of culture and cultural assets as I mentioned earlier was 2013. In the year before that, I put forth a proposal for its extension. After that, the Senkaku Islands was nationalized. The Japan-China relations were suddenly strained. The anti-Japan violent demonstrations were carried out in more than 100 places across China. The cooperative projects I had undertaken were given impact in one way and another. Since the extension of the awards was not approved, I could not help giving up at the 15th awards. I had tried to be patient, thinking that the chance of resumption would emerge if things get better. In 2016, the Xinjiang side offered the proposal of extension. I agreed with all of my heart, indeed. I signed the memorandum of understanding to extend and increase the award value in September upon my visit there.

We should put a high priority on the intention of the counterpart because the main stage is situated overseas when it comes to international cooperation. Nothing proceeds only in a Japanese style. The response that should have been received today takes several days, or sometime a few weeks. I have made a point of restraining myself time and again and then soliciting cooperation.

Patience is a vital ability for a large-scale research in a desert. It is an unpopulated region. You have to carry in food stuff and researching devices by desert vehicle and camel. The pertinent period for research is limited in terms of weather like only one month from October through November, which has required our research to take longer years. The daily life there was extremely punitive as described on page 214. You would not be able to persevere without a strong sense of mission, outstanding mental and physical strength, and cooperativeness.

⑨ 継続する

筆者がシルクロード新疆で国際貢献を開始して早くも36年、よくぞもったものと振り返っている。中国が独特な国であることは度々報じられている。先方からすれば日本も独特な国である。投げ出したくなる事も多々あった。その度ごとに「大愛無疆」精神で継続した。『新疆世界文化遺産図鑑』日本語版の序で段躍中氏は「毛沢東主席は次のように述べた。一人の人間が一回良いことをすることは難しくない。難しいのは一生続けることだ」と記しているが、まさにそうであろう。

活動は表面的・一時的・資金的な付き合いではなく、人と人との付き合いを重視し、至誠・感謝・縁・義理・人情といった琴線にふれる交流を続けてきた。このような実践が実績を生み出し、継続が信頼へとつながった。口や頭だけでなく、心の交流こそ重要である。

継続のため注意してきたことのひとつに特殊な関係にならないことがある。ともすれば複雑で面倒な国際協力、社会通念を超えた土産などを提供したりすればスムースに進行することもある。しかしそれは一時的な関係にすぎない。筆者が新疆で活動したこの36年間にトップの中国共産党新疆ウイグル自治区委員会書記は王恩茂・宋漢良・王楽泉・張春賢・陳全国へ五代、新疆政府主席も鉄木尔・達瓦買提・阿不来提・阿不都熱西提・司馬義・鉄力瓦尔地・努尔・白克力・雪克来提・扎克尔へ五代の代替わりがあった。外事弁公室や文化庁・文物局・档案局・文物考古研究所・新疆大学・ウルムチ市政府なども同様である。このように人が交代しても友情に近いかたちで国際協力を継続できたのは、決してその場限りの「裏交渉」をしなかったからであり、「特殊な関係」にならなかったからである。もしそうなっていたら人事異動後その機関との関係は断絶していたことであろう。

VII 国際協力の意義　255

朝日新聞 2008.5.9

タクラマカン遺跡　日中共同調査

息の長い交流で信頼築く

単眼複眼

中国・新疆ウイグル自治区で、仏教大学の「ニヤ遺跡学術研究機構」などが進める発掘調査の報告書が出た。タクラマカン砂漠の南部に埋もれた二つの遺跡報告書から

古代都市から出た仏教関連の壁画や装身具、住居、工房、墓地跡などがわかった古代仏教寺院の遺構が明らかった古代仏教寺院の遺構が明らかにされた。ガラス工房跡をはじめ、遠く地中海・イランなどから運ばれたらしいサンゴ、貝、トルコ石など広域交易の遺物も紹介されている。

『ニヤ遺跡学術調査報告書第3巻』は96、99年に続く3冊目。紀元前1世紀～紀元5世紀に栄えた都市国家「精絶国」だったニヤ遺跡の調査は、故田辺昭三氏らが参加した88年から始まった。これまでに約250カ所の遺構が確認された。今回は、新

中国社会科学院考古研究所新疆考古隊が調査、同自治区の大規模な仏教遺跡の中の七世紀の壁画の図版もある。

両遺跡の調査は、同自治区の西、約1500㎞で2年間かけて調査。尼雅の遺物も紹介されている。

1896年にスウェーデンの地理学者ヘディンが紹介して有名になった5～8世紀を中心とする遺跡群。高さ3㍍ある粘土づくりの壁が残る円形城壁遺構（直径約100㍍）や寺

キジル千仏洞の修復保存などに佛教大の小島康誉氏が寄金や技術面で貢献した縁で始まった。『丹丹烏里克』だ中国西端の奥地で、息の長い交流で中国側と信頼関係を築いてきた意義を、2冊の報告書は語っている。

「西域のモナリザ」とも呼ばれる中国・丹丹烏里克（ダンダンウイリク）遺跡出土の壁画＝同遺跡報告書から

院、住居、果樹園跡など計70カ所へ。

問い合わせは佛教大宗教文化ミュージアム（電話075・8873・3115）へ。

（天野幸弘）

多くの仏教壁画の中には、砂に埋もれて極彩色をとどめたものもある。ヒンドゥー教系の神々に囲まれた仏や、笑みをたたえた如来の図などが注目された。所の分布が分かった。

継続の重要性を報じる朝日新聞
报道了持续之重要性的朝日新闻
Asahi Shimbun reporting the importance of continuity

⑨ 持续

笔者在丝绸之路-新疆开始国际贡献转瞬已经36年了，回头想想"真坚持下来了！"。经常有报道说中国是独特的国家。对方看日本也是一个独特的国家。也曾多次想过要放弃，但是每次都在"大爱无疆"精神指引下坚持了下来。段跃中先生在《新疆世界文化遗产图典》日语版序言中写到"毛主席说过，一个人做一件好事并不难，难的是一辈子做好事"，的确如此。

活动不流于表面的、一时的、金钱的交往，要重视人与人的交往、坚持推进拨动至诚、感谢、缘分、义理、人情之琴弦的交流。这些实践产生成果、持续与信赖相连，不只是口与脑，心灵的交流才是最重要的。

为了持续下来，笔者一直注意一点，就是不要陷入特殊的关系。有的时候，赠送超越社会理念的土特产会令复杂而繁琐的国际合作顺利进行。但那只能造就短时间关系。笔者在新疆活动的36年间，最高领导人中国共产党新疆维吾尔自治区委员会书记有过五届更换，

先后是王恩茂、宋汉良、王乐泉、张春贤、陈全国；新疆政府主席也先后为铁木尔·达瓦买提、阿不来提·阿不都热西提、司马义·铁力瓦尔地、努尔·白克力、雪克来提·扎克尔。外事办公室、文化厅、文物局、档案局、文物考古研究所、新疆大学、乌鲁木齐市也是一样。即使出现这样的人事变动，依然可以以近乎于友情的形式继续国际合作，就是因为没有进行特定的"背后交涉"、没有形成"特殊的关系"。否则，出现人事变动后，与那家单位的关系也就断了吧。

⑨ Continuing Efforts

36 years have already passed since I started international contributions in Xinjiang on the Silk Road. Looking back all these years, wonders will never cease. It has been reported in Japan more often than not that China is a peculiar country, and vice versa. There have been many cases that I wish to give up. But I have continued my efforts on each occasion based on the principle of "No Boundaries for Love of Humanity." In the preface of *The Pictorial Book of the World Heritage in Xinjiang* (Japanese version), Mr. Duan Yuezhong says, "Chairman Mao Zedong once told that what's easy for humans to do one good thing, but what's not easy is to continue to do it for life." That should definitely make sense.

In my activities, I have placed a premium on people-to-people exchange, avoiding interacting superficially, temporarily, and financially, and have continued socializing with people to get to their heart with such manners as faithfulness, appreciation, bond, obligation, and humanity. To continue these kinds of actual practices have produced remarkable results, which added up to reliability in the end. Not just talks and intelligence, but hearty communion is exactly what it takes.

One thing I have kept in mind is not to have a special relationship. People are given to offering a socially unacceptable gift in the context of complicated, troublesome international cooperation, which sometimes happen to work well. But that is only a temporary relationship. During my 33-year undertakings in Xinjiang, the five generations of Secretary of the Xinjiang Committee of the CCP, or the uppermost echelon, include Wang Enmao, Song Hanliang, Wang Lequan, Zhang Chunxian, and Chen Quanguo. And the five generations of the Xinjiang Governor are Tiemuer Dawamaiti, Abulaiti Abudurexiti, Simayi Tieliwaerdi, Nuer Baikeli, and Shohrat Zakir. The same goes with the Foreign Affairs Office, the Cultural Agency, the Xinjiang Cultural Assets Bureau, the Archaeological Institute, the Archives Center, Xinjiang University, the Government of Urumqi city, etc. The reason that I have been able to keep a close contact with each person is that I have never negotiated ad hoc behind the curtain or fallen into a special relationship with anyone. Otherwise, my relationships with those organizations would have been severed after personnel reshuffles.

⑩ 感謝する

国際協力も極言すれば「人間力」が決め手であろう。相手との縁をありがたく頂き、相手への感謝を感じ、義理と人情で接し、口や頭だけでなく心で行動するように努めた。科学技術がいかに発展しようと人と人の信頼こそが国際協力の決め手である。

外国との事業は思いようにいかないことも多い。利益がともなう経済活動であれば双方が利益という明確な目標で協調しやすいが、金銭的利益がともなわない文化活動では継続は難しい。一過性の貢献は多数見てきているが、続かないのは遭遇する各種困難を乗り越えられないからである。

引退した人たちとも交流を続けている。数年前の新疆政府主催の筆者訪問30周年記念活動時の感謝宴には退職者多数も招いた。新疆生産建設兵団司令・新疆政府副主席・党宣伝部長などである。在職中はその重責により影響力をふるった方々も退職し10年20年経ち、誰も訪ねて来なくなっている。「散歩して、テレビ見て、小説読んでいるだけだ。よく招いてくれた」と。ハグし友情に感謝した。先日も20年数前に新疆文化庁文物処長を定年退官した83歳の老人を訪ね昔話をひととき楽しんだ。キジル千仏洞への個人寄付時の相手方である。

⑩ 感谢

国际合作说到底是"人格魅力"决定一切。我力求：感恩与对方的缘分，心怀对对方的感谢，以义理和人情交往，不只停留在嘴和脑而是用心行动。无论科学技术如何先进，人与人的信赖关系才是国际合作的决定因素。

与外国的事业经常无法如愿推进。如果是伴随利益的经济活动，双方以明确的利益为目标，很好协调，但是没有金钱利益的文化活动就很难持续。一时性的贡献很常见，之所以不能持续就是因为无法克服遭遇的各种困难。

与卸任后的人们也保持联系。在几年前感谢新疆政府为笔者举办访问新疆30周年纪念活动的答谢宴上，笔者邀请了很多退休人员。原新疆生产建设兵团司令、原新疆政府副主席、原党委宣传部长等。即使在职期间职务很高、影响力很大的领导退休10年、20年以后就没有人来看望了。"每天就是散散步、看看电视、读读小说，感谢您叫我们来"，拥抱、感谢友谊。前几天，笔者还去拜访了20多年前任新疆文化厅文物处长、现在已经退休的83岁老人，我们共叙旧情、度过了愉快的时光。他是我个人捐赠克孜尔千佛洞时的接待方。

⑩ Appreciating

Extremely speaking, a decisive factor of international cooperation may be human qualities. I have tried to appreciate the connection with the other person, feel gratitude for others, and behave not verbally or wisely, but sincerely. No matter how science technology would progress, trust between people is the last resort to nurture international cooperation.

Sometimes, a project overseas does not work well as you might expect. If it is a business project seeking profit, cooperation relationship is easy to develop because of sharing explicit goal. Continuation is quite hard to attain when it comes to a cultural activity entailing no monetary profit. Whereas I have seen many success stories about temporary contributions, the reason that we have been unable to continue is the failure to have overcome various hardships we have encountered.

I have kept in touch with those who retired. A number of retirees were invited to the thank you party at the time of the 30th anniversary of my visit sponsored by the Xinjiang Government several years ago. Those retirees include the Commander of the Xinjiang Production and Construction Corps, the Vice-Governor of the Xinjiang Government, the Chief of the CCP Public Relations, and others. Those who once were pretty influential and powerful coming from their heavy responsibilities are now visited by no one in 10 to 20 years. They said, "I walk, watch TV, and read novels, that's all. I really appreciate for this invitation." We hugged each other and I thanked for their friendships. The other day, I visited an 83-year-old man who took mandatory retirement as the Director of the Xinjiang Cultural Agency 20 or more years ago and talked about the good old days. He was my counterpart when I personally made a contribution to the Kizil grottoes.

VIII 36年略年譜

（諸氏ご協力による 新疆36年略年譜）

1982
- 新疆初訪問、トルファン参観、人々の温かい心と豊富な文化遺産に魅せられる
- ウルムチ仏教協会へ寄付、以後各種寄付実施

1986
- キジル千仏洞初参観、修復保存資金個人寄付
- 新疆大学に小島奨学金設立

1987
- 日中友好キジル千仏洞修復保存協力会を設立

1988
- 日中友好キジル千仏洞修復保存協力会第一次贈呈
- 各種代表団派遣開始
- 新疆文化庁と調査覚書、第一次日中共同ニヤ遺跡学術調査実施

1989
- 日中友好キジル千仏洞修復保存協力会第二次贈呈
- 『鉄木尔·達瓦買提詩集』（日本語版）出版　以降各種出版・講演
- 日中両国で新疆および新疆文化財保護重要性の広報開始

1990
- 日中双方の各種仲介開始

1992
- 文部省科研費助成開始、国家文物局正式許可、第四次日中共同ニヤ遺跡学術調査実施

1993
- 中国文物保護基金会に奨学金設立
- 新疆の各方面訪日代表団招聘開始

1994
- 国家文物局発掘許可をえて第六次日中共同ニヤ遺跡学術調査実施
- 佛教大学にニヤ遺跡学術研究機構設立

1995
- 新疆ウイグル自治区成立40周年祝賀寄付
- 第七次日中共同ニヤ遺跡学術調査で王墓発掘、1995年中国十大考古新発見に

1996
- 『王恩茂日記』（日本語版）出版
- 『日中共同ニヤ遺跡学術調査報告書』（第一巻・日中両文）出版
- 楼蘭を参観し過去の探検隊などのゴミ回収

1997
- 第九次日中共同ニヤ遺跡学術調査実施、現地調査終了
- 日中調査隊、佛教大学でニヤ遺跡調査国際シンポジウムと文物展開催

1998
- 希望小学校建設開始

1999
- 小島新疆文化・文物事業優秀賞設立
- シルクロード児童就学育英金設立
- 『日中共同ニヤ遺跡学術調査報告書』（第二巻・日中両文）出版

2000
- 中国歴史文化遺産保護網設立
- 日中調査隊、ウルムチでニヤ調査国際シンポジウム開催

2001
- 新疆ウイグル自治区人民政府「小島康誉氏新疆来訪20周年記念大会」開催
- 『近代外国探検家新疆考古档案史料』共同出版

2002
- 第一次日中共同ダンダンウイリク遺跡学術調査、「西域のモナリザ」など壁画発見

2003
- 日中共同でダンダンウイリク壁画保護開始

2004
- 「新シルクロード展」交渉などで14回訪中、内11回が新疆

2005
- 新疆ウイグル自治区成立50周年祝賀切手セット贈呈
- NHK「新シルクロード」放送、NHKなど「新シルクロード展」開催

2006
- 第四次日中共同ダンダンウイリク遺跡学術調査実施、現地調査終了
- 『中瑞西北科学考察档案史料』共同出版

2007	• 『日中共同ニヤ遺跡学術調査報告書』（第三巻・日文）・『日中共同ダンダンウイリク遺跡学術調査報告書』（日文）出版
	• 『スタイン第四次新疆探検档案史料』共同出版
	• 平山郁夫ユネスコ親善大使宅を盛春寿文物局長と訪ね、世界遺産申請の示唆をえる
2008	• 改革開放以来の新疆の巨大変化を反映した『見証新疆変遷』（第一巻）出版
2009	• 『見証新疆変遷』（第二巻）出版、8都市で「新疆改革開放成就広報万里活動」実施
	• 日中調査隊、北京大学で「漢唐西域考古国際シンポジウム」開催
	• 日中調査隊、『丹丹烏里克遺跡－中日共同考察研究報告』（中文）出版
2010	• 『清代新疆建置档案史料』共同出版
2011	• 清華大学創立100周年記念「ガンダーラからニヤ」写真展共同開催
	• 新疆ウイグル自治区人民政府「小島康誉氏新疆来訪30周年記念活動」開催
2012	• 大英図書館国際フォーラムで「世界的文化遺産保護研究を使命として」発表
2013	• 『新疆での世界的文化遺産保護研究事業と国際協力の意義』出版
	• 佛教大学でシンポジウム「新疆の世界的文化遺産保護研究と国際協力の意義」開催
2014	• キジル千仏洞「世界文化遺産」登録　同時登録6遺跡を再訪し、祝意と感謝を表す
	• 北京大学カローシュティー研究会で発表、内外教授らとニヤ遺跡再訪
	• 新疆文物考古研究所『新疆文物・ニヤ文物特集号』刊行
2015	• 雪克来提・扎克尓新疆ウイグル自治区主席に自治区成立60周年祝賀5項目報告
	• 民生改善活動「訪恵聚」に呼応し、井戸掘削・学校修理・街路灯設置
	• 『新疆世界文化遺産図鑑』（中国語版）・「絵葉書セット」出版
2016	• フジテレビ系列「天山を往く－シルクロード物語」放映
	• 『新疆世界文化遺産図鑑』（日本語版）・『Kizil, Niya, and Dandanoilik』出版
2017	• NHK「シルクロード・壁画の道をゆく」放映
2018	• 天津テレビ「泊客中国」筆者特集3番組「大愛無疆」「五星出東方利中国」「西域蒙娜麗莎」放映
	• ニヤ調査30周年記念として、日本側本書出版と市民講座開催、中国側報告書出版と文物展開催
	• 本書校正完了後決定活動：第33回新疆大学奨学金・第20回児童育英金・第18回新疆文化文物優秀賞を授与（9月末）、クチャ希望小学校へ備品類寄贈（9月末）、『中国改革開放40周年記念－邁進新時代』出版し新疆各方面へ贈呈（中国語・10月末）

新疆政府主催「日本友人小島康誉氏新疆来訪30周年記念大会」
新疆政府挙办"日本友人小島康誉先生来新疆30周年紀念大会"
The Xinjiang government hosting the 30th anniversary of Mr. Kojima's visit to Xinjiang

  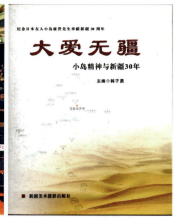

新疆訪問20周年大会を報じる新疆経済報、大会会場、訪問30周年記念誌『大愛無疆』
报道访问新疆20周年大会的新疆经济报，大会会场，访问新疆30周年纪念册《大爱无疆》
Xinjiang Economic Daily reporting the 20th anniversary of my visit to Xinjiang　Anniversary venue　*No Boundaries for Love of Humanity*, 30th anniversary issue of my visit

各位协助下的新疆36年简略年谱

1982	• 初次访问新疆，参观吐鲁番，被人们的温暖之心和丰富的文化遗产所吸引
	• 向乌鲁木齐佛教协会捐款，之后实施各种捐款
1986	• 初次参观克孜尔千佛洞，个人名义捐赠修复保存资金
	• 在新疆大学设立小岛奖学金
1987	• 成立日中友好克孜尔千佛洞修复保存协力会
1988	• 日中友好克孜尔千佛洞修复保存协力会第一次捐款
	• 开始派遣各类代表团
	• 与新疆文化厅签调查备忘录，第一次中日共同尼雅遗址学术调查
1989	• 日中友好克孜尔千佛洞修复保存协力会第二捐款
	• 出版《铁木尔·达瓦买提诗集》（日文版），之后各种出版、讲演
	• 在中日两国开始宣传新疆及保护新疆文化遗产的重要性
1990	• 开始日中双方各种斡旋
1992	• 文部省科研费助成开始，国家文物局正式许可，第四次中日共同尼雅遗址学术调查
1993	• 在中国文物保护基金会设立奖学金
	• 邀请新疆各方面代表团访日
1994	• 获得国家文物局发掘许可，实施第六次中日共同尼雅遗址学术调查
	• 在佛教大学成立尼雅遗址学术研究机构
1995	• 为祝贺新疆维吾尔自治区成立40周年捐款
	• 第七次中日共同尼雅遗址学术调查发掘王族墓地，入选1995年中国十大考古新发现
1996	• 出版《王恩茂日记》（日文版）
	• 出版《日中/中日共同尼雅遗址学术调查报告书（第一卷　日·中文）
	• 参观楼兰，捡拾以前探险队等丢弃的垃圾
1997	• 第九次中日共同尼雅遗址学术调查，实地考察结束
	• 中日考察队在佛教大学召开尼雅考察国际研讨会和文物展
1998	• 开始建设希望小学
1999	• 设立小岛新疆文化·文物事业优秀奖
	• 设立丝绸之路儿童就学育英金
	• 出版《日中/中日共同尼雅遗址学术调查报告书》（第二卷　日·中文）
2000	• 创办中国历史文化遗产保护网
	• 中日调查队在乌鲁木齐召开尼雅调查国际研讨会
2001	• 新疆政府召开"日本友人小岛康誉先生来新疆20周年纪念大会"

- 共同出版《近代外国探险家新疆考古档案史料》
2002　• 第一次中日丹丹乌里克遗址学术调查，发现"西域的蒙娜丽莎"等壁画
2003　• 开始中日共同保护丹丹乌里克遗址壁画
2004　• 为交涉"新丝绸之路展"，14次访问中国，其中11次是去新疆
2005　• 祝贺新疆维吾尔自治区成立50周年捐献套装纪念邮票
　　　• NHK播放"新丝绸之路"节目，NHK等主办"新丝绸之路展"
2006　• 第四次中日共同丹丹乌里克遗址学术调查，实地考察结束
　　　• 共同出版《中瑞西北科学考察档案史料》
2007　• 出版《日中/中日共同尼雅遗址学术调查报告书》（第三卷 日文）、《日中共同丹丹乌里克遗址学术调查报告书》（日文）
　　　• 共同出版《斯坦因第四次新疆探险档案史料》
　　　• 与文物局盛春寿局长拜访世界教科文组织亲善大使平山郁夫，获申遗提示
2008　• 出版反应改革开放以来新疆巨大变化的《见证新疆变迁》（第一卷）
2009　• 出版《见证新疆变迁》（第二卷），在8座城市举办"新疆改革开放成就宣传万里行活动"
　　　• 中日考察队在北京大学召开"汉唐西域考古国际研讨会"
　　　• 中日考察队出版《丹丹乌里克遗址－中日共同考察研究报告》（中文）
2010　• 共同出版《清代新疆建置档案史料》
2011　• 共同主办清华大学建校100周年纪念"从犍陀罗到尼雅"摄影展
　　　• 新疆政府举办"日本友人小岛康誉先生来新疆30周年纪念活动"
2012　• 在大英图书馆国际研讨会上发表题为"以保护研究世界性文化遗产为使命"的演讲
2013　• 出版《保护研究新疆世界性文化遗产与国际合作的意义》
　　　• 在佛教大学召开"保护研究新疆世界性文化遗产与国际合作的意义"研讨会
2014　• 克孜尔千佛洞成为"世界文化遗产"，再次访问同时申遗成功的6处遗址，表示祝贺和感谢
　　　• 在北京大学佉卢文研究会上发表，与海内外学者再访尼雅遗址
　　　• 新疆文物考古研究所《新疆文物 尼雅文物特刊》出版
2015　• 向新疆维吾尔自治区雪克来提·扎克尔主席祝贺自治区成立60周年并汇报5项工作
　　　• 为响应民生改善活动"访惠聚"号召，挖掘水井、修缮学校、安置路灯
　　　• 出版《新疆世界文化遗产图典》（中文版）、明信片
2016　• 富士电视台播出"穿越天山 丝绸之路物语"节目
　　　• 出版《新疆世界文化遗产图典》（日文版）、《Kizil, Niya, and Dandanoilik》
2017　• NHK播出"丝绸之路 探寻壁画之路"节目
2018　• 天津电视台"泊客中国"份播出本人的专题三集节目"大爱无疆""五星出东方利中国""西域蒙娜丽莎"
　　　• 为纪念尼雅考察30周年，出版本书及报告集、举办文物展和市民讲座
　　　• 在完成本书校对后决定开展以下活动：九月末举行第33次新疆大学奖学金、第20次儿童助学金、第18次新疆文化文物优秀奖的颁奖典礼和库车希望小学日常用品赠送仪式。10月末出版《纪念中国改革开放40周年 迈进新时代》图典并向新疆各界赠送

A chronological record of my 36 years in Xinjiang having been supported by various people

1982　• The first visit to Xinjiang; Sightseeing at Turpan; Attracted by warm-hearted people and abundant cultural assets
　　　• A contribution to the Urumqi Buddhist Association; Afterwards, making various contributions
1986　• The first visit at the Kizil grottoes; A personal contribution for restoration and conservation
　　　• Establishment of the Kojima Scholarship Awards at Xinjiang University
1987　• Establishment of the Japan-China Friendship Association to Restore and Conserve theKizil Grottoes
1988　• The first donation by the Japan-China Friendship Association to Restore and Conserve the Kizil Grottoes
　　　• Launching the dispatch of various delegates
　　　• The memorandum of agreement with the Xinjiang Cultural Agency; Conducting the first Japan-China joint Scholarly Research of the Niya ruins

1989	• The second donation by the Japan-China Friendship Association to Restore and Conserve the Kizil Grottoes

1989
- The second donation by the Japan-China Friendship Association to Restore and Conserve the Kizil Grottoes
- Publication of The Poetry Anthology of Tiemuer Dawamaiti (Japanese version); Afterwards, publication of various books along with lecturing
- Launching the public relations campaigns both in Japan and China to inform Xinjiang itself and the importance of preserving cultural assets in Xinjiang

1990
- Beginning to serve as an intermediary between Japan and China in various affairs

1992
- Beginning to receive the subsidy from the Education Ministry; The official authorization by SACH Chinese, Conducting the fourth Japan-China joint scholarly research of the Niya ruins

1993
- Establishment of the Chinese Cultural Relics Protection Foundation
- Beginning to invite various groups in Xinjiang to visit Japan

1994
- Conducting the sixth Japan-China joint scholarly research of the Niya ruins having been authorized to excavate by SACH Chinese
- Foundation of the Academic Research Organization for the Niya Ruins, Bukkyo University

1995
- Offering a contribution on the occasion of the 40th anniversary of the Xinjiang Uyghur Autonomous Region
- Discovery of the royal graveyard during the seventh Japan-China scholarly research of the Niya ruins which became one of the 10 greatest discoveries in China in 1995

1996
- Publication of The Diary of Wang Enmao (Japanese version)
- Publication of The Report of Japan-China Joint Scholarly Research of the Niya Ruins Vol. 1 (Japanese and Chinese versions)
- Picking up litter left by past explorers when visiting Loulan

1997
- Conducting the ninth Japan-China joint scholarly research of the Niya ruins which is the last research on site
- The Japan-China joint team holding the international symposium of the Niya ruins research and the exhibition of cultural assets at Bukkyo University

1998
- Initiating the construction of Kibou Primary School

1999
- Foundation of the Kojima awards for outstanding performances among Xinjiang cultures and relics
- Foundation of the Silk Road Scholarship for Grade-schoolers
- Publication of The Report of Japan-China Joint Scholarly Research of the Niya Ruins Vol. 2 (Japanese and Chinese versions)

2000
- Establishment of the website to preserve Chinese historical, cultural heritages
- The Japan-China joint team holding the International symposium of the Niya ruins research in Urumqi

2001
- The Xinjiang Government hosting the 20th anniversary of Mr. Kojima's visit to Xinjiang
- Joint publication of The Archives of Modern, Foreign Explorers in Xinjiang

2002
- The first Japan-China scholarly research of the Dandanoilik ruins in which the murals such as "The Mona Lisa in the Western Regions" was discovered

2003
- Initiating preservation of the murals through collaboration between Japan and China

2004
- Visiting China 14 times for the negotiations of The New Silk Road Exhibition and others, out of which 11 times leaving bound for Xinjiang

2005
- Donation of the commemorative stamps to celebrate the 50th anniversary of the Xinjiang Uyghur Autonomous Region
- NHK broadcasting The New Silk Road, The New Silk Road Exhibition being held at NHK and others

2006
- Conducting the fourth Japan-China joint scholarly research of the Dandanoilik ruins and having completed the research on site
- Joint publication of The Archives of Chinese-Swedish Scientific Studies on Northwest China

2007
- Publication of The Report of Japan-China Joint Scholarly Research of the Niya Ruins Vol. 3 (Japanese version) and The Report of Japan-China Joint Scholarly Research of the Dandanoilik Ruins (Japanese version)
- Joint publication of The Archives of the Stein's Fourth Expedition to Xinjiang
- Visiting UNESCO Goodwill Ambassador Ikuo Hirayama at his home with Cultural-Assets Bureau Director Sheng Chunshou to receive a meaningful suggestion about the World-Heritage application

2008	• Publication of Witnessing the Transition of Xinjiang Vol. 1, which reflects tremendous changes made in Xinjiang after the reform and the door-opening policies
2009	• Publication of Witnessing the Transition of Xinjiang Vol. 2; Conducting the campaign, "The long journey to celebrate the achievements of the reform and the door-opening initiatives in Xinjiang" in eight cities
	• Japan-China joint team holding the international symposium on the Western Regions in the ages of Han and Tang from the archaeological perspective
	• Japan-China joint team publishing The report on the China-Japan joint studies and research on the Dandanoilik ruins (Chinese)
2010	• Joint publication of The Archives of Xinjiang Province in the Qing Dynasty
2011	• Holding the photo exhibition under the title of From Gandhara to Niya jointly at Tsinghua University to celebrate the 100th anniversary of its foundation
	• The Xinjiang government hosting the 20th anniversary of Mr. Kojima's visit to Xinjiang
2012	• Making a presentation under the title of "The Significance to Conserve and Research World-class Cultural Heritages in Xinjiang" at the international forum of the British Library
2013	• Publication of The Projects to Preserve and Research World-class Cultural Heritages in Xinjiang and the Significance of International Cooperation
	• Holding the symposium at Bukkyo University: The Significance to Conserve and Research World-class Cultural Heritages and International Cooperation in Xinjiang
2014	• The Kizil grottoes being registered as the World Cultural Heritage; I revisited six ruins simultaneously registered to express my congratulations and appreciation
	• Making a presentation at the Kharosthi Study Association, Peking University; Revisiting the Niya ruins with professors from various countries
	• The Xinjiang Archaeological Institute's publication of a special issue of Xinjiang Cultural Relics featuring the Niya antiquities
2015	• Reporting five celebrating items to commemorate the 60th anniversary of the establishment of the Autonomous Region to Governor of the Xinjiang Uyghur Autonomous Region Shohrat Zakir
	• Digging wells, repairing schools, setting street lights to accommodate the initiative to enhance people's livelihood called Fanghuiju
	• Publication of The Pictorial Book of the World Heritage in Xinjiang (Chinese version) in set with postcards
2016	• The Fuji TV network broadcasting the program: Journey over Tianshan–The Silk Road Tale
	• Publication of The Pictorial Book of the World Heritage in Xinjiang (Japanese version) and Kizil, Niya, and Dandanoilik
2017	• NHK broadcasting the program, Journey over the Silk Road to go after Murals
2018	• Tianjin TV's program, China Right Here featuring me through a series of three parts titled: No Boundaries for Love of Humanity; Five Stars Appearing in the East Bring Good Fortune to China; and The Mona Lisa in the Western Regions
	• To commemorate the 30th anniversary of the Niya research, publishing this book and the report, holding cultural assets' exhibitions, and giving public lectures
	• The followings are activities which have been decided to initiate after proofreading this book: Awarding the 33rd scholarship for Xinjiang University, the 20th scholarship for grade-schoolers, and the 18th prize in outstanding performances for Xinjiang culture and relics (the end of September); provision of school supplies to Kuqa Hope Elementary School (the end of September); publication and donation of *The 40th Anniversary of the Chinese Reform and Door-Opening Policies — A New Era to Forge Ahead* to various groups in Xinjiang (the end of October/Chinese)

日中友好から日中理解へ 日中共同へ 新時代へ

本書は約840点の写真・資料が示す日中共同で実践してきたその軌跡

中日友好走向中日理解、中日共同、新时代　本书记录了中日共同的实践轨迹

From Japan-China friendship to Japan-China mutual understanding, and further to Japan-China collaboration in the future
This book following the track of Japan-China collaboration in action

提唱つづけている「日中友好から日中相互理解へ日中共同へ」を報じる人民日報と中日新聞

人民日报和中日新闻报道了我一直提倡的"从日中友好走向日中相互理解、日中共同"

People' Daily and *Chunichi Shimbun* reporting my long advocated theme: From Japan-China friendship to Japan-China mutual understanding, and further to Japan-China collaboration

（第3種郵便物認可）　2003.8.17　中日新聞

CULTURE

タクラマカンの古代都市　保護研究を使命として

ニヤ遺跡

着手14年、日中理解の礎に

小島　康誉

こじま・やすたか　一九四二年、名古屋市生まれ。佛教大学ニヤ遺跡学術研究機構代表、浄土宗僧侶、ツルカメコーポレーション名誉会長。同社社長時代から仏教を学んで得度。九六年に社長を退き、九八年には念仏行脚脚下日本縦断を成就した。一方でニヤ遺跡を中心とするシルクロードの遺跡研究・保存に執念を燃やしている。著書に『シルクロード・ニヤ遺跡の謎』『人生の道・経営の道』など。

日本をはるか離れた中国西北部タクラマカン沙漠に「ニヤ遺跡」と称される約二千年前の古代都市遺跡が残存している。西域三十六国のひとつ「精絶国」である。その規模は周辺を含めて東西約七㌔、南北約二十五㌔と名古屋市の縦三分の一に相当するほど巨大だ。

一九〇一年一月、のちにイギリスに帰化した探検家スタインがウイグル族青年の案内で発見した。スタインは四回にわたり調査し、約七百点のカローシュティー木簡を主とする大量の文物を収集し、当時としては卓越した研究を行った。その存在が明らかにされるや西域探検熱が高まり、大谷探検隊実施のひとつの契機ともなった。十八歳の若さで第二次大谷探検隊に参加した名古屋の僧侶橘瑞超師もニヤ遺跡の約三十㌔南の小オアシスを発掘したが、あまりの暑さのためニヤ遺跡への進入は断念したと当時のイギリスの新聞が報じている。

中国四大石窟のひとつである「キジル千仏洞」の修復保存のために日本で浄財を募り新疆ウイグル自治区政府へ寄贈した折に「ニヤは非常に重要な遺跡だが本格的調査が行われていない」と聞き、共同保護研究を提案した。西域一帯は過去に日本人を含む外国探検隊が文物を持ち出した経緯もあり、なかなか許可は下りなかったが、交渉を経て一九八八年より「日中共同ニヤ遺跡学術調査」を開始した。日本側は佛教大学ニヤ遺跡学術研究機構、中国側は新疆文物局・新疆文物考古研究所が中心となり、双方とも多くの研究機関の参加を得て実施してきた。九回の現地調査を行い現在も研究は続いている。既に十四年が経過し、日中間の文化財保護研究事業としては最大規模である。二〇世紀中国考古大発見「一〇〇」のひとつにも選ばれた。約二百五十カ所の遺構を発見し、正確な遺跡分布図を作成、住居址や墓地を発掘し、中国の国宝中の国宝六十四点のひとつに指定された文物をはじめ、国宝級文物多数をも検出するなどの大きな成果もあり、昨年末には関連調査としてダンダン・ウイリック遺跡に日本人として初到達し、国宝級壁画を発見、研究を開始している。仏教東漸解明に貴重な情報をもたらすものと期待されている。

タクラマカン沙漠は日本とほぼ同じ面積であるが、大沙漠での調査は困難を極める。例えば六十人の調査隊が三週間に必要とする水は顔を洗わず風呂もなく食器も洗わずといった耐乏生活でも六㌧が必要である。あるものは千㌔、あるものは数百㌔南の民豊から運び込む。日本各地や北京から参加する研究者たちの交通費も人数が多いため少額ではない。結果的に大金が必要となる。

ありがたいことに文部科学省や佛教大学からの補助金も頂いているが、不足する部分は提唱者であり推進者である私が負担せざるをえず、名古屋の高級住宅街から三重の妻の実家に居候させて頂いている始末である。

資金以上に大変なのは日中間の共同事業である点だ。すべての面で国家管理の厳しい中国であり、考え方も調査手法も異なる。その調整は簡単ではない。顔を合わせての交渉が重要であるので、新疆へは約九十回も訪問した。

そこまでして何故ニヤ遺跡保護研究に執念を燃やすのかと絶えず問われる。第一に世界的文化財を保護するためである。世界に例をみない最大規模の国家都市遺跡である。次には日中共同で行っているのでなく、日中共同を実践すべき時代と考えているからである。戦後六十年近くを経過した今、いつまでも日中友好と叫ぶ、多くの方が日中友好のレベルに留まっているのでなく、日中共同を成し遂げ、世界遺産への登録など次の世代へバトンタッチしたいと考えている。今後とも多くの方のご支援頂きながら微力を捧げたい。　合掌

砂漠での調査には今でもラクダは欠かせない。左から2人目が筆者

安田暎胤薬師寺長老「小島さんほど新疆を愛し、実際に貢献された人はいないじゃないかと思います。阿倍仲麻呂は長安で亡くなった。小島さんも新疆で亡くなったら本望でしょうね」、筆者「そうです」（天津TV「西域蒙娜麗莎」Web放映を撮影）
药师寺长老安田暎胤说"象小岛这样热爱新疆，并且作出实际贡献的恐怕别无他人，阿倍仲麻吕在长安去世，小岛希望能在新疆瞑目吧"，我回答说

"是的"（摄于天津电视台"西域蒙娜丽莎"网络播映）
Patriarch of Yakushiji Temple Eiin Yasuda said, "I have never seen anyone like Mr. Kojima who loves Xinjiang and has really contributed to Xinjiang. Abe no Nakamaro died in Changan. Dying in Xinjiang must make your dream come true, right?" I answered, "I hope so." (Screenshot of Tianjin TV's *The Mona Lisa in the Western Regions*)

おわりに―使命として

　合掌　ありがとうございます。キジル千仏洞修復保存からニヤ遺跡調査、ダンダンウイリク遺跡調査、同壁画保護、関連活動を含めて豊富な成果をあげることができた。この機会に永年にわたりご指導ご協力いただいた関係機関と関係各位に心からの感謝を改めて表わすものである。なかでも沙漠での過酷な現地調査そして日本やウルムチでの保護研究や報告書刊行に尽力いただいた日中双方隊員諸氏には深謝している。

　調査保護研究事業には、多くの方々の膨大な熱意・時間・英知・資金が投入された。キジル千仏洞はすでに「世界文化遺産」となり、ニヤ遺跡もやがて「世界文化遺産」に登録されるであろう。

　不思議なご縁に心から感謝している。後半生の殆どを物心両面にわたって投じたが、悔いはない。今後も「命」をかけて新疆ウイグル自治区を中心に、文化遺産保護研究、人材育成と日中間相互理解促進に老残微力をささげ、次世代へ引き継ぎたい。共同通信から「活動の幅がひろくどう表現したらよいのか」と問われて、「国際貢献手弁当長期実践家とでも」と答えたことがある。関係各位の更なるご指導ご協力をお願いするしだいである。

　36年間、提供しつづけてきたのは「至誠」。新疆各族の皆さんにはささやかな喜びを提供したにすぎないが、筆者は大きな幸せを頂戴した。第二の故郷である新疆の人々、そして輝かしい成果をともにあげてきた日中双方の方々の益々のご多幸を祈ります。

　　　陽はのぼり陽はしずみ花がさき花がちり夏がきて冬がきて
　　　嗚呼！新疆36年迷い迷いときに悟りすべてのすべてありがとう
　　　　　骨はタクラマカン沙漠に埋める　頓首再拝

结束语－我的使命

　合掌　衷心感谢！从克孜尔千佛洞修复保存协力开始，包括尼雅遗址、丹丹乌里克遗址考察及其壁画保护、其他相关活动都取得了重大的成果，借此机会，向多年来对我给予指导、协助的有关单位和个人表示衷心的感谢，特别要向在沙漠中完成艰苦的实地调查、在日本和乌鲁木齐进行保护研究、为研讨会和报告书的出版贡献了力量的中日双方的队员们表示深深的谢意。

　　要进行调查保护研究事业，需要众多人士投入极大的热情、时间、智慧和资金，克孜尔千佛洞已经申遗成功，相信尼雅遗址也会成为世界文化遗产。

　　衷心感谢这不可思议的缘分，无论是物质还是内心，我几乎投入了自己后半生之所有，人生无悔。我已下定决心，以新疆维吾尔自治区为中心，以文化遗产保护研究、人才培养、增进日中间的相互理解为使命，继续贡献绵薄之力。共同通信社问我"活动范围很广，我们怎样来表达好呢？"，我说"就叫'自带盒饭国际贡献长期实践家'"吧。期待各位给予进一步的指导和协助。

　　36年来，我献出的是"至诚"。只是向新疆各族人民送上了一点点的喜悦，却收获了巨大的幸福。祝愿我第二故乡的新疆人民以及共同取得了辉煌成果的中日双方的各位更加幸福。

日起日落、花开花谢、暑往寒来
呜呼！新疆36载、迷散悟醒、感恩所有
要将骨灰埋在塔克拉玛干沙漠　叩首再拜

As a conclusion

I thank you all very much with joining my hands in prayer. My missions to restore and conserve the Kizil grottoes, to research the Niya ruins, and to research the Dandanoilik ruins to conserve its murals have made bountiful accomplishments, let alone the associated undertakings. I would like to take this opportunity to express my appreciation to those people and organizations for having advised and cooperated with me over the years. Above all, I deeply feel obliged to Japan-China joint team members who have made a tremendous effort to conduct research on site in a punishing condition, preserve and study in Japan and Urumqi, and issue the reports.

A great deal of eagerness, time, intelligence, and capital has been poured in for the projects of research, restoration, and studies. The Kizil grottoes has already become the world cultural heritage site and the Niya ruins will be registered as the world cultural heritage site in time.

I am always thankful for a mysterious arrangement from the bottom of my heart. I have devoted most of the second half of my life psychologically and materially for Xinjiang, which I have no regret about. From now on, as well, I have made up my mind to exert my last bit of life for conservation and studies of cultural assets, development of human resources, and betterment of mutual understanding between Japan and China. Once Kyodo News asked me, "How should I describe such a person like you practicing a wide range of activities?" I replied, "A lifelong volunteer for international cooperation or something like that." I would like to ask you all to lead and help me even further for some time to come.

For 36 years, what I have kept offering is heartfelt sincerity. While I might have offered only a bit of joy for the people of various races in Xinjiang, I have been bestowed the greatest happiness ever from them. I wish all the best for the people in my second home, Xinjiang, and those Japan-China joint team members who have achieved outstanding performance with me.

The sun rises and sets, flowers blossom and fall, the summer comes and the winter comes
Oh, having strayed for 36 years in Xinjiang to at times find enlightenment,
I thank you all for everything
Bury my ashes in the Taklamakan Desert
Respectfully yours

国際貢献手弁当長期実践家と報じる佐賀新聞、共同通信配信で各地方紙に掲載された
报道自带盒饭国际贡献长期实践家的佐贺新闻，刊登在经共同通信社配发的各个地方报纸上
Saga Shimbun covering me as a lifelong volunteer for international cooperation; The Kyodo News Service has distributed this phrase to the various local media

一部活動を報じる新疆日報
新疆日报报道了一部分活动内容
Xinjiang Daily reporting part of my activities

皆々様

ありがとうございます

衷心感謝！

Thank you so much !

小島康誉

1942年生まれ。66年24歳で「宝石の鶴亀」（後にツルカメコーポレーション・あずみと社名変更、現As-meエステール）を創業。93年株式上場。96年創業30周年を機に社長を退任。一方で、87年得度し僧籍に入る。88年佛教大学卒業。中国新疆へ82年以来、150回以上訪問しキジル千仏洞修復保存協力、ニヤ遺跡やダンダンウイリク遺跡を日中共同で調査するなど文化財保護研究・人材育成・相互理解促進の三分野で多くの国際協力を実践している。2006年から11年まで佛教大学客員教授、現在は佛教大学内ニヤ遺跡学術研究機構代表や新疆ウイグル自治区政府顧問などを務めている。編著『日中共同ニヤ遺跡学術調査報告書』『日中共同ダンダンウイリク遺跡学術調査報告書』『シルクロード・ニヤ遺跡の謎』『念仏の道ヨチヨチと』『新疆世界文化遺産図鑑』『Kizil, Niya, and Dandanoilik』など多数。（ADC文化通信より）

小岛康誉

1942年3月出生于日本名古屋市，毕业于日本佛教大学，净土宗僧侣。1966年创立鹤龟宝石公司，并成功将公司打造上市，1996年从社长职位引退。自1982年以来，访问新疆150多次，在经济交流、文化、文物、教育、扶贫、档案管理等领域推动了100多个项目。曾任日本鹤龟宝石公司社长、佛教大学客座教授，现为新疆维吾尔自治区人民政府文化顾问、乌鲁木齐市荣誉市民、新疆大学名誉教授、佛教大学内尼雅遗址学术研究机构代表、中国历史文化遗产保护网理事长、中日共同尼雅遗址/丹丹乌里克遗址学术考察日方队长。编著有《清代新疆建置档案史料》、《中日共同尼雅遗址学术考察报告书》、《中日共同丹丹乌里克遗址学术考察报告书》、《丝绸之路·尼雅遗址之谜》、《见证新疆变迁》、《迷路悟道》、《新疆世界性文化遗产保护研究事业和国际合作的意义》、《斯坦因第四次新疆探险及其始末》、《新疆世界文化遗产图典》、《Kizil, Niya, and Dandanoilik》等。多年的努力赢得了中日两国的盛赞，全国人大、文化部、新疆维吾尔自治区人民政府、清华大学、中国人民对外友好协会、中国文物保护基金会、日本政府等都对小岛康誉给予了表彰。被《人民日报》誉为"当代的阿倍仲麻吕"。(来源：中国历史文化遗产保护网)

Yasutaka Kojima was born in 1942 and currently works as a Buddhist monk. Kojima is a representative of Academic Research Organization for Niya, Bukkyo University and a special, cultural adviser to Xinjiang Uygur Autonomous Region Government, China. He has visited Xinjiang more than 150 times since 1982 and contributed there in the fields of 100 or so, including preservation and research of cultural assets, human resources development and the promotion of mutual understanding between Japan and China. Those contributions have been released to the public through international symposiums as well as various reports. His thesis, titled "The Whole Story of Sir Marc Aurel Stein's 4th Expedition to Xinjiang in Central Asia", and "Kizil, Niya, and Dandanoilik" was recently publicized.

中国新疆36年国際協力実録
キジル・ニヤ・ダンダンウイリク

2018年10月30日　第1版第1刷発行

編　者‧‧‧‧‧‧‧‧‧‧‧‧‧‧‧‧‧‧‧‧‧‧‧‧‧‧‧‧‧‧‧‧　小 島 康 誉
　　　　　　　　　　　　　　　 Yasutaka Kojima

発行者‧‧‧‧‧‧‧‧‧‧‧‧‧‧‧‧‧‧‧‧‧‧‧‧‧‧‧‧‧‧‧‧　稲 川 博 久

発行所‧‧‧‧‧‧‧‧‧‧‧‧‧‧‧‧‧‧‧‧‧‧‧‧‧‧‧‧‧‧‧‧　東方出版㈱
　　　　　　〒543-0062 大阪市天王寺区逢阪2-3-2
　　　　　　Tel.06-6779-9571 Fax.06-6779-9573

印刷所‧‧‧‧‧‧‧‧‧‧‧‧‧‧‧‧‧‧‧‧‧‧‧‧‧‧‧‧‧‧‧‧　亜細亜印刷㈱

©2018 Yasutaka Kojima, Printed in Japan　ISBN978-4-86249-348-4

本書の全部または一部を無断で複写・複製することを禁じます。
落丁・乱丁のときはお取り替えいたします。